THE BOOK OF
ST ERVAN
The Story of a Rural Parish

MOIRA TANGYE

HALSGROVE

First published in Great Britain in 2006

British Library Cataloguing-in-Publication Data.
A CIP record for this title is available from the British Library.

ISBN 1 84114 494 0
ISBN 978 1 84114 494 8

HALSGROVE

Halsgrove House
Lower Moor Way
Tiverton, Devon EX16 6SS
Tel: 01884 243242
Fax: 01884 243325
email: sales@halsgrove.com
website: www.halsgrove.com

Frontispiece photograph: *The carved wooden angel fixed to the outside of the porch door in St Ervan Church.*

Printed and bound in Great Britain by CPI Bath Press, Bath.

Whilst every care has been taken to ensure the accuracy of the information contained in this book, the publisher disclaims responsibility for any mistakes which may have been inadvertently included.

Foreword

In an age which is becoming more and more specialist, Moira Tangye is refreshingly different: a real all-rounder. She has served various Cornish causes – and served them well. Meeting her is a tonic and reading her words is equally rewarding.

The fact is, she belongs to a literary dynasty. Her husband, Nigel, produced a string of good books, including a collection of short stories written in Paris, while her brother-in-law, Derek Tangye, was the author of the best-selling Minack chronicles.

Now Moira makes her debut as an author and St Ervan is fortunate to have such a gifted historian. A literary Miss Marple emerges, uncovering a rich mine, fascinating facts and figures.

Her research is deep, proving our villages and hamlets, despite their calm surfaces, have enough drama to pack a novel.

Reading these chapters we understand how and why a wordsmith like Mr Winston Graham, a mutual friend, found so much inspiration in Cornwall. Even today, along this jagged North Cornwall coast, in places we catch a whiff of Poldark.

A contrasting cast parades here: the Revd Henry Nowell Barton, parson and squire for six decades, Richard Brewer, yeoman, miller and maltster, the St Ervan cricketers playing 'overseas', a trip to Scilly; James Rundle, who died aged 53, leaving a wife and 14 children, the travelling preacher Elizabeth Dart, another cleric, Hugh Molesworth, who did so much for the weekday schooling of local children – and many others.

Wonderful names pepper the pages: Curgenven, Trevaskis, Brenton and Kessell are just some of them.

Moira Tangye has been having a love affair with St Ervan for 30 years and the esteem in which she is held is mirrored in the fact that she has obtained over 250 photographs. They range from a prehistoric longstone to a prizewinning scarecrow at the Royal Cornwall Show in 1983. We see Mr Sandry with his newly purchased fleet of Morris lorries in 1935 and a Methodist Sunday-school treat around 1910.

The older images, in particular, are hugely evocative, recalling a mood and way of life that have gone – and will never come back. Looking at them, we realise the old-school editors were correct: a good picture is worth a thousand words.

But we need this caring scribe to interpret the stories behind the picture. Moira's words and these illustrations combine to make a marvellous cocktail. A joy for us today and coming generations.

Michael Williams
St Teath, North Cornwall

Frederick Hawke (1894–1964) with adoptive parents Mr and Mrs Hawkey in St Columb.

Accident in the lane leading down to Rumford from the north, c.1930s. A visitor has misjudged the width of the road and pushed William Lobb's car into the hedge.

CONTENTS

Acknowledgements

I remember with affection the late Dorothy Bennetts, Sidney Bawden, Stewart Buscombe, George Hawke, Gwenny Hawke, Winnie Lobb, Christine Sandry and T.H. Sandry, who generously shared their love of the parish with me and lent me old photographs to copy.

I owe much to discussions with the late Dr F.L. Harris, whose classes developed my interest in local history ('Look at the lives of the ordinary people'), the late Revd T. Shaw, Methodist historian, whose collection in the Courtney Library is such a wonderful resource, and with Methodist historian John C.C. Probert. I have to thank Cornwall Family History Society, especially the founders, for setting me on the correct path of family history research into the families of the parish, which proved so interesting. I wish I could have spent more time talking music with Michael O'Connor.

I thank Terry Knight, Librarian, and all the staff at the Cornish Studies Library, and Angela Broome, Librarian of the Courtney Library, Royal Institution of Cornwall, for their cheerfulness in looking out books and documents for me, and Dr Jennifer M. Freeman, Director of the Historic Chapels Trust, for photographs of the refurbished Penrose chapel.

I am very grateful to all those who spared time to talk to me and/or search out photographs, especially those who are so busy because they live and work in the countryside. They include: Caroline Arnold, Ted Ball, Fernley and Nancy Banbury, Alan Bennett, Hilda Bennett, Roger and Susan Biddick, Denis Brewer, Nina Brewer, Len and Beth Carhart, Roger and Rose Clemens, David and Edith Cowling, Millicent Curgenven, John Deacon, Margaret Eustice, Gillian Fisher, Diana Ford, Alberta Gregor, Jill Hagley, Rod and Sally Harvey, Betty Hawke, Graham Hawke, Les Hawke, Michelle Hawke, Howard Hawken, Joan Henwood, W. John James, David Kempthorne, Pat Kent, Roger Lacey, Sara Louise Lobb, Reg and Jenny Middleton, Michael and Tina O'Connor, Larry and Jenny Old, Susan Old, T. Henry Old, Alan Plester, Hilda Plester, Charlie Powell, John Reskelly, Bill Rowe, Michael and Freda Salmon, Peter Sandry, Jeremy and Sally Simmons, Trevor and Linda Simpson, Ken and Mary Skinner and John, Adam and Zoe Turner, Errol Walling, William and Annette Wood.

A big 'thank-you' to Malcolm McCarthy, whose computer skills enabled me to return precious photographs to their owners quickly.

I am most grateful to Dr O.J. Padel for supplying the translation of medieval place-names, and to Donald Rawe for permission to use his delightful poem, 'June Evening, St Ervan'.

Finally, all errors or misinterpretations of any aspect of the history of St Ervan are entirely my own.

Introduction

If you stand on the highest point in St Ervan, just 560ft above sea level, you can survey the gentle sweep of the farming landscape against a distant backcloth of sea.

St Ervan lies not quite on the north coast of Cornwall, to the south of the Camel river which runs out into the Atlantic Ocean by the port of Padstow, and the parish is disturbed by no main road running through it from anywhere to anywhere.

Its pocket-sized 3,000 acres, broken up by shielding Cornish turf or stone hedges into irregular-shaped fields, tuck into the folds of land rising from 200 to 400ft above the sea, and are surrounded and enclosed by similarly agricultural parishes. The few trees, unless within the protective embrace of the narrow valleys, stand stripped of foliage, their branches bowed before the savage salt winds from the west.

It feels remote and deeply peaceful.

The dozen farmhouses snuggling in their groups of outbuildings are discreetly withdrawn from one another and mostly hidden from our view. From here there is no sign of the clusters of fewer than 20 houses which make up each of the two villages.

From this ridge, follow the winding road down through the farmyard on the lower edge of the moor, drop right down into the valley and discover the tiny cruciform church hidden in the trees on the bank of the stream. Surrounded by greenery, facing the sunlit, steeply rising slope opposite, the little stream pursuing its familiar course in front of the old mill and cottages, the whole is a scene of tranquillity. God's peace, God's beauty pervade this spot.

I entered this small church one winter's day with no great expectations. As I opened the heavy south door with its carved-wood angel I was conscious of February dankness and at the same time of careful tending. In each pew, prayer and hymn books were thoughtfully set out in readiness for worshippers. Perhaps their number showed optimism, but how hospitable and welcoming.

Then I had a surprise, for adorning the plain walls, all around the church, in the nave, the transepts and the chancel, are magnificent memorials, simply decorated but finely carved in dark slate, plus two more elaborate ones in alabaster, to people who lived and died in St Ervan 300 years ago. No high aristocracy but no mean men either:

Richard Hore Gentleman
William Pomeroye Esquier
Humphrey Arthur yeoman
Richard the sonne of Richard Lovis Gent.
John Tom of Treleigh yeoman

A good sprinkling of lower gentry, men of of substance in such a small community.

I looked through the window across the cleft in the soft hills to the village beyond and to the farmhouse on the crest of the hill and wondered about these people whose memorials, surviving three centuries, now begin to flake in submission to the persistent erosion by time and the gentle mists of Cornwall.

I was intrigued, and my hunt to unravel the secrets of this mysterious, obscure and tiny Cornish parish had begun.

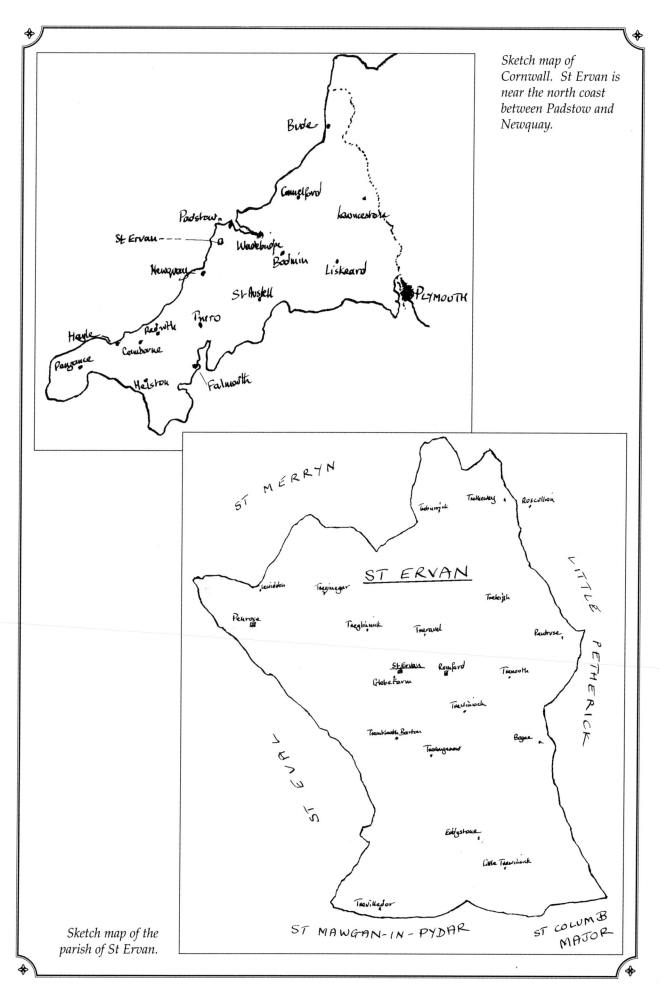

*Sketch map of
Cornwall. St Ervan is
near the north coast
between Padstow and
Newquay.*

*Sketch map of the
parish of St Ervan.*

✦ CHAPTER 1 ✦

Saint, Church, Rectors, Recusants

We know that the church has been dedicated to St Hermes since the Middle Ages, but we do not know for certain who he was. There was a Roman martyr of the second century called Hermes and this is possibly an instance of the Roman Church, when it brought the Christians in Britain under its control, adapting an ancient British dedication to the close-sounding name of a saint in the Roman Calendar. Who, then, was St Hermes, the subject of the first dedication? Probably the same Celtic saint who also has dedications at St Erme and Marazion in Cornwall and in Wales and Brittany, but about whom nothing certain is known.

By the west end of the church are three springs, one of which feeds the 'holy well'. Is it simply the proximity of this well to the church which has earned it the label 'holy', or was it a shrine for ancient pagan worship? The well, an opening in the bank of the lane, is romantically fringed with delicate foliage filtering the sunlight, its roof the roots of an elm rising high into the sky above, its floor encircling a pool of water, ice-cool and crystal clear.

It has never been listed by the authorities on holy wells. Even the long battle for recognition waged on its behalf by the scholarly Prebendary Johnson (rector from 1915 to 1955) was unsuccessful. Holy or not, its waters have never run dry, even in the severest

drought. The grateful parishioners do not concern themselves too much with the genuineness of its claims to holiness but happily use the pure water for baptisms.

Was Saint Ervan a Celtic hermit who came here to pray and live where he could find shelter from the Atlantic gales and be close to an abundance of that vital element for life, water? The stream rushes by even today. Or could it have been Erbin, who occurs in the royal genealogies of Cornwall? Scholars continue to argue about his identity.

Not far from here is the town of Padstow on the Camel estuary, centre of the pilgrim landings in the Dark Ages, when Christians who had sailed from Ireland and Wales traversed Cornwall from the north coast by following the waterways of the River Camel and then the River Fowey to the south coast, where they could take another boat across the sea to Brittany. Petroc was a sixth-century Welsh evangelist who landed in the Camel estuary (Trebetheric – 'farmstead of Petroc') and established a wide area of influence. His main settlement was Padstow and later he founded an important sub-monastery at Bodmin – 'the dwelling of the sanctuary'. Perhaps Erbin was among those fired with fresh Christian zeal by the powerful influence of Petroc to found his own community, on this spot by the three springs on the ground sloping down to the river.

Whatever the nature or identity of the founder of the first Christian community in this place, we know that the land around was settled by man long before then.

The southern boundary of the parish lies along a ridge at 500ft above sea level, and on the downs dropping away from this ridge there still remain several of the humps so familiar in the Cornish landscape, Bronze Age burial mounds. Thus we have evidence of man, in the area we now know as St Ervan, in the period 3000BC to AD500, burying his cremated dead in stone chambers heaped over with great circular mounds of earth.

These barrows do not feature in the more fertile landscape further down. The richer soil below the moor would have grown trees in which wolves could lurk, and if man did at any time live in the wooded valleys of the several streams which cross the parish, any evidence has long since been ploughed away by the cultivation of centuries. The farm name Trembleath is Cornish tre + an bleth, 'the farmstead of the wolf', indicating the presence of wolves on the lower ground as late as the seventh century.

The prehistoric longstone, unmoved by centuries of cultivation all around it.

9

Music Water caravan park.

We shall probably never know the precise nature of the earliest setlements here. As if to emphasise the point, near the foot of the downs stands a longstone, or standing stone, of unworked white quartz 3.6m. high tapering from almost 2m. 'square' at the base, as if defying our attempts to fathom its mysteries or to bridge the impassable gulf which separates us from it and those who erected it. We can only wonder what religious or commemorative significance it may have had. In some cases where standing stones in Cornwall were excavated last century, evidence of burial has been found. If this is so in this case, what manner of man must he have been who merited a grave which this huge stone has so spectacularly marked for hundreds of years? What must have been the skill and strength of the men who erected it to stand so steadily for so long? It dwarfs the modern farmer manoeuvring his tractor around the base of the archaic monument and, like a brooding hunched giant, it looks across the tops of the lichened trees, below which lie concealed the ruins of nineteenth-century field workers' dwellings, to glimpse the twentieth-century holiday caravan site in the field beyond.

We then have to take a great leap forward in the darkness of historical ignorance of the early centuries after Christ's birth. We know there was a busy traffic of people – Petroc did not travel alone – coming across the sea from Ireland and Wales to land in the Camel estuary just to the north of the present-day parish of St Ervan. Around the Camel estuary and well upriver the farm names reveal the impact of this traffic on the surrounding land. Almost without exception they begin with tre, 'farm', 'farmstead', 'estate', denoting an agricultural settlement created in the period 500–1100.

St Ervan farms have all retained their old Cornish names. They have also remained in the old Celtic pattern, small farms scattered over the parish, rather than only a few larger farms, and no large town or village. In the past each farm had a labourer's cottage or two within its group of buildings. The Celts did not live in groups and even the 'villages' of Penrose and Rumford today are only hamlets. Rumford, from the lack of a Cornish element in its name, appears to be a comparatively modern upstart

Place-names and their meanings:

Penrose: 'end of the upland', **pen** 'head, end' + **ros** 'moorland, upland, hill-spur'. The hamlet is situated near the end of a two-mile ridge of land between streams.

Pentruse: seemingly a new residence created in the later-nineteenth century (before 1884). Penatruse is found earlier (in 1841) as the name of a field in Trenouth, but its meaning is obscure; presumably Cornish **pen** 'head, end'.

Rumford: English, probably 'roomy ford, wide ford', with reference to the stream-crossing here.

Bogee: 'lord's dwelling', **bod** 'dwelling'+ **yuf** 'lord'.

Lewidden: obscure, for lack of early references.

tre: 'farm, farmstead, estate', denotes an agricultural settlement. Names beginning with Tre- were mostly created in the period 500–1100, and many of the places may have fitted into a native system of land-tenure which preceded the manorial system current under the Anglo-Saxons and Normans. Very often the second word following **Tre-** is a man's name, presumably that of an early occupant of the farmstead, of whom nothing else is now known.

Treginegar: originally *Tregeneder* 'farm of a man, Keneder'.

Treglinnick: 'farm at a holly-grove, **tre + kelynnek** (from *kelyn* 'holly-trees').

Trenouth: 'new farm', **tre + nowyth** 'new'.

Treravel: probably 'farm of a man, Rovel'.

Tregwinyo (spelt Trevengenow on some maps): probably 'farm in the downs', **tre + yn + gonyow**, plural of goon 'downland'.

Trewinnick: either 'farm of a man, Gwynnek', or Gwynnek might instead be a former name of the stream which flows round Trewinnick to the east and north-east, through Rumford.

Trembleath: 'the farm of the wolf', **tre + an bleth** 'the wolf'.

Trevilledor: this place cannot be traced back before 1841, and it seems to be a modern place, created out of part of Bear's Downs, and named after the older Trevilledor in the adjacent parish of Little Petherick. (That older place is probably 'farm of a man, Eleder'.)

Treleigh: originally *Tre-nans-le*, which is obscure; it might mean 'farm of the lesser valley' (**nans** 'valley', **le** 'lesser'), if that makes any sense on the ground, or possibly 'farm of the valley of *Le*', if *Le* was once a local stream-name.

Trethewy: 'David's farm', **tre** + *Dewy*, Cornish for David.

Treburick: originally *Trebrichok* or *Trebruek*, **tre** 'farm' plus unknown word or name. To be distinguished from Treburrick in St Eval parish, two miles away.

(The author thanks Dr O.J. Padel for supplying these interpretations.)

Milestone on the southern bound at Five Turnings.

Milestone on the eastern bound of the parish.

anyway, but Penrose, from its name and its layout has more ancient beginnings in times of communal agriculture. The church<u>town</u> never had more than six dwellings, including the rectory, around the church, <u>town</u> in Cornish having a different meaning from modern English. The <u>townplace</u> on a farm, for example, is simply the farmyard. At Penrose <u>Lowertown</u> was one farm down the hill from, hence lower than, the main part of the village.

By the ninth century the important manor of Pawton (the lands of Petroc) included all those lands along the south bank of the Camel from the coast to the head of the estuary. After King Egbert the Saxon defeated the Cornish in AD835 he presented this manor to the Saxon Bishop of Sherborne in Dorset, thus driving a wedge into the stronghold of Petroc's successors, isolating the principal Petroc monastery at Padstow from its subject community further inland at Bodmin.

A sketch of the Pawton title down through the years shows it being granted and leased and exchanged until in 1748 it was purchased by Sir W. Morice, Secretary of State to Charles II. At a cost of £16,000 he became lord of all three manors – Pawton, Trevose and Ide – and controlled their advowsons. Having descended to Sir Nicholas Morice, the last baronet, the title then passed to his sister Barbara, who brought it in marriage to Sir John Molesworth, Bart. By the 1870s, it was the property of the heirs of the late Sir William Molesworth Bart of Pencarrow in nearby St Breock parish. With it came the patronage of St Ervan Rectory which was to stay with the Molesworths of Pencarrow until the mid-nineteenth century.

Throughout this time, the churches and parishes within the manor, including St Ervan and all the parishes immediately adjoining to the west, north and east of it (seven in all), remained ecclesiastically directly subject to the Bishop of Exeter (they were

Bishop's Peculiars) so were not supervised by his archdeacon in Cornwall. The Peculiars ceased to exist when Cornwall regained its own See in 1877.

Thus we see the close link through the centuries of land ownership and patronage of Parish Churches within the manor of Pawton. The act of the Saxon monarch, Egbert, in handing Pawton manor to the See of Sherborne in the middle of the ninth century decided both the manner in which the parishes were governed ecclesiastically and the ownership of the greater part of the land in those parishes, including St Ervan, right down to the middle of the nineteenth century.

St Ervan remained quietly agricultural. If the size of the parish, determined in the Middle Ages by its capacity to support the material needs of the rector, is anything to go by, then St Ervan was a fertile parish. It shared in the general increase of prosperity of Cornwall and along with the rest built its church large enough to accommodate the entire population of the parish and with good sturdy walls of the abundant local stone. The font, crudely hexagonal, could be as old.

In the fourteenth century a west tower was added, a plain structure with battlements, but without pinnacles or buttresses, possibly also the south porch. Certainly three bells were hung in the tower. In the fifteenth century it was not enlarged by the addition of side aisles, as most Cornish churches, but was simply rebuilt retaining the same sturdy walls of the first plain cruciform structure of two centuries earlier. If only it had been more sensitively restored it would present us with a good example of what Cornish Parish Churches were like before the fifteenth century.

Important landowners in the fourteenth century were the Arundell family, who owned the chief place in the parish, the manor of Trembleath. This was the property whose name had been taken by the family

De Trembleth and which had been acquired through marriage by the Arundells, who lived here before removing to Lanherne in the neighbouring parish of St Mawgan, when Trembleath became a dower house.

On 5 May 1329 'Joan de Arundelle Lady of Trembleythe' was granted a licence for her oratory within the said manor provided the rector of the parish gave his consent. He appears to have done so, for there is a tenement of 28 acres in Trembleath still called 'Chapel Ground', and the site of the chapel is marked on Ordnance Survey maps. There is no trace of it now but just to the south of the site can be seen on the ground a rectangular platform and associated terraces. This could well be the site of the original manor-house and is a much more likely position than the present farmhouse site.

Relations between the Arundells and the rectors of the parish were good at this period in history, for one gave his consent for a licensed oratory, and another acceded to an agreement whereby the 'estate of Trembleathe paid a modus of ten shillings to the rector in lieu of all tithes.' (This right was maintained until the commutation of tithes in the nineteenth century.) By the sixteenth century, however, there was unprecedented upheaval in Cornwall, which held out longest against the religious changes under Elizabeth I. The rectors of St Ervan bowed to the winds of change, but this branch of the Arundells remained staunchly Roman Catholic, so were branded 'popish recusants' and fined heavily for not attending the English Church.

In 1551 two members of the Hore family, dependants of the Arundells, were still in the Fleet prison. The Hore family became wholehearted recusants. We see the result. The manor of Trenouth was their seat for many years and is noted as such by Norden on his map made at the end of the sixteenth century (Norden shows only one other property of note, Trewinnick), but by the time Hitchins and Drew published their *History of Cornwall* in 1824 the estate of Trenouth had 'long since ceased to be considered a manor.' The Hores had been men of substance, now they had lost their money in paying the huge fines for not attending the English church services.

A Richard Hore, who made his will in 1556, desired to be buried in the 'Church of St Ervyn, in the somytory before the picture of St Erasme' and he left 13s.4d. for his name to be put on the parish Bede-Roll. This shows how keen Richard was to practise the old usages once the Catholic Queen Mary came to the throne. A later Richard Hore died in 1619. His memorial is cut in slate in the church:

Be holde thy Sealfe By me
The Like was I as Thou
And Thou in Tyme Shalt be
Turn dust as I am now.

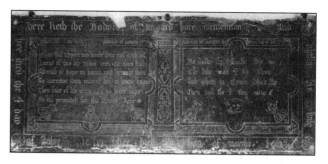

Slate memorial to Richard Hore, gent., and family. He died in 1619.

A close-up of the Richard Hore slate, showing the beautiful script.

Another recusant was George Beare, no stranger to troubles. In February 1620 he had married Rebecca, daughter of Ralph Keate, gent. His father-in-law, shortly before his death, was a prisoner in the Fleet prison. The will he made while there reads:

In the name of God Amen. I Ralph Kete being a prisoner of the fleete in the Citty of London gent. being of perfect mynde and memorie having given and bequeathyd in my former will or willes larger Legacyes than my estate can performe by reason of my falling into decay by reason of these late troubles, doe this present fifty day of August Anno Dni 1634 revoke all former wills and Testaments.

The following year he added a codicil telling us he was in 'St Ervyn'. He died there in April 1636.

It was 36 years before his epitaph was erected in the church, but we can let its inscription tell the story:

*Here lyeth the Body of
Ralph Keate Gent Eldest Sonn
of Ralph Keate Second Sonn
of William Keate of Hagborn in Barkshire
Esq. hee had by his first wife Ann the
Daughter of William Arscott of Holsworthy
Esq. three sonnes William John and Ralph
and as many Daughters, Rebecka, Elizabeth
and Ann by his second wife hee left noe
Surviving Issue hee dyed Aged 69*

The Keate monument, before it was restored in 2006.

and was buried the 14 day of Aprill 1636
Here lyes he dead Whose yet Surviving good
Like flames by night shines through Ingratitude
We vertue present loath when gone its pris'd
King Charles was murther'd first then Cannonis'd
His Country foe his offspring and the poore
Doe owne his benefits findeing such noe more
Which long in after time (the Just mans doome)
Revive'd his memory and Rays'd his toombe
Anno Domini 1672.

The tomb to the memory of Ralph Keate could not be raised until the political and religious climate had changed.

Revd Richard Russell, rector 1633–54, would never have countenanced the sympathies for King Charles I expressed on Ralph Keate's monument. When he died in 1654 his memorial called him 'Minister' and was the only one surviving at St Ervan from the Commonwealth period. It was also the most elaborately decorated of all those in the church, and the inscription the most elaborate in style:

Richard Russell, Minister of this Parrish who was
buried the eleventh day of December 1654
Looke on this living Saint, this Matchles summ
So comprehensive a Compendium
A learned Scholler, Painfull Labourer
A Faithfull Shepherd, True Embassadeur
An untir'd watchman, & A shining Saint
A Burning Taper, Beauty without Paint
Bright Gem hath left its casket, to be sett
By God into a Nobler Coronett
Ripe Grace Now ends in Glory: so is he
Sounding Triumphs, with the Hierarchy.

Richard Russell was rector in the year 1641 when Parliament, in its struggle for power with King Charles I, organised a protest against the possible imposition of 'an arbitrary and tyrannical government'. It took the form of a declaration promising to support and maintain the Protestant religion as expressed in the doctrine of the Church of England. In St Ervan 75 male parishioners 18 years and over took the oath, plus the two constables, two church-wardens and two overseers. Those who 'tooke it not' also had to sign their names or make their mark. There were six: John Pierce, gent., Thomas Pierce, gent., Philip Pierce, gent., John Tom, Richard James, William Dinnicombe.

In all Cornwall only 200 recusants declared themselves, and when one looks at the adjoining parishes and finds two in St Eval out of 80 names, four in Little Petherick out of 28, six in St Mawgan out of 197, it can be seen that a stronghold of the old faith still flourished here around the Arundells of Lanherne, in spite of the fact that Lanherne was in decay and Arundell influence had waned as a result of the severe recusancy fines of £300, later £400, a year imposed for their refusal to attend the English service. The Arundell Rental Roll of 1678 includes among the conventionary tenants (i.e. tenants paying rent), 'Thomas Pearse 40 years Elizabeth his wife 36 years and Richard their son 14 years at St Ervan Churchtown.' They were farming the land right on the rector's doorstep!

During this restlessness there were more respectable citizens among the social hierarchy who managed to conform to what both the State and the Church expected of them, and whose respectable lives earned them a monument in their Parish Church.

Only one stood higher socially than the 'gentlemen', William Pomeroy Esq. 'who departed this life on the thirde day of June An'o Domini 1622 Memento Mori.' Crudely carved in low relief, his full-length figure, wearing a doublet and knee breeches, looks every inch the Esquire, and the shield by his head displays the arms of the Tregony Pomeroys. (No connection has been found between him and St Ervan.)

One slate commemorates the death of William

Arthur, yeoman, in 1627 and informs us 'Hee had issue 5 sonnes And 3 daughters.' His wife and the eight children are all lined up beside him. The man wears a plain doublet and knee breeches and a spade beard. His five boys are dressed exactly as their father, while his wife and daughters wear identical wide-brimmed hats and simple gowns with ruffs at the neckline.

Another Arthur, Humphrey, has several slates. Humphrey Arthur, yeoman, died in 1676 and though he was not young his wife Elizabeth survived him for a further 30 years. Both are commemorated in slate. The verses inscribed on these memorials emphasise their human mortality, the necessity of leading virtuous lives here on earth in case called without warning to the next, and the importance attached to the virtue of looking after the poor.

Of Humphrey Arthur they said:

Here's one (whome yet wee hope to bee in bliss)
Scarce to be found on earth whose equall is
But having found may not bee like in this.
Near sixty years he kept good hous on earth
Within his family was never dearth
But att his door the poore had allwayes mirth
Thank God for such A father yee his seed
Bless him yee poore that did you dayly feed
And all good Christians follow him indeed.

And the memorial to Jane Brewer, wife of Nicholas, who was 'buried the 11th day of Februarie... An'o 1642', asserts:

Ever remember to call on God for grace
Repent thy sinns, in heven thou shalt have place
Farwell sweete husband, & my children three
Doe good on earth, in heven shall you see.
Remember the poore.

After Minister Russell's stewardship had ended with his death in 1654 it seems another Commonwealth disciple could not be found to take his place. Only after nine years, shortly after the Restoration of Charles II, do we learn of the presence of Revd Richard Harvey in the rectory.

The rectory was the most spacious house in the parish, having six hearths. In 1663 the church-wardens reported that the 'Parson's house is in good repair', which was fortunate because the rector's responsibility in the church itself, the chancel, 'was decayed before our Minister came to ye place and he desires time to new built it till ye next Visitation.' The churchwardens, too, had their problems: 'Our church was repaired but ye Last wind did blow som part of ye Tiles off which wee are repairing and desire to have half a year's time.'

They are optimistic: 'We shall provide workmen speedily to repair our church and churchyard.'

In addition, they had to make good the ravages of Puritan rule: 'We shall provide a flagon for ye Communion.'

The rector set to work and two years later his initials 'R.H.' and the date '1665' were carved in granite on the chancel wall outside, beside the south window. He 'fought a good fight, he hath ranne well his race' before dying 2 September 1666.

Richard Harvey was succeeded by Richard Vivian, possibly from a local family – early Vivians from St Eval and St Issey had leased tenements at Penrose. He was in his twenties when he came to St Ervan, where he would be one of the longest-serving rectors of the parish. His children were born here, including John, who succeeded his father in March 1709. We know nothing of Richard Vivian's academic attainments (rectors usually had a BA or MA degree or a degree in law) but his son gained the Matric for Exeter College, Oxford, when he was 15 years old and his BA degree a few years later. His epitaph to his parents is the only surviving one with an inscription in Latin:

Hic requiescunt in Domino
Richardus Vivian Hujus Ecclesiae Rector
Et uxor dilectissima Eleanora Vivian
Nullo no digni Elogio
Eo vero digniores, quod nullo se dignes Aestimarerint
Foelieem proestolantes Resurrectionem,
quam suo demum tempore bonus dabit Deus.
Amen...

They died in 1707 and 1708. John's use of Latin hints at a yearning for the return of the old faith and, interestingly, the material he chose for the monument, alabaster, and the style in which it is fashioned, are replicas of those of the monument to Ralph Keate.

Revd John Vivian's own death in 1712 is simply recorded in St Ervan parish register: 'John Vivian Rector of this parish died Launceston, buried there 15 7ber.'

Just as undramatically he brought the parish into the eighteenth century.

✦ CHAPTER 2 ✦

The Eighteenth-Century Farmer, His House and His Accounts

In 1712 John Day, BA, from a local clerical family, came to St Ervan as rector. His entries in the church registers are characterised by precision and a neat hand. One of his first acts is to record in the baptism register:

Memorandum, That all the leaves that are wanting in this Book were Cut out Before It came to my Hands in the year 1712 When I was Instituted and Inducted to the Rectory of St Ervan.

John Day.

(Could he have been anticipating the frustration of later genealogists at finding gaps in the register?)

In 1727 a detailed description of the glebe property was required and John Day was the man to give it. Richard Harvey's repair work in the chancel is obviously still good because John Day makes no comment.

The parsonage was stone built with a slate roof. There was a parlour, 15ft x 16ft, in which the 'south wall is ceiled, and painted, and the other walls plaistered with lime.' The floor was boards. There was a hall, 15ft x 20ft, partly floored with boards and partly lime ashes. A little parlour, 12ft x 10ft, floored with boards and papered, and two other chambers were plastered with lime. The kitchen was 16ft x 16ft. In six of these rooms was a hearth. Probably no house in the parish was as grand as the rector's.

At the west end of the parsonage was a tenant's house consisting of three little rooms, which was also stone built but had the more common thatch roof. All the farm outbuildings were listed, and the fields of the glebe land described in detail.

As well as enjoying the produce from his own farm and hop garden and fruit from the orchard, the rector's living benefited from the produce of all the other farms in the parish. A tenth part, or tithe, had to be handed over for the upkeep of the rector and his family. John Day tells us that the owners and occupiers of the land in his parish had for the last 20 years compounded their tithes and were now in composition for great and small tithes. The farms here were fertile, the living a good one. However, that ancient agreement between the church and the Arundells was now working very much to the rector's disadvantage. This must have been particularly galling in view of the Arundells' continued obstinacy in remaining outside the Church of England. The formal language in which is couched the official return made by the rector to his superior conceals any feelings of resentment John Day might have felt.

He says simply:

The Barton of Trimbeth – the land of the heirs of Sir John Arundell – in lieu of which tithes There hath Been Customarily paid from year to year only 10sh. on Easter day at the Communion Table after morning service.

Inflation had rendered this amount the equivalent of a peppercorn. It would now buy just one bushel of wheat, under two bushels of barley or six quarters of mutton.

On Martyn's map of Cornwall (1748) there were only three places in the parish in the eighteenth century which were likely to compete in size of dwelling-house with the rectory, the three 'seats of nobility or gentry': Trewinnick, Treravel and Trenouth. Martyn calls all the other places 'villages'. Penrose and Rumford were then no more than hamlets, and the 'villages' of Treginegar, Treburthick (Treburrick), Treglinnick, Trembleath and Bogief (Bogee) were merely two or three farmhouses or a farmhouse and farm labourers' dwellings grouped together at the centre of a group of tenements making up a larger farm.

The farmhouse at Treginegar had a hall, a parlour, a cellar, and there was a chamber over the parlour and cellar, and adjoining the hall was a linney – or linhay – house and dairy, but it was still much smaller than the rectory. By 1760, however, a new farmhouse had been built against the old one which had a hall, parlour and cellar with chambers above, and kitchen with dairy above. The outhouses included a barn and oxen stall, but the addition of stables reflects the improvement in the standard of

Treginegar farmhouse, c.1890.

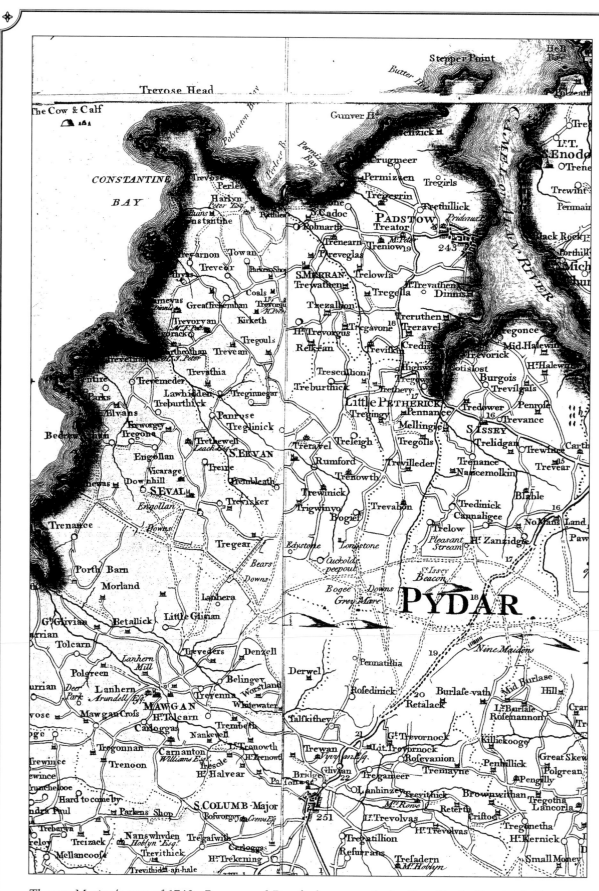

Thomas Martyn's map of 1748. Penrose and Rumford are named, also Trembleath, Trewinick, Trenowth, Treravel, Trigwinyo, Bogief, Treleigh, Treburthick, Treginnegar, Lawhidden and Edystone. The Longstone is marked, and nearby a place called Cuckolds Peepout!

living indicated by the building of the new dwelling. Treginegar was now a house approaching the size and grandeur of the rectory. It was stone built and roofed with slates taken from the small quarry of 'heling' or roofing stone on the farm.

As with all farms there was a mowhay, a place to put the hayrick, and the occupant had 'commons in the townplace', a right to make use of the farmyard or open space at the centre of the buildings.

Surveyor Thomas Martyn 'survey'd and plotted' Trenouth in 1732. He numbered and named each field. At that time Trenouth consisted of 551 acres, including Penalewes or Pentruse. Only three fields are described as 'good land', another has one part good land but part indifferent, some is 'tolerable', some ordinary, there is coarse land and furze (gorse)-growing land, but mostly there are 'moory [marshy] lands, sometimes partly in tillage but of no great value per acre.' Martyn found no trees of any value, but there was a tiny hop garden not far from the house, and fields called 'Bee Park', familiar to most farms. The fiercely burning salt winds from the sea inhibited the growth of most plants of any height, but the gorse thrived and it was gorse that nurtured the honey bees. Before sugar was imported honey was the only available sweet food. The historian Polwhele claimed that bees were sacred in Cornwall. Certainly great efforts had to be made, even in the comparatively warm, mild winters of Cornwall, to protect the bee hives, or skeps of straw. The farmer built a wall with beehive-shaped niches into which the skeps could be placed. At Trenouth a stone wall had a row of seven bee boles and remnants of more. The wall faced south to catch the pale warmth of the winter sun and was sheltered by the house and outbuildings from prevailing winds. Very snug the bees must have been in their purpose-built winter homes.

The farmland was much less intensively cultivated than later. Much of the ground was still swampy and in need of draining. It was a complex mixture of arable, meadow, pasture, furze and waste, the quality varying from field to field and within each field. (A modern farmer says that even today he has fields in which the soil varies within the same field.)

In 1790 Francis Roberts, yeoman, of Penrose sold a variety of stock and implements which show the

Bee boles in a garden wall at Trenouth in the 1970s.

range of activities by one farmer. He needed to borrow £30 and had to take out a bond of £60 to secure the debt. The security was:

All the cattle, Sheep, Corn, household goods hereinafter mentioned...
32 oxen One Grey Mare One Bay Gelding one Brown Calf 25 Sheep and ten Lambs and 1 Pigg 5 acres of Wheate 3 Acres of Barley and 3 Acres of Pease now growing on Trevethan in St Eval and One of Wheate growing on Little Treviscar in St Eval, and 3 Acres of Wheate now growing on Perose in St Ervan
2 feather beds furnished
Eight Pewter Platters
12 Pewter Plates
7 brass pans and kettles
2 brewing Keives
4 Barrells now in the house of Fras Roberts at Perose together with a Weigne [cart] and wheels
2 Butts and Wheels
a Plow
and 2 Harrows now at Trevethan in St Eval.

(On this bond the signature has been cut out, signifying that the £30 was repaid.) The variety of farming revealed by this list is appropriate to the variable land and the contents of the house are such as one would have found at the rectory, Treginegar and any other substantial farmhouse.

Francis Roberts was living in Penrose farmhouse, which had earlier been enlarged and improved by Nicholas Leverton (1700–58). Nicholas was the son of Henry Leverton who, in 1678, was the tenant renting the principal property in the parish, the barton farm of Trembleath. In 1716 he sold Common Close plus another tenement in Penrose to his son, Nicholas. In 1727 both father and son are among the 16 signatories to Revd John Day's glebe terrier.

Nicholas's farm accounts are muddled and scarcely legible but we can pick out some of the things that occupied a yeoman in the mid-eighteenth century. He was farming Penrose Farm and part of Treginegar and for 'one half a yeare' the tithes cost him £3.8s.6d., in addition to which he paid altogether 11s.11d. church rate. Other payments had to be made in connection with his half of Trevengenow. Smaller taxes on goods had to be paid. The receipt for one of these is written in the account book:

Received of Mr Leverton the Sum of Fifteen Shillings being Composition money for making malt for his Family's Uses only one year pending midsummer 1742 He having only three heads in his Family as pro his Entry.

£0.15.0   Jno Singleton, Offr St Columb Dn.

The 'three heads' in Nicholas Leverton's family were himself and his wife and Cleare Docton, who had

Penrose village, c.1920. John Henry Lobb is standing by his horse. May Bate, from Trevisker in St Eval, is in the middle of the picture, and Winnie Lobb is sitting on the granite trough holding a little dog. Penrose farmhouse is just showing a corner, top right.

begun to serve an apprenticeship with him. Docton received board and lodging and '£1.15.0 for one yeare'. Other labour was employed by the day, for weeding, loosing [sic] of stones or pounding of apples.

Nicholas Leverton was one of the parish's wealthy farmers, as revealed by more domestic items in his accounts:

Paid for Silk frenge & to Tasels & making
Paid for 3 quarters and half quarter of Velvet
Paid for 3 quarters and half quarter of fine Silk
Paid Mrs Tanner for postage and Carrige of velvet & silk
Paid for the Shammi Skins and Silk & Thred

The total for these was £2.15s.10½d., and he then 'bought a Clock of Mr John Belling of Bodmin, £5.0.0.'

In 1736 it was his turn to disburse the church rate. These accounts are in the back of his farm ledger. It was his responsibility to purchase the Communion wine, candles and oil for the bells, and to pay for keeping the register. He also gave money to 'severall poor Destrised persons' (on several occasions) or to 'severall pore Travelors'. The largest sum went to 'ye Rector and Churchwardenes Dener 6sh'.

Nicholas Leverton of Penrose, gent., died in 1757. His widow placed an affectionate slate memorial in the churchyard but he was best remembered by the late Tom Sandry as builder of the west side of Penrose farmhouse. These rooms have high ceilings, wide doorways and a lovely staircase rising very gently two and a half inches at a time. The high spot is the moulded cob (clay) ceiling around the staircase and around three walls of the sitting-room. This fits a man whose signature is a great flourish across his account book.

Another farmer at Penrose, Thomas Stribley, has left a fuller account book (1795–1823), from which we can follow the farmer's calendar of work, although

sketchily, as these are the daily payments made for work done by casual labourers. Threshing wheat, barley or oats was done at most times of the year, as also was hedging, i.e. repairing and building up the earth and stone Cornish hedges enclosing the fields. Potatoes were set in April, in May the furze was cut, in June cabbage plants set, grass mown and dung turned, in July turfing, in August reaping and mowing barley and selling barley by the peck or bushel to individual purchasers, including his casual labourers, and to market, September binding and mowing barley, dressing the ground, October spinning ropes, November drawing potatoes, and December, January, February and March continuing with the threshing and hedging and making ropes, in the absence of seasonal tasks or when the main farm-work could be managed by the regular workforce.

Stribley was an overseer to the poor and responsible for drawing up a list of freeholders for the justices. His record of these duties are in his farm account book.

From the papers of a landowner such as Lord Arundell we see they had lands scattered in many different parts of Cornwall and several other counties. Deeds show that one farm or estate could be divided into plots of varying size, even as small as one field only, among several lessees. Also, an individual lessee or tenant farmed land scattered over the parish or in different parishes. We can readily agree with Worgan, writing on agriculture in Cornwall in 1811, that 'property is very much divided, subdivided and vexatiously intermixed...'

This is beautifully illustrated by R. Thomas's survey of Richard Binny's lands at Penrose in 1803 or 1809. The property of this one man was scattered across Penrose in six different places. Even fields making up one tenement, e.g. 'Roberts Tenement' (the name lingering on after that tenement had been tenanted by Francis Roberts and his son William) are not to be found in one block but in four different places. When he made his will in 1838 even he had difficulty defining all his lands:

All that my messuage or Dwelling House Malthouse and Premises in Lowertown And all that Orchard called the Quarry Orchard part of Eplett's Tenement And Also all that other Orchard called Hawke's Orchard And Also all that DwellingHouse and Garden parcels of Eplett's Tenement...

and later: 'All those my several Tenements by several names of Cadnor's Tenement Roberts Tenement and Hicks's Tenement all in the village and fields of Perrose.'

The eighteenth century was one of improvement, and it might seem that all was calm in the countryside of St Ervan, but religious dissension would once again interrupt the peace before the end of the century.

CHAPTER 3

Early Methodism

John Wesley, founder of Wesleyan Methodism, a movement for the deepening of spiritual life within the Church of England, first came to Cornwall in 1743. He preached to tin and copper miners and fishermen who all had one thing in common, grinding poverty relieved only by drunkenness. John Wesley made frequent visits to Cornwall – he went 21 times to St Ives, where men earned a scant living from mining or fishing – and his impact on those communities, which numbered thousands, was enormous. It was some years before meeting-places were licensed in less populated rural districts.

Methodism did not establish itself in the country areas around St Ervan without opposition. At Wadebridge gunpowder was placed under the doorstep of the meeting-place, and at St Breock the rector persuaded shopkeepers to adopt economic sanctions towards Methodists. This action was successful and there was still no Society there as late as 1784.

On 16 March 1798, the Bishop's Court in Exeter granted a licence registering for worship a room on the ground floor in a dwelling-house at the 'village of Treglinnick' in St Ervan. The application was signed by William Henwood, yeoman, the occupant who had leased the farm in 1787 for a term of 14 years, and by Thomas Cradock, Richard Wood, a Port Isaac preacher, Nicholas Sibley, a travelling preacher, and John Boyle, a Methodist minister in the St Austell circuit. It was the custom for influential Methodists to join in a new venture to help it off the ground.

In March 1804 Richard Trefry was travelling and preaching in the area, and recorded in his journal: 'March 12 preached at St Ervin from Hebs:11:5... we have a good prospect here'.

By 1812, when a list was drawn up of existing Methodist chapels, St Ervan was not among them. In 1820 Malachi Spear made his will in which he left:

... unto Ten Poor Widows in the parish of St Ervan the sum of 1s. per year each... to be paid yearly on 6th of July out of the Methodist Chaple situated in Rumford in the parish of St Ervan during the Lifes on the said Premises.

He was a man of material substance, but his slate headstone in the churchyard has a more pious note than most:

Sacred to the Memory of Malachi Spear of this Parish who yielded up his soul into the arms of his Merciful

Redeemer on the 20th day of May in the Year of our Lord 1820 Aged 81 Years.

The only other record of this early Wesleyan chapel is in Revd William Molesworth's answers to the Bishop of Exeter's pre-Visitation Queries of 1821: 'There is one licensed Meeting House belonging to the Wesleyan Methodists – and two private Houses frequented by the Bryanites, unlicensed.'

Wesleyanism was now well established in Cornwall. In 1831, about 90 years after John Wesley's first visit, when Bishop Phillpotts, newly arrived at Exeter, surveyed his diocese, he declared that Wesleyanism was the established religion of Cornwall. The reformatory nature of Victorian Methodism must be remembered. John Gilbart, banker, wrote in 1861:

The effects of Cornish Methodism in making the drunkard sober, the idle industrious, the profligate moral, and in inducing men to provide decently and comfortably for their families, and to give a suitable education to their children, can be attested by thousands of witness.

In 1830 the Wesleyans built a chapel by the bridge on the road that runs through the village of Rumford. The trustees were all substantial men in the community. They put up the money for the building. The land was usually purchased at a nominal price from a sympathiser, in this case Thomas Key of St Breock, yeoman.

All that spot or piece of Land or Ground at or near Rumford Bridge containing by admeasurement Thirty feet long and Twenty two feet wide with all the wastrel in front of the same bounded on the W and N by the River on the S by a House in occupation of Silvester Key on E by Rich. Brewer's Orchard together with ladder-room in the Garden for building or repairing any House or Building which may be erected on the Premises...

The trustees were Thomas Sandry (a St Issey cousin of the family living in St Ervan), Gregory Tom, the 50-year-old farmer at Trethewey, Malachi Spear, son of the Malachi who had died in 1820 and brother-in-law to the miller Richard Brewer, Robert Higman, a 40-year-old farmer at Penrose, Thomas Hawke and Francis Hellyar of St Eval, and Robert Bazeley of St Columb Major, yeoman.

It was in communities of related people, humble

Wesleyan chapel, Rumford, pre-1907. It was built in 1830.

for the most part, that Methodism became an ancestral faith. Those esteemed higher in the social scale, merchants, bankers, mine agents, yeoman farmers, blacksmiths and carpenters – in St Ervan's agricultural society Gregory Tom, Malachi Spear – were the natural leaders among them.

In his replies to the Bishop's Queries in 1821 the rector had also written that there were in the parish:

Some Wesleyan Methodists, also followers of Bryan – Bryanites. A class leader of each sect resides in the Parish, neither of them licensed. Two occasional preachers visit the Parish, one licensed, the other not.

In the same year the clergy of Devon and Cornwall reported Bible Christians active in ten Devon parishes, mostly around Shebbear, and in 30 Cornish parishes. William O'Bryan, born 1778, son of a surface miner and farmer, was a member of the Methodist Society, but he was a wayward and independent individual who wanted to preach in rural areas rather than to the miners and fishermen. His conduct resulted in his exclusion by the established Methodist church in 1810. In October 1815, while he was preaching at the home of John and Mary Thorne, Shebbear, North Devon, 22 members were enrolled in his class. Thus was founded the Bible Christian movement, 'taking the Bible as my Rule, and Christ for my Example.'

William O'Bryan penetrated the remoter rural areas where none had gone before, including St Mawgan, St Eval and St Mabyn. In 1820 St Ervan already appears as the head of a circuit in the Bible Christian Minutes of Conference, with two itinerant preachers, William Reed and Mary Ann Soper. This circuit covered an area encompassing Padstow, Wadebridge, Rosenannon, Whitemoor, St Dennis, Fraddon and St Mawgan. St Columb was the geographical centre but the fact that St Ervan was

chosen as the head of the circuit indicates that membership was stronger there.

The established and respectable Methodist church continued to flourish in St Ervan. However, a new vitality in religious experience was introduced into the parish in June 1818, when Bible Christian preacher Elizabeth Dart made her way across the moor from Camelford to preach. The Bible Christians became more charismatic in ethos than traditional Wesleyans, seeking to be open to the leading of the Holy Spirit and at the same time suspicious of His working through forms and ceremonies and church authority. Her visit was reported thus:

The Lord made bare his arm in the salvation of many. No sooner did one of the first persons set at liberty begin to pray in his family than his wife cried for mercy, and in less than half-an-hour was rejoicing in a sin-pardoning God.

A few weeks later the evangelist found the people 'hungering and thirsting for the bread and water of life.'

Elizabeth Dart's biographer, F.W. Bourne, describes her as possessing 'a transparent simplicity of character, a quaintness of manner, and a power of sympathy.' What a contrast to the typical Victorian parsons, sons of landed gentry and university educated. It appealed to Richard Brewer, miller, who was undoubtedly one of the first persons 'set at liberty', and his wife Ebbett, daughter of Malachi Spear, both already practising Wesleyan Methodists.

Elizabeth Dart's preaching had more vitality in it, and more saving power, than had all the refined and critical teaching of men with LlB, BA or MA after their names. By 1820 Richard Brewer was leading a Bible Christian class (meeting) at Rumford and it was in one of his fields near the mill at Rumford that a small hut served as their first chapel. The Bible Christian movement, new and vibrant, made its greatest impact on those lower down the social scale: Richard Brewer, miller and shopkeeper, the first to accept the new power, became leader, to be joined by smallholders, shoemakers and agricultural labourers. He was a typical Bible Christian leader. He was rooted in the parish, being at least the fifth generation of Brewers in the St Ervan records. He was of the people and lived and worked among them. It is probable that he was already living at Millingworth mills in 1818 when Elizabeth Dart came to preach and he and Ebbett were converted – he was at that time approaching his fortieth birthday – so once again the Anglican clergyman in the rectory next door had to endure dissent right on his own doorstep. In the seventeenth century it had been tenants of the Roman Catholic Arundells who occupied land to the east of the rectory – the so-called 'popish recusants'.

Elizabeth Dart preached in St Ervan in 1818. The

Bible Christians, concentrating on rural areas, among small farmers and agricultural labourers, found their leaders among the middle class of that society, the craftsmen. By 1820 Richard Brewer was the established leader of the class at Rumford in St Ervan, at the spiritual centre of the St Ervan Bible Christian Circuit, and in the following years the Bible Christians went from strength to strength. In 1826 the St Ervan Circuit enjoyed 'great increases'. This did not take place without opposition. There was strong disapproval of the noisy behaviour of some of the more eccentric followers of William O'Bryan. A report in *The West Briton* of 5 October 1827 tells us:

BRIANITES – For some weeks past the town of St Columb has been disturbed by frequent assemblies of Brianites, in a room over the market-place. What with the ravings and shrieks of the preachers and their disciples within, and the shouts and laughter of the crowds without, the place has been a perfect Babel, and a complete stop has been put to the comfort and repose of the more rational inhabitants of the neighbourhood.

In 1834, the St Ervan Circuit was 'specially favoured with revival influence and power'. Revivals were occasions of conversions on the grand scale, in a highly charged atmosphere of intense religious feeling. In 1835 the Circuit added 223 persons to its membership. A year later William Courtice wrote from St Ervan: 'The Lord is working gloriously in many places in this Circuit; sinners are crying for mercy and we are expecting a larger outpouring of the Holy Spirit.'

Then, in 1839, the Rumford class suffered a personal tragedy. On 18 September 1839, James Rundle senr died. The Rundle family farmed Roscullion, across the parish boundary in Little Petherick parish. Their fields adjoined those of Trethewey. The Rundles were from St Eval but James Rundle senr was born at Penrose in St Ervan parish, where his father farmed for a time. At the age of 26 he married Betsy Paynter and took his own small farm, Roscullion. His Memoir in the *Bible Christian Magazine* of 1839, written by Francis Bullock, a relative, tells us much about his life and personality, and gives an insight into the life of the Bible Christians in and around Rumford at the time.

He was a regular attendant at the parish church, and constrained his family to do likewise.... he not only read the word of God at home, and heard it preached at the parish church; but he also went to hear the Methodists... After some time, the Bible Christians coming into the neighbourhood he attended to hear them... In 1822, he began in earnest to seek the Lord, and soon found what his soul longed after. He joined himself to the Bible Christians and very soon after he obtained the pardon of all his sins. Then he was able to rejoice in God his

Saviour... In 1826, he was appointed to lead a small class at Highlanes in Little Petherick about half a mile from his house.

When the Highlanes class in 1832 was broken up by disruptive elements, James Rundle returned to his old Society that he first met with at Rumford and was joyfully received by brother Brewer, his first Leader. In May 1839 he was taken ill of an inflammation of the lungs, with an enlargement of the liver, and died on 18 September 1839 aged 53, leaving a wife and 14 children.

James Rundle's son wrote:

I believe my Father was free from worldly anxiety: for the things of the world by no means interrupted his mind; and unless absolutely necessary, he did not converse about worldly matters... He could commit us [family] to the Lord; and I doubt not he felt the assurance that the Lord would keep what he had committed to His trust.

Five of the children were members of the Bible Christian Connexion, and one, the eldest, James, became a zealous local preacher in the St Ervan Circuit. Eleven of the children were lifelong teetotallers.

But in September 1842 James became ill. The doctor thought at first he had water on the brain, but it was soon declared to be typhus fever. Typhus was a most unpleasant and painful infection, resulting in high fever, delirium and hallucination. The infection could be carried by rats, and since these were present on any farm and at the corn mill near the Bible Christian meeting-place in Rumford, even people leading an open-air life could be struck down by it. He died on Friday, 23 September 1842, aged 28.

On Sunday morning, the 25 September his remains were conveyed to St Eval church yard [the family burying ground]... I never recollect seeing so large a funeral procession, in so thinly populated a neighbourhood... The parish church was filled to over-flowing, and many could not gain admittance.

Allowing for the subjective extravagance of the writer, and remembering the funeral was on a Sunday, the one day of freedom from work, this gives a good idea of the large number of Bible Christians and other Methodists in the area. Though they had mostly ceased by now to attend their Parish Church in addition to their own chapels, the Parish Churchyard was the only burial-ground available.

According to Methodist historian J.C.C. Probert, there was:

... a Methodist custom going back to John Wesley's day of giving a funeral oration on the dead person and using it as a moral example so that others might see what God had done for them and follow their example.

Young James Rundle was given one funeral oration by the writer of his Memoir on the following Sabbath, and a second one by another preacher the next Sunday. He preached from the text: 'Be ye therefore also ready' to a large and attentive congregation. What added to the solemnity of the funeral tale was the announcement by the preacher of the death of Sarah, sister of the deceased, who had died that morning, just six weeks short of her seventeenth birthday.

Her father's cousin, Francis Bullock, wrote an account of her short life:

From a child she was brought to read and understand the scriptures, and took great delight in reading religious books. She also regularly attended both the Methodist and Bible Christian preaching, and the word preached was not in vain... In January, 1841, she attended the public means of grace in the St Ervan Chapel... the spirit of God arrested the congregation; seven were constrained to cry aloud for mercy... her cries were truly affecting, and there was every mark of sincerity. 'Her chains fell off, her soul was free' for her sins were all forgiven, and she could now rejoice.

This brief extract gives a vivid picture of the people who found joy in a religious discipline having come to God through a conviction of sin, prayer and

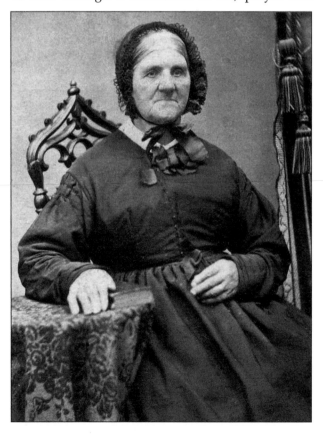

Betsy Rundle (née Paynter, 1790–1878), in 1869 at Platteville, Wisconsin, USA. She and 11 of her 14 children emigrated to America after the death of her husband, James Rundle.

receptiveness, and who lived their faith positively and fervently. They discussed their relationship with Christ and their growth in spiritual life without inhibition or false modesty. They supported each other, visiting sick neighbours daily, a Wesleyan sitting all night and praying with a dying Bible Christian. They spent long hours in prayer with each other and for each other. They rejoiced at the conversion, or 'new birth', of another.

The three deaths in the Rundle family, of James the father, whom he had known so well in his own classes at Rumford, then of the young James, whose first preachings he had doubtless heard, whom perhaps he had even advised and helped in memory of his father, then Sarah, whose 'conversion' had taken place at Rumford and which he had possibly witnessed, were all bitter blows for Richard Brewer and, coming so swiftly upon one another, must have severely tested his faith.

In 1853 several of the surviving Rundle children sailed with their widowed mother from Padstow via Quebec to settle as farmers in Wisconsin. (Two other deaths from typhus occurred mid-nineteenth century in St Ervan – Richard Tippett, son of William of Penrose, was buried on 12 July 1843 aged 14, and James Ball, 33-year-old farmer at Trevilledor, died of typhus fever on 15 February 1853.)

Richard Brewer's third son, also Richard, aged 33, in July 1841, married Jane Tom, daughter of Gregory Tom, sheep farmer at Trethewey, a Methodist and trustee of the Wesleyan chapel at Rumford. They had two sons, William, born 1842, and Gregory, born 1844, and Jane was pregnant with their third child when Richard became another victim of typhus. He had been running the mill at Rumford for his father and it is possible that the disease came to him from the mites harboured by the rats. The records trace the tragic course of events. The miller's account book was being kept by Richard junr – the last entry is dated 2 May 1845. Richard was buried, aged 38, on 30 June 1845. Their third child, Mary, was born 27 July 1845.

The overall fervour, ardour, zeal and enthusiasm of the Bible Christians, whose lives were infused by the light of faith, resulted in 1844 in the building of a chapel to replace the hut in Richard Brewer's field. This was only 14 years after the Wesleyans had built a new chapel in Rumford, for a total population of 477 people. Methodism, both the Wesleyan and the Bible Christian varieties, was very strong and one might well ask what the Anglican Church was up to at this time. The Established Church, descended into complacency, could not satisfy the spiritual zeal and passion of these people. In St Ervan's Parish Church, the young curates supplied by the rector, Revd William Molesworth, to look after his parish while he resided at St Breock, had no doubt done their best to serve the people well. They had the disadvantage of not being of the people, and they provided only one service each Sunday of which the formality inhibited expression of feeling. Children were catechised, but adults were treated to abstruse academic theological dissertations. There was no opportunity for the lower classes to open up their hearts and discuss matters spiritual. Indeed, if the Revd William Polwhele (curate 1834–41) had followed the guidance of his father, the historian, on the composing of homilies, he would have delivered a finely polished piece of profound theology. At least there was no sectarian bitterness. The Methodists simply felt disappointment with the Church of England for its neglect of their spiritual hunger and did not go so far as to refuse Church Rates.

The rector of St Ervan, from his parsonage at St Breock, of which he was also rector and where he resided, knew very well what was happening in the parish. When his eldest son, Hugh Henry, had been received into Holy Orders in 1842, he was immediately put in charge of the parish as resident curate. He was a young bachelor aged 24 and a breath of fresh air. From that moment on, enthusiasm and activity in the Parish Church equalled that of the Dissenters. He was local in the sense of having been born at St Breock, although educated at Eton and with a BA degree from Cambridge University and destined to become the 9th Baronet in the Pencarrow family in succession to his cousin in 1855. Immediately on arrival he recorded in an exercise book that: 'The St Ervan Sunday School was begun November 1842.'

In the parish register he wrote: 'Planted a yew tree in the Churchyard Dec 1842. Hugh Henry Molesworth, Curate', and was honest enough to add: 'which died 1846'.

His Sunday school fared better. Vestry account records show the existence of a Sunday school in 1821 and again in 1833, though with only 16 children compared with 61 children receiving some sort of schooling in the three day schools, all at their parents' expense. Revd Hugh Molesworth brought changes. He started his Sunday school with two assistants, signing the announcement of its commencement thus:

Hugh Molesworth   Curate
The Clark   Assistants
Prudy Lobb

– a telling indication of the social niceties, even in a small parish of only 470 people. The curate is a young man and Prudy, a matron of 53 years, wife of Henry Lobb, carpenter, and mother of five children, ran a dame-school. When her pupils were outside playing she swung a donkey shoe suspended on a string like a pendulum. When it stopped swinging it was time for the children to come in.

Hugh Molesworth's first Sunday-school book in St Ervan records a strong start, 70 boys and girls, aged between 3 and 12 years; two divisions for boys,

two for girls, and the move to the higher division was generally made at the age of nine. It would be interesting to know how the Anglican curate persuaded 70 children from such a strongly Methodist parish to attend his Sunday school from the first Sunday of his residence in St Ervan, achieving a huge jump from only 16 Sunday-school pupils just ten years before. Of 15 farmers with children in the appropriate age group, only four did not send their children, and of 28 agricultural labourers, only seven kept their children away. The carpenter Thomas Brewer, second son of the miller and a named trustee on the 1844 Bible Christian Chapel Trust Deed, had three children, a two-year-old and Jane (8) and Maryann (6), who both attended the Sunday school regularly. Notable Wesleyans attending were Joseph, Jane and Samuel Higman, children of a farmer at Penrose and related to the Higmans of Roche, who provided a President of the Methodist Conference. Their elder brother, William, became a local Methodist preacher a few years later.

There were two sessions each Sunday, recorded in the Attendance Book:

Order
Reading the Text in the Morning
Cathechism heard and explained in the Afternoon.

In the Sunday school of the 1840s, under Hugh Henry, the children learned the Catechism. By adding a morning reading (probably 'reading round' by rote) the curate not only reinforced the lesson, but also demonstrated how the Church had come to add reading to make elementary education for the poor. By December 1844, when this register finishes, the number of children attending had risen to 84.

Every Sunday school had its annual tea-treat:

June 29th 1843
Had my Sunday School treat
72 children present
Distributed prizes. Prayer books & Testaments &c.
Prudy and Henry Lobb, Jinny Hicks, Thaby and John Green partook of tea also.

Former Bible Christian chapel, Rumford.

See how this young curate gets everyone involved, Prudy was joined by her carpenter husband, Henry, by Jinny Hicks, widow in her late fifties of the former sexton, and by John Green, who was the other assistant with Prudy. He lived at Churchtown and his signature is often found as a witness in the marriage register.

Hugh Henry writes personal comments about some of the pupils in his register, but in French, such as 'tres bon', 'tres bonne et belle', 'sanguissant mais bien intentionne', 'un garçon tres vivant', and of William Vivian, who obviously proved difficult, 'Arcades ambo!'.

The Sunday-school register, with its record of activity and personal comments in Hugh Henry's hand, identifies him as a young man not merely filling a post procured for him by his family so that he could benefit from the living and not be a financial burden on them, but serious in his vocation, enjoying his faith in God and enthusiastically spreading the word to all his parishioners. After Revd Hugh Henry Molesworth left the parish of St Ervan in 1847, never again would the number of children attending school, day school or Sunday school, reach such dizzy heights.

His influence on the weekday schooling of the parish children had been just as powerful. In 1846, in answer to the General Inquiry of the National Society, the reply showed the combined total of children attending two day schools was 90, which must represent a high proportion of the total number of eligible children in the population. His personality clearly united vigour with amiability, by which he was able to achieve so much in such a short time in a parish already given over to Methodism in one form or another. At his death the *Western Journal* described him thus: 'By the urbanity of his manners, and by his readiness to assist in every good work, he had endeared himself to a very large number of persons of all classes.'

From St Ervan he removed to Little Petherick parish as curate under his father Sir William, the rector, and succeeded to the baronetcy in 1855, but in 1862, at the age of 44, he succumbed to the Pencarrow Molesworths' affliction of early mortality.

It is a good moment to take stock of the parish.

We have seen how, with Hugh Molesworth's departure, the enthusiasm for Sunday-school attendance and even daily schooling faded. The ecclesiastical census of 1851 is revealing. All the force of Hugh Molesworth's personality had not stopped the tidal wave of Wesleyan and Bible Christian Methodism in the parish. The emotional and spiritual satisfaction provided by these churches was not

to be deplored, for they had served to turn many away from drunkenness and other destructive behaviour. The Bishop of Exeter had recognised that Methodism was 'the established church in Cornwall' now, but at the same time he must have been disappointed that Hugh Molesworth's work in the improvement of attendance at the Parish Church failed entirely to be maintained by any subsequent curate. In a church with 300 sittings, only 92 people attended the afternoon service on Sunday, 30 March 1851, whereas 120 went to the Bible Christian chapel that evening (over 26 per cent of the population). In the morning there were two services in St Ervan, one at the Parish Church and one at the Wesleyan chapel. A total of 19 went to church, 30 to chapel, and perhaps others were at prayer- or class-meeting in the Bible Christian chapel, also held in the morning. In addition to the Sunday service, nearly every chapel in the St Ervan Bible Christian Circuit had a service with a preacher on one weekday.

The Bible Christian return to the Ecclesiastical Census was signed by Richard Brewer Elder. Aged 71, he was now living at Churchtown with his wife Ebbett, 70, their daughter Rachel, 28, 10-year-old grandson Richard and a granddaughter, 18-year-old Jane. Also living in the house was 22-year-old John Higman from Penrose, wagoner, who married Jane in September. In December Rachel married Robert Higman, miller, and went to live in St Columb at Killiworgie Mills. The Higmans were farmers, millers and Methodists. A sister, Maria, married James Ball and their son, William, born in 1851, was a future Methodist minister.

Richard Brewer had left the running of the mills at Rumford to his eldest son, John (who technically had inherited the lease from his Uncle, Edward Spear), together with brother, William. Brother Edward, with his wife and six children, had moved to Churchtown. A third family living in Churchtown was Ebbett Brewer's nephew, the Methodist Thomas Spear, with six children, and James Key, the innkeeper, who was the son of a Methodist. There was only one other house in that corner of the parish, occupied by William Bennett, a groom, and his young family. Almost every one of the curate's immediate neighbours was a prominent Dissenter.

The fact that Brewer was the name of the zealous Bible Christian leader, and Brewer was the name held by 10 per cent of the parish population must have been an irritation to the curate. Worse still, as shown by the 1851 Ecclesiastical Census, one-third of the parish attended the two Methodist chapels, a far higher percentage than the regular congregation of his Parish Church.

✤ CHAPTER 4 ✤
Landowners and Tenant Farmers

In the early 1800s the principal landowners were all non-resident owners of large estates in Cornwall and beyond:

Lord Arundell	*Sir John Morshead Bart.*
Mr Prideaux	*Sir Arscott-Ourry Molesworth Bart*
John Phillips Gent.	*Henry Peter Esq.*
Mrs Esther Day	*Sir Christopher Hawkins*
Geo B Collins Esq.	*John Hicks Gent.*

By 1842 the Tithe Award shows that Francis Cross of Crediton, who had bought the last remaining Arundell lands in 1802, had become by far the biggest landowner in the parish, having acquired 740 of the parish's 3,200 acres, comprising the Trembleath estates, which included lands at Penrose and Churchtown and Trevengenow. John Paynter Esq., of the St Columb family of lawyers, owned 463 acres, Treleigh and Bogee. Treleigh was farmed for his own profit and Francis Paynter occupied the barton farm of Bogee. Thomas Tremain owned all Treginegar, totalling 292 acres. Sir William Molesworth, the eighth baronet, still one of the biggest landowners, owned Treburrick's 204 acres. George Wightman Esq., living in Truro, owned Trenouth's 192 acres, and Francis Hearle Esq., living at Mawnan in south Cornwall, owned 155 acres at Treravel. Mary Werry owned Treglinnick's 150 acres. The last of the non-resident major landowners was the rector, Revd William Molesworth, living at St Breock, who owned the 78 acres of glebe land and the three acres adjoining the rectory in Churchtown which were farmed by his curate.

Thus in the mid-nineteenth century, of 3,200 acres, 2,274 were still owned by non-resident landowners,

Side view of 1827 farmhouse at Trewinnick.

leaving just under 1,000 for the smaller landowners who lived in the parish.

Jonathan Bennett owned the freehold of Trewinnick barton farm (108 acres), where he lived. Most of the remaining Trewinnick manor lands were owned and farmed by members of the Key family. Gregory Tom owned 66 acres at Trethewey and farmed a further 28 acres elsewhere. Richard Binny at Penrose owned 43 acres, which he farmed with his brother, John.

When landownership and the patronage of the church were so intimately linked (in 1842 Sir William Molesworth of Pencarrow in Little Petherick held the title of Pawton manor together with Trevose and Ide manors, which between them embraced all the land in St Ervan parish, his cousin, Revd William Molesworth, was the rector, and the rector's son, Hugh Henry Molesworth, was the curate) the rector, or the curate as his representative, occupied the top position in the social hierarchy within the parish, especially in the absence of a mansion and squire. Those who will play the most significant part in our story are not the non-resident landowners but tenant farmers leasing the bigger farms and resident landowners of small farms. They lived, worked and employed labourers in the parish. They were obliged, in proportion to their tenancy, to play a major part in the government of local affairs. As major ratepayers, it was their money that was being spent on the poor, on keeping law and order, on keeping the parish roads in repair. By reason of their wealth they had the power, indeed the duty, to run the parish, to decide the annual rates (subject to the law and agreement of the justices) and how they should be spent.

The names of the men who farmed Trembleath, Trevengenow, Trewinnick, Bogee, Trenouth, Treravel, Treleigh, Treglinnick, Treburrick, Treginegar and Penrose Farm appear in the lists of 'principal inhabitants' who sign important documents, such as the glebe terrier requested by the Bishop of Exeter in 1821. This recorded in detail the church, church furnishings and fees, the extent of the parsonage and the lands belonging to the church. It was the same men who filled the offices of overseer to the poor, assessor, constable and waywarden, who signed the minutes of the annual general meeting of the Vestry, who in effect were the local government of the parish. The names Bennett, Biddick, Binny, Brewer, Hawke, Hawken, Key, Old, Poyner or Rowe, Sandry and Tom dominate the records of the government of

Trenouth farmhouse.

parish life through the nineteenth century.

The men who signed the 1821 glebe terrier were headed by a young man, George Biddick, one of two churchwardens. One of the wealthiest men in the parish, he farmed Trenouth's 192 acres plus 155 acres at Treravel, where he lived.

As well as a churchwarden, George was for several years one of the two constables. In 1837, when the Board of Guardians of St Columb Union, which took over responsibility for the poor from the parish Vestry, was formed (the Union was an amalgamation of 16 parishes under one Board of Guardians), George Biddick was the first 'Guardian' representing St Ervan. His eldest son, George, born in 1820, carried on the tradition, acting as overseer to the poor, even acting occasionally as chairman of the annual general meeting of the Vestry when Revd Barton was rector. As occupier of 342 acres altogether, he was a major ratepayer and as such headed the parish upper class.

At first Richard Williams, George senr's wife Ann's kinsman, farmed their other farm, Trenouth, though her eldest son, George, was the tenant until 1845, when George junr took the lease of its 195 acres of 'very good land' for a 14-year term at a yearly rent of £150. By 1851 Trenouth was farmed by George senr's fourth son, William, now married and with a small child, and employing four men and two women. Two of the labourers and one female servant lived in with the family in the 'commodious farmhouse'.

The second eldest son, Matthew, went out to Queensland, Australia, where he died in 1868 at the age of 46.

Though there is a Biddick family farming Treravel in 2006, there has been a long interruption in the continuity of the name in St Ervan. George and Ann's eldest son, George, married and had two children in Feock in 1860 and 1863. His brother Matthew's son, also George, born at Little Petherick in 1843, married a Fowey woman, Thirza Jacobs, and their two children, George and Mary Jane, were born at Polruan in Fowey parish in 1868 and 1871. This George had a son George, born in 1904 at the Ship Hotel, Polperro. In the meantime, Treravel was farmed by a Sandry family. We still do not know how George Biddick, born 1904 in Polperro, and Ruth Rundle Sandry, born 1911 at Treravel, met and married and established the name of Biddick once again in St Ervan parish.

The second churchwarden signing the 1821 document was a much older man, 72-year-old William Hawken. The Hawken family is interesting because it swept into such a dominant position as yeomen farmers at the beginning of the nineteenth century, was so prominent in the Vestry (no fewer than three James Hawkens among the six signatories at the Annual Vestry Meeting in 1863) and yet had completely disappeared from the parish by the end of the same century.

There was John Hawken at Treginegar, James at Treginegar Mill, Joseph at Treburrick and two more Hawken brothers farming the glebe lands. In addition, members of the Hawken family owned one property of 33 acres at Penrose, another of 27 acres there, and 14 acres at Rosa Parks, alongside Rumford village. Their widowed sister, Mary Key, leased Treglinnick's 150 acres. This generation of Hawkens had made a clean sweep of land occupancy across the north of the parish.

Also in St Ervan was a kinsman, John Hawken, miller at the Trewinnick manorial mill in Rumford, who met an unfortunate end. The *Exeter Flying Post* of 12 January 1792 reported: 'John Hawken, miller of St Ervan, slipped when pulling out the plug from the millpool, fell in and was drowned.' His body was returned to his root parish, St Merryn, for burial.

William Hawken, churchwarden, was a butcher but owned a little land near Rumford and leased the five-acre Treginegar Mills tenement.

Those five leasehold acres were the beginning. They gave him a toe-hold in the fertile northern land in the parish and his sons took full advantage. The youngest, Thomas, farmed 100 acres in St Issey, but Joseph, James, William and John stayed to make their mark in St Ervan. In 1832, of the 23 men who signed an 'agreement to prosecute felons', four were the Hawken brothers, and throughout the Vestry records they are seen playing a full part over many years because of their occupation of land. By 1841 the four brothers occupied between them a great part of Penrose, all Treginegar, a great part of Churchtown, Treburrick and Four Turnings and Rosa Parks; their sister, Mary Key, was at Treglinnick, and their younger sister, Ann, married another member of the Key family who farmed Trewinnick, making a great sweep across the north of the parish, occupying between them over 700 acres of it. By 1841 there were seven households containing 31 people named Hawken. In 1844 James added further to the Hawken grasp on land in St Ervan by purchasing two freehold lots, four acres and eight acres, being sold at auction by John and Stephen Binny at Penrose, for which he paid £740.

In 1845 John, the tenant of Treginegar, took the lease for a seven-year term from the landowner Thomas Tremain, of Brabyn's Tenement (Great Treginegar – 146 acres previously occupied by a Mr Brabyn, whose very smart table grave is in the churchyard), at a yearly rent of £110 and also Martyn's and Peter's Treginegar for a further yearly rent of £300.

By 1851 William had died. The three remaining brothers were Joseph, 73 years, farming 150 acres with his son James and employing five men and two women, his son Joseph junr farming his own 55 acres at Penrose and employing two labourers; James, 72 years, farming Penrose and employing three labourers and his nephew James (William's son); John, 63 years, farming Treginegar with his son James and employing eight men, two women and a boy. The other sons of the deceased William were carrying on the butcher tradition, William at Penrose and Samuel at Churchtown, where he was also landlord of the Churchtown Inn. Both also rented three or four acres of land at about £2 per acre per annum.

In 1855 and 1859 the two elder brothers, James and Joseph, died. The eldest, Joseph, who had seven surviving children out of 11 births, had bought some freeholds at Penrose. His son, James, continued farming at Treburrick and inherited the residue of his father's estate, after a couple of other bequests. To his married daughters, Ann Old, Mary Paynter, Maria Old, Elizabeth Key and Kitty Paynter, Joseph bequeathed £19.10s. each, but to his youngest daughter, Fanny, who was married to John Hawke (son of Philip Hawke of Trevengenow), he left £45. Fanny's husband was Philip Hawke's eldest son, but he had not risen above 'agricultural labourer' by the 1851 census so her brothers were looking after her. Joseph Hawken also left £15 to each of his daughter Sarah's four children, payable when they reached the age of 21. Sarah died while they were infants.

James Hawken senr was married but had remained childless, which possibly explains how he managed to leave 'effects under £600'. In James Hawken we find wealth comparable to that of George Biddick, who died in 1819. Neither had children.

The only brother of this Hawken generation not to leave a will was William, who farmed only a few acres at Rumford Four Turnings.

Let us look again at the founder Hawken brothers, Joseph, James, William and John, and some of their descendants.

Joseph Hawken (1777–1859). His sons were successful farmers. An unfortunate grandson, James,

spent a hot July day mowing hay with a scythe, then took a dip in the mill pool to cool off. The water was icy cold, he caught pneumonia and died within three days. His mother was heartbroken, never smiled again and died the following April.

James Hawken (1779–1857) had no children and left a fortune.

William Hawken (1784–1845) left nothing of value, but he had started with the smallest farm and had the biggest family, 12 children. His eldest son, William (1811–90), married Sarah, daughter of Joseph, and they had four children when Sarah died. William then married Mary Ann Knight, who had a daughter, Jane. William and Mary Ann had nine more children. Through these have passed down to us tales of their father, who carried on the tradition of butcher in the Hawken family and was also a cattle dealer, and could tell the weight of a beast by running his hand over its back. Drink was his weakness – his horse found its own way home from market with his master slung across his back. Fortunately for the family, Mary Ann had acquired enough education to help in the school and was also a hardworking and clever seamstress. She often went to Tywardreath, her birthplace, to work as a sewing mistress. She had a gift for treating sick animals. By William's death in 1890 his sons had had enough of the difficult life in agriculture, and all moved away to London, taking their mother with them. By 1901 her daughter Jane had married Alfred Osborn, saddler, from St Columb. Living with them were Mary Ann, 63, working as a monthly nurse, Harry 21, working as a salesman in fancy goods, and Ernest, 19, working as a saddler with Alfred.

William's third son, James (born 1826), was the executor and residual legatee of his wealthy but childless uncle James's will of 1858. It seems that James shared his brother's liking for the beer, and soon became bankrupt. In 1880 (he was 54 years old) his 50 acres of land at Penrose were put up for auction. His cousin, James Hawken, a successful auctioneer,

Top: *Samuel James 'Jim' Hawken (born 1868) a big man, he stood no nonsense from his drunken father (1811–90).*

Above: *Bible Christian minister Revd William Hawken, born 1819, son of yeoman farmer John and Martha Hawken at Treginegar, St Ervan, died 1903 Devonport, Devon. 'Wherever he was he would always make himself felt; he was that kind of man – an irrepressible man – because he had one great passion and that was to save and win souls.'*

Pentruse farmhouse, c.1922, just after Albert Henry Key and wife Anna (née Old) moved in. The farmhouse was built c.1870 by James Hawken, auctioneer, when he made this part of Trenouth Farm land into a separate farm.

Pentruse Cottage in the twentieth century. In the 1870s it became the lodge to Pentruse Farm.

Late 1800s farm buildings at Pentruse – shippen with loft and adjoining hen house and pigeon loft.

divided the land into 13 lots. The auction was held at the Lowertown Inn, and the idea was to give the potential buyers a good dinner with plenty to drink first. If the prices pencilled in on the copy of the sale poster by the late John Henry Lobb are what was paid, James Hawken earned £3,245 for his 50 acres, which at £60 per acre was about the price his uncle had paid for some of the same fields when he had bought them 36 years before. The family removed to St Merryn, where his three sons farmed very successfully.

John Hawken (born 1788) disappears from St Ervan after 1851. His eldest son, William, directed his energies to leadership in the spiritual field as a Bible Christian minister. He died in 1903 in Devon. A funeral tribute declared: 'Wherever he was he would always make himself felt; he was that kind – an irrepressible man – because he had one great passion and that was to save and win souls.'

John's second son, James (1828–1900), managed Treginegar for him until he married in 1857. He was especially successful. By 1861 he was farming

Trenouth's 192 acres and by 1871 he had built the farmhouse and outbuildings at Pentruse. The rest of Trenouth land was farmed by a kinsman, Henry Hawken, from St Merryn. James was also a successful auctioneer. He died at Pentruse in 1900 aged 70, having served many years as manager of the School Board. His eldest son, Alfred James Grigg Hawken, gained his Master of Arts degree at Oxford University.

All these Hawken sons (except the cattle dealer) and grandsons (except the Bible Christian minister), even the drunken James of Penrose, occupied land, therefore paid rates, therefore filled posts in the Vestry and played a part in the parish government. Indeed, no other single family name occurs so frequently in the nineteenth-century Vestry records, a Hawken occupying at least one, if not two or three of the four official posts each year. In 1861, out of a total population of 437, there were 42 people named Hawken, nearly 10 per cent of the population. Thereafter their numbers within the parish of St Ervan declined.

After the churchwardens, the next 'principal inhabitant' to sign the 1821 documents was John Hawke of Trevengenow (120 acres). He died aged 84 in 1830. He was a man of substance. Apart from a money bequest, he left to his daughter Joan: 'such one of my Beds properly furnished as she shall make choice of, except the Bed in the parlour Chamber, and my Chest of Drawers.'

One daughter married into the Key family, another wed Gregory Tom of Trethewey; John's seventh child and younger son, Philip, born in 1793, was to be his heir, and the executor of his will.

John was a churchwarden in 1805. His daughter Elizabeth married staunch Methodist Gregory Tom that same year, and two of his grandsons, i.e. Philip's sons, George and Robert, married daughters of the Methodist families of Higman and Spear respectively, and James married Philippa Brewer, granddaughter of miller and Bible Christian leader Richard Brewer. Philip, however, continued as churchwarden and as tenant at Trevengenow. In 1851 his household included 13 persons.

Philip played his part in the Vestry over the years, and was churchwarden from 1851 to 1856, after which there is a gap until his second son, Philip, a bachelor, appears among those signing the minutes of the annual general meeting. None of Philip's other sons ever took part, since none became an independent farmer. We know from the Trembleath sale particulars of 1855 that Philip Hawke senr rented Trevengenow and other land on short leases, all due to expire at Michaelmas 1858. His sons remained agricultural labourers.

The eldest, John, who married Fanny Hawken, and who might have been expected to follow his father, became instead 'engine driver to a threshing machine', a position which carried real status in the nineteenth century but gave him no investment in land. John and Fanny had nine children, including James, born 1847, who became a devoted Bible Christian, and George, born 1858, who became a shopkeeper at Penrose. He died aged 91 in 1949, and was buried in the Nonconformist cemetery. These were known as the Penrose Hawkes.

Philip senr did not renew the lease on Trevengenow. His health was failing and his sight was going. He died in 1872 aged 79 at Bogee, where he lived with his son James and family.

The Hawke family had entered St Ervan in the mid-eighteenth century and until the mid-nineteenth century was among the wealthiest tenant farming yeomen families in the parish. Those who did not die in infancy often lived to a good old age, and their numbers increased, but their wealth diminished and they rejoined the ranks of the agricultural labourers. The St Ervan Hawke line continued into the twentieth century but then died out through lack of male issue. Miss Mary Gwendoline 'Gwenny' Hawke was the end of that line. She was born and lived all her life in the tiny cottage built by Peter Sandry on the side of Rumford House. She died in 1997 aged 84.

The next principal inhabitant's signature in 1821 was that of 75-year-old Silvester Key. Silvester and his wife Susanna had 11 children. Their fourth son, Nicholas, married Mary Hawken, sister of the older generation of Hawken brothers, but died 12 years later aged only 36, leaving Mary with five daughters and a son, Silvester, aged 6 years. His will, made five weeks before he died, left his estate to his father to look after Mary and their son until Silvester reached 21, when they would share it equally: 'provided my said wife Mary Key lives single but if she marry again One Shilling only in Money and the Bed which was formerly hers...'

Nicholas Key's surviving brothers increased their land holdings bit by bit until between them they owned or occupied most of Trewinnick manor and almost two-thirds of the common on Bear's Downs. Of the brothers who were active and resident in the parish in the 1820s, it seems that Thomas, born 1774, needed help from Silvester and James. The land they occupied at Trewinnick abutted on to the farmhouse of Trevengenow and in the corner made by a bend in the road on the north side of the farmhouse they

Albert Henry and Anna Key with one of their beloved dogs at Pentruse Farm, c.1935.

Kathleen Key with pony and trap at Pentruse, c.1930.

left bequests totalling £775, which included money for the 'education and maintenance of her present Son' to a widowed sister-in-law, and: 'to my kinswoman Ann Gill who now lives with me, £105, together with the Bed she sleeps on, fully furnished, and my best set of China Ware.'

James Old, who was 79 when he died in 1840 at Treleigh, leaving over £400, stated in his will:

If it should happen at any time that my Wife cannot live comfortably with my Executor that he my Executor [their youngest son, William, farming Treleigh] shall provide her a House to live in during her life at his own expense [i.e. not out of her annuity].

And if my Wife shall be under the necessity to go from my Executor to live I give to her the Bed and Bedding on which we now sleep and one other turn up Bed and Bedding which she may chuse. And such other Articles of household furniture as she shall stand in need of.

carved out New House Tenement. The sale deed from Silvester to Thomas was dated 18 January 1825:

... contracted for sale to said Thomas Key for the sum of £35... ALL that New built Cottage or Dwellinghouse and Garden and two Closes of Land containing altogether about One acre adjoining the high road lately built and inclosed on a Wastrel belonging to Loveys Tenement in Trewinnick... now in occupation of said Thomas Key together with waters and watercourses, pasture and turbary...

The cottage was two up, two down, built of stone. Thomas and his wife brought up their daughter and two sons there.

The 'pasture and turbary' rights on the common might seem a nonsense for such a tiny property but would prove valuable in 1839 when Thomas, now described as a labourer, was allocated a strip of about an acre in Well Park as his share following enclosure of Trewinnick common. By this time he had also converted the wastrel by his house into 'garden and meadow'. He died in 1852 leaving little money but his 'property including my Freehold House and lands' to his wife Mary and daughter Nancy to share and share alike. In 1864 Mary, her daughter Nancy and son Thomas emigrated to America.

Meanwhile, Nicholas's widow, Mary, farmed Treglinnick's 100 acres, between her brothers' farms at Treginegar and Treburrick, helped by three nephews. Four of her five daughters married, the two youngest to the Sandry brothers, Peter and John.

George Biddick, James Hawken, Nicholas Key, his brother Silvester, John Hawke, Jonathan Bennett, Gregory Tom and James Old all left sums of money in their wills from £450 to £800. A bed and its bedding was an important item worth specific mention in the will of a wealthy farmer.

When bachelor George Biddick died in 1819 he

Once again the hierarchy of the first half of the nineteenth century, as established by the substance of their wills, confirms the tenants of the principal farms to be the upper class. These families, Biddick, Hawke, Hawken, Key, together with a William Brewer of a branch of Brewers not prominent in St Ervan, and Thomas Roberts, a substantial farmer in Penrose, were the major farmers and therefore 'principal inhabitants' for official purposes in the early-nineteenth century. They were the largest ratepayers. A major landowning family such as the Hawkens could dominate the decisions made at the annual general meeting of the Vestry if they so willed. They were the officials carrying out those decisions on a week to week basis. At no time have I found any suggestion in the records that the overseers of the poor in St Ervan were anything but fair and just, even generous, by the standards of the day.

Farmers were also important as employers of the greatest number of people. In the 1831 census there were 16 employers of 54 agricultural labourers (and probably many more casual labourers). In 1851 the bigger farms were responsible for the employment of 36 men and nine women between them, and several younger boys and girls as well. The young people were taken into the farmhouses to do the general work, outside on the farm, inside the dairy, or inside the house. Young boys were sometimes employed specifically as ploughboys. Older men and women who remained unmarried were employed as agricultural labourers or domestic servants and given accommodation in the farmhouse. Married men were employed on a casual basis, but they usually rented a few acres of their own to supply their needs.

These families also lived in the biggest houses, though from the brief description of the number of rooms at Treginegar we can see that even the larger farmhouses were not large by today's standards.

The farmhouse at Trevengenow in the 1970s.

Nineteenth century farm buildings at Trevengenow Farm in the 1970s.

The 1830 will of John Hawke specifies that his daughter Joan may choose a bed 'except the bed in the parlour', which explains how 12 people in 1851 could fit so well into a house, Trevengenow, with only a main living room 17ft x 13ft, an 8ft linney behind and a parlour 13ft square. The cottage, a basic rectangle of 18in.-thick walls, was built in the late-seventeenth/early-eighteenth century in cob, divided by post and panel partitioning, giving three bedrooms on the upper floor. At some stage a 7ft deep outshut dairy, in cob and with sloping linney roof of ragstone, was added.

It was not until the latter half of the nineteenth century (possibly in Joseph Strongman's time) that the 8ft linney room behind was extended a further 8ft in stone to provide a separate kitchen 16ft square with a new deeply recessed open fireplace which continued up into the bedroom above. A dog-leg staircase led to three double and one single bedroom. Behind the kitchen a further 9ft x 16ft room housed the pump, and the brewing furnace. Most farmers had their own brewing furnace, a hatch in the floor of the loft almost immediately above the furnace providing easy conveyance from storage to manufacture.

Treginegar and Penrose farmhouses were built during the eighteenth century, and Trenouth was extended in that period. Treburrick is termed a 'good farmhouse' in a nineteenth-century advertisement

for sale, while Trenouth headed the list for grandness, being called 'a commodious farmhouse' in a sale advertisement. Jonathan Bennett built a new farmhouse against the side of the old one at Trewinnick in 1827, in stone and slate roofed. It was on a scale only slightly larger than the old one. The stone came from quarries at Trewinnick or at Tredinnick in Little Petherick parish.

Rumford House, built by blacksmith and farmer Peter Sandry in 1828, was not only built of Trewinnick quarry stone but must have formed an imposing feature at the top of the street looking down over Rumford village. It had four rooms on the ground floor and four above and the walls were extra thick. The stone was carried on a stretcher because the less bumping and bruising the stone suffered the more waterproof it remained. This house compared well with the only two farmhouses about which we know any detail at that time, Bogee and Treleigh.

At Treleigh, a new farmhouse was built in 1859 by Ann Paynter, also new farm buildings after the old house had been demolished. It is described in a Sale Advertisement as:

Large stone-built and slated Dwelling House containing Entrance Hall, Dining Rooms, Drawing Room, Six Bedrooms, Boxroom, Kitchen, Dairy and usual domestic offices.

A new farmhouse was built at Bogee about this time, though slightly smaller. It was stone-built, with slate roof, with two living-rooms, five bedrooms and domestic office.

These, then, were the big houses in the parish, on the larger farms of about 150 acres.

The manors of Trembleath and Trewinnick embraced a number of much smaller holdings, mostly found in the south of the parish. Often the men who farmed these came in from parishes to the south of St Ervan, men like Philip Strongman from St Columb. He married Susanna Strongman of the St Ervan family and, when their first six children were baptised between 1814 and 1823, his occupation in the church register was given as 'labourer'. In 1824 Philip Strongman leased 9 acres at Iron Gate on a 99-year lease, the annual rent being £3, the three lives being his own and his two elder children, nine-year-old John and ten-year-old Ann. This entitled him to be called 'Farmer – Trewinnick Lane' in the baptism register when the seventh and youngest child, Betsy, was baptised in 1826. At the same time he was farming 11 acres at nearby Kestle.

The complexity of landownership is seen in Philip Strongman's holdings. The 1845 Tithe Schedule shows Philip's steady intrusion into St Ervan land. He lived at Bear's Downs and was the landowner of:

Striving Parks   *4 acres arable + house*

Kestle	1 acre arable + house
Barn Ground	6 acres arable
Trewinnick Common	2 acres

These 13 acres were part of Trewinnick manor and committed Philip to a yearly tithe rental of £1.15s.11d. It varied in quality. Striving Parks was said to be arable land, but later earned the more significant name 'Empty Purse'.

From Trembleath manor Philip leased Iron Gate (9 acres) plus a further 9 acres which were shared with Sam Clemow, who owned neighbouring Eddystone Farm. The fields were interspersed alternately, a last residue of ancient strip farming, until Philip Strongman bought out Sam Clemow in the 1850s.

Philip was 74 when he died in February 1855. He could still sign his will with a mark only, yet he left nearly £200. He left to his five daughters, three of whom were married, annuities of £1 each for ten years, to be charged on his 'Dwelling houses, Lands and Tenements'. His younger son, Joseph, aged 31 and as yet unmarried, was his principal legatee and executor. To him Philip left all his:

... freehold and leasehold messuages, lands, heredita-ments and real estate... also all his household furniture farm and implements money securities goods chattels and personal estate.

He had come a long way since leasing 17 acres 30 years before.

Joseph Strongman continued to build on this legacy and when the lease on Trevengenow, 100 acres, expired at Michaelmas 1858, he took it over from Philip Hawke. By 1871 he had increased his tenure to 150 acres. He was now a substantial ratepayer, occasionally acting as churchwarden. Thus, at Trevengenow, Joseph Strongman had not only built on his father's progress to take over the land formerly farmed for several generations by the Hawke family, but had replaced them in the Vestry and as churchwarden.

In the Hawke and Strongman families of St Ervan of the nineteenth century we see the opportunity for a slow but steady rise which lay in the existence of small groups of fields of variable quality and there-fore rental in the southern parts of the manors of Trewinnick and Trembleath, provided the beginner was prepared to break in the ground and work them by hand.

Another who came from outside was James Ball. James, born in St Minver, and his wife Grace, born in Little Petherick, had their first five children baptised in the parish of St Mawgan and the last two in St Ervan, in 1825 and 1828. Between these last two their father has risen from labourer to farmer at Bear's Downs.

James Ball began in 1824, aged 37, by leasing 24 acres of arable and coarse pasture from Trembleath manor on a 99-year lease determinable with three lives, his own and two of his elder sons, William, nine, and James junr, four, and by annual rent of £6. In 1828 he leased a further 69 acres adjoining, a mixed bag of coarse pasture, furze and arable, again on a 99-year lease, and on his own life and his two younger sons, George (aged six) and Joseph (a few months old), yearly rent £14. Although nothing more than enclosed common, this plot had a 'watering place' which was so important to farmers pasturing their cattle along the downs.

In later years James Ball took his place in the Vestry, as overseer one year and assessor another. When he died in 1861 he was in a position to leave his widow, Grace, in the smaller farm and, after cash legacies to his other children, he left the leasehold of the larger farm to his youngest son, Joseph. For Maria, the widow of his son James, who had died in 1853 of typhus at the age of 33, he left 1s. each to her two sons – he had obviously made provision for her earlier. The eldest of her three infant children was an imbecile. Her other son, William, left home to become a Methodist minister. There is a touching tribute to his mother, who had been widowed when William was only two years old, in his obituary in the minutes of the Methodist Conference, 1942:

To be a minister in the church he loved was the dream of his early years... His mother was an old-fashioned Methodist saint to whom under God he owed every-thing.

These examples have shown the great mobility of the agricultural labourer/small farmer, moving from parish to parish, gathering up small plots of land, with good fortune, good health and hard work climbing steadily higher.

The small farmers, those farming 20–30 acres of the poorer soil in the south of the parish, or in the vicinity of Penrose and Rumford, lived in cottages built of cob. The base of the outer walls of the basic rectangle was built like a Cornish stone hedge. Large 'grounders' made the foundation, and rows of slate, one row sloping to the left, the next to the right, faced both sides of the inner filling of earth and small stones. This foundation was about 2ft high, then topped with cob to make a second storey. Cob is a mixture of clay, gravel, and horse or cattle hair. It has to be limed on the outside and, if kept dry, provides good insulation and will last hundreds of years. The windows were small, so the rooms were dark, but cool in summer and warm in winter. The roof was slated or covered with ragstone, the floor beaten earth, possibly planched or boarded. The inside measurements were 11ft x 22ft overall, a thin wood partition dividing the length into two rooms, with the front door opening into one. At one end down-stairs an open fireplace would jut into the room. Inside this was a clome oven in one corner which would be fired with furze and kept hot with turves. Opposite the door, immediately as one stepped inside, rose a steep flight of wooden stairs. The beams which supported the first floor were unceiled and at a height of 6ft from the ground. When cob cottages are left unoccupied and rain is allowed to penetrate the outer limewash, they deteriorate rapidly, the walls bulge out and collapse like an avalanche.

The Tithe Map of 1842, when the population of St Ervan was at its highest, shows little communities clustering in places like Bogee Downs (Mid Bogee one cottage, Outer Bogee one, Pleasant Streams one, Music Water two, New Barn one, Mount Misery one) and on Trewinnick Downs around Eddystone (Iron Gate one, Osborne three, Mount Charles one, Cluckey five, Trewinnick Lane four) and Trembleath or Bear's Downs (Lower Trembleath one, Middle Trembleath one, Higher Trembleath one, Trevilledor one, Rye Parks one). Labourers and smallholders lived very near the fields they worked. Of these 27 cottages not one remains today. With the decrease in population after 1841, a decrease which accelerated after 1871, and developments in agriculture, these small cob cottages were the first to be deserted. Having fallen quickly into a ruinous state, they soon merged their fabric with the soil from which they had risen. Only a discoloration of the earth, a lumpiness, or a greater stoniness in the corner of a field, reminds us of the existence of these former dwellings.

From the account book (1832–45) of Richard Brewer, miller, also a smallholder, we get a good idea of their lives. They had to 'bet, burn and scade' the poor ground on the downs to break it for a small crop; and they had to carry any produce from Trembleath or Bear's Downs to the mill at Millingworth, or from Trewinnick and Bogee Downs to the mill at Rumford. They spent a hard time cutting the prickly furze and bundling it into faggots in May, and cutting turves in July for their fuel. They grew potatoes for the family and kept a pig, even a cow, for food for the family's consumption. While the children were tiny, other labour was employed, but once a boy was 10 or 11 he had to help his father. A girl of 12 went into service, often in the house of a relative.

From two sales of stock at Eddystone Farm, in 1841 and 1843, we see the varied nature of livestock held by such a smallholder. The farm had about 23 acres: there were ten items, including ewes, oxen,

cow in calf, heifer in calf, horses, pigs, withers and lambs. A smallholder on the downs worked with cattle, oxen, horses, sheep, pigs and hay.

Between the census returns of 1841 and 1871 there is continuous movement among the inhabitants of these smaller 'villages'. Seldom do they stay in one place or even in one parish for two decennial census counts. These smallholders discredit the theory of stagnant family residence in an agricultural parish. Even those occupying the larger farms cannot be said to be rooted in the parish over centuries. Migration is the keynote of the period.

The big farms remained occupied, but while the labourer might occupy the modern cottage next to the farmhouse the cottages scattered further afield fell into disrepair as the numbers of agricultural labourers employed in the parish declined. After 1871 farms like Bogee gathered into their holdings the tenements on Bogee Downs; Eddystone developed into a larger farm by taking in Iron Gate and Bear's Downs; Rye Parks, now called Trevilledor, took in land to the north including Little and Middle Trembleath; Trembleath barton farm took under its own control tenements to its south, and Trewinnick swallowed up Cluckey and Trewinnick Lane to its south.

In common with the pattern in North Cornwall agricultural parishes, the population of St Ervan reached its peak, 477, in 1841, and then, again in common with other North Cornwall parishes, declined. The drop was fairly steady between 1841 and 1871, from 477 to 449. Several families are known to have emigrated to America. Instead of being able to find work by moving into a neighbouring parish, they now had to go much further afield, to leave Cornwall altogether and venture to London (as many did to work in warehouses), the industrial areas of the Midlands, or overseas.

In the next decade, approaching the agricultural depression of the 1880s, the population declined by 12 per cent, and if one compares the population at peak in 1841 with that of the last census before the First World War – in 1911 – then one sees the depopulation by the agricultural worker at a rate of 44 per cent. In 1911 only 265 people lived in the parish of St Ervan.

The number of land workers, who had seized the opportunity to work a smallholding and thus earn a living considerably above that of the labourer, were, before the century was out, beaten back by the force of national and international events.

Rumford village, c.1895. The girl is Emma Chapman, who is living with her grandparents, Thomas and Dorothea Rabey, the old couple on the right. Her parents and siblings are living in Portsmouth. Emma married Jack Tippett and their daughter, Dorothy Bennetts, was a teacher at St Ervan School for many years.

✦ CHAPTER 5 ✦

The Poor

In the nineteenth century the majority of households in the parish, about 75 per cent, were headed by an agricultural labourer. Most families remained in this class. Some acquired land piece by piece until they had sufficient to call themselves 'farmers'. Others escaped from the labouring classes by learning a craft. For example, Henry Brewer was apprenticed to Thomas Brewer, carpenter, John Strongman to shoemaker William Pope. But still the labouring class made up the greater part of the parish population and the majority all shared the same financial plight. As long as they, their wives and their children were strong and healthy, and they had access to a plot of land for a garden to grow vegetables and to keep a pig, they could sustain an adequate standard of living. Water was in excellent supply, fuel in the form of furze and turf was plentiful. Nevertheless, incapacity to work through illness or old age, or misfortune and fluctuations of trade, could pitch men and their families into frightening poverty. Those who had no other source of income and who could not work were classed as paupers, the poor and destitute.

The basis for Poor Law administration for the seventeenth and eighteenth centuries and into the nineteenth century was the Act of 1601. Under its provisions, in each parish substantial landholders served as overseers of the poor. Paupers were to be maintained and set to work, the funds provided by taxes exacted from the inhabitants and holders of land. The overseers were to erect poor houses for the incapacitated poor.

The records for St Ervan survive from 1827 to 1837. They show that the Vestry had an average annual expenditure of £210 to maintain the poor, to pay all the expenses incurred in feeding, clothing and sheltering them, in caring for them in sickness, in putting them to work as parish apprentices, to pay the expenses of journeys to St Columb to consult solicitors and deal with the magistrates in obtaining warrants and 'swearing oaths to paternity'. The men who, under the chairmanship of the rector, administered this money during these ten years included in turn all the farmers on the big farms, plus the blacksmith Peter Sandry and (for two years only) Richard Brewer, miller. The Vestry consisted of 24 men (or women, e.g. widow Mary Key), of whom 12 were elected each year to fill the official posts.

As one of the two overseers in the year March 1832 to March 1833 George Biddick dispensed relief of all kinds, regular weekly payments to aged and disabled, weekly relief to widows, occasional payments of wheat to infirm elderly, payments to unmarried mothers for their children, the occasional cash disbursement, payment to a woman for 'tending', i.e. nursing, a sick pauper, and the funeral expenses for a parish pauper. He dispensed parish rates for fuel and clothing, he paid house rents and for repairs to the parish poor house at Bogee. He chased up one young man to make a contribution, £2.17s., 'on account of a base child', and he had had to pay 13s.8d. to Mr Collins, solicitor, St Columb and 3s.6d. to Mr John Hellyar on account of this same young man.

The parish overseers preferred to give food, fuel and clothing to help the poor and cash only occasionally to stave off the day when regular weekly payments became necessary. The staple diet was barley, sometimes the more expensive wheat, occasionally mutton.

If the pauper was living out, i.e. not in the parish poor house, their house rent was paid direct to the landlord. House rents were paid, for example, for William Parsons's family, £1.10s., Joseph Bennett's family, £1.15s., Humphrey Hicks's family, £1.10s. The rent for a one-up, one-down cottage was £1.10s., and each of these families had several children. Joseph Bennett had ten children between 1813 and 1838, Humphrey Hicks had ten children between 1810 and 1832, and William Parsons had four children. Not all the children would be living at home at one time. As soon as a child reached 12 years of age, if not before, he or she was apprenticed to a farmer as a labourer in the fields or servant girl in the farmhouse. The children of a pauper family were apprenticed out by the Vestry at the age of nine. In 1805 the fourth of Francis and Candacia Brewer's ten children, Jane (born 1796), was sent to Trewinnick Farm to learn to be a domestic servant in the household of William Eplett.

The system was, of course, open to abuse, but an instance of generosity was Peter Sandry in 1831 leaving his apprentice girl £5 for when she reached the age of 21.

When pauper women had babies the Vestry paid the costs of the birth. 'Oct 1827 Pd Mary Rawling for delivering a child... 5s.0d. Mary Hicks for the lying-in of Ann Hicks... £1.10s.0d.'

Ann Hicks's child died and was buried before he was a month old.

Tending, i.e. nursing or sitting up at night with a sick person, was paid for at the rate of 4d. a day or 6d.

THE BOOK OF ST ERVAN

a night. Often this was a woman in need of financial support herself.

Mr Matthew Trevan, Licentiate, Society of Apothecaries, living at Padstow, was the doctor retained at a salary of £2 a year, £3 in 1829, to care for the sick of the parish. He sometimes charged extra. For caring for William Parsons on one occasion Dr Trevan was paid an additional £2.

Beer was the medicine in a variety of circumstances: 'Dec 1827, 2 qts of beer in curing Martha Cowle's child, 1/-.'

The child was a three-month-old boy! It seems to have done the trick. We find him labouring in the fields at the age of 14. 'Mar 1828, Beer for William Parsons on account of his sore leg, 5s.10d.'

Gin, rum and brandy also had medicinal uses: 'July 1831, For brandy for the sick people, 2s.6d.'

If, however, rum was ordered, then look out. It was an indication that the end was near. Honor Johns, widow, was receiving 2s.6d. a week, and a woman was paid 1s. a week for 'tending' her. Honor was 84. In January she was given a blanket, in February half a pint of rum (1s.), in May shoes (only 1s.9d., so they must have been a light slipper), and a shift (1s.9d.), in July 1 pint of rum, in August another half pint, in October 2 pints, also 100 faggots of furze, candles and tea (9½d.), in November a new blanket and 3½ pints of rum. In November the final entry concerning Honor Johns concerns her funeral expenses, £2.14s. The burial register records: 'Honor Johns, buried 25.11.1827, 85 years old of Bogee Common.'

The supply of liquor did not always finish with the death of the sick person. In April 1829 61-year-old Mary Gill was buried: 'Funeral charges... £2.10s.0½d. For liquor for the funeral... 3s.9d.'

A child's funeral cost about £1.8s. Whether it was the equivalent of three weeks or five weeks of the father's wages, it was a heavy sum for a labourer to find, and impossible for a pauper.

Mr Trevan, 'surgeon to the poor of St Ervan', also treated the family of farmer Gregory Tom at Trethewey. The bill for this one family, for the three years from January 1837 to March 1840 came to £3.18s. and was mainly for ointment, pills and bleeding. Nor was the account settled promptly. The last treatment was in March 1840. The account was settled in May 1842.

Some families could, by their number, long lives and disability, keep the overseers very busy. Such a family was that of Francis and Candacia 'Candy' Brewer. Francis Brewer married Candacia Strongman on 24 April 1791 and son John was born on 9 May, the first of their ten children. It was a family which, for the next 18 years, was well known to the overseers. We see something of the lives of eight of the ten children from the accounts concerning the poor (records of the other two have not been found):

1. John, born 1791, remained unmarried, worked on farms and in 1841 had his widowed mother living with him at Rumford. In 1848 the overseers recorded: 'for conveying John Brewer to Union Workhouse – 3s.6d'.
2. William, born 1793, while a parish apprentice aged 18 under John Hawke at Trevengenow, absconded. An advertisement in accordance with official requirements was inserted in the *Royal Cornwall Gazette* on 9 February 1811 publicising his disappearance. He was described as 5ft 6in. high, with light hair and sallow complexion and wearing a blue coat and hat covered with an oil case. No reward was offered for his return!
3. Jane, born 1796, was indentured as a parish apprentice at the age of 9.
4. Nancy, born 1798, received occasional parish relief.
5. Thomas, born 1801, died aged 27 in 1829 at Bogee (possibly in the parish poor house).
6. Grace, born 1803, had an illegitimate son.
7. Henry, baptised in 1805, was the one child who made good. We'll learn more of his story later.
8. Lancelot, baptised in 1807, was buried in 1815, aged 8.

When the overseers' accounts open in 1826, their father, aged 58, is receiving relief varying from occasional provision of wheat to regular weekly payments of 2s.6d. to 4s. a week 'for Francis Brewer and wife'. In 1831 Francis and Candy receive a peck (6 gallons) of wheat every month, shoes, furze and turves, but the overseers also get some work out of Francis.

1830 Nov	Cord and wire for Francis Brewer 6d. + 2s.	
Dec	Cord and wire for Francis Brewer to catch moles	6d.
1832 Dec	Francis Brewer for mole traps	2s.6d.

Towards the end of 1833 there is obviously trouble in the Brewer household. In addition to their weekly 3s. they started to receive extra cash relief on frequent occasions. Then in April comes the warning signal: '16s. in extras + liquor... 1s.10½d.'.

On 11 May Francis was buried, aged 66. The overseers did not pay for his funeral. Up until March 1834 Francis had been running a very small account with Richard Brewer, miller, for mutton mainly, which his son Henry settled on his behalf. Henry probably paid for his father's funeral.

Widow Candy received relief at 1s.6d. a week. She was 63 when widowed but was able to work a little. Her son, Henry, may well have partly supported his mother by carrying on the account for mutton with Richard Brewer. However, Henry married Rebecca Hosken and they started a family. He had more financial commitments now.

In 1837 the parish became part of St Columb Union. In April 1839 the St Columb Union Board instructed the clerk: 'to write the overseers St Ervan to obtain summons against Henry Brewer to show cause why he does not support his mother', and in

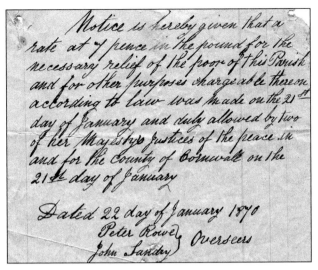

Peter Rowe and John Sandry, Overseers, sign the notice of the rate to be levied for the relief of the poor in 1870.

May they chased them up, to make Henry pay 1s. a week. Two years later, on 31 March 1841, two Justices of the Peace made an Order on Henry Brewer:

... requiring him to maintain Candy Brewer his mother, who is poor and unable to work, so as to maintain and support herself, and chargeable to the... Parish of St Ervan, he the said Henry Brewer being a person of sufficient ability to maintain and provide for his said mother.

He was ordered to pay 6d. a week 'for and towards the sustention, relief, maintenance, and support of the said Candy Brewer his mother...'

In 1841 Candy is living with her eldest unmarried son, John, an agricultural labourer. Henry is also an agricultural labourer, with a wife and two children to support, so why should he be picked out to support his widowed mother? Obviously the eldest brother, John, was not strong, as he went to the Union Workhouse a few years later. William had absconded and Thomas and Lancelot had both died. This left Henry. As a carpenter he could command more money and, in addition, his wife Rebecca was a dressmaker. In the 1844 Electors' List he was qualified to vote in Parliamentary elections by virtue of being the freeholder of 'houses and garden in Rumford'. Later he leased a five-acre arable field in Churchtown. The overseers had no choice but to demand a contribution towards his mother's maintenance.

The field leased by Henry Brewer, carpenter, is next to fields farmed by Thomas Brewer, carpenter. They were cousins. Through his mother, Henry was first cousin to John Strongman, master shoemaker and fervent Bible Christian and chapel trustee, also living in Rumford. Thomas Brewer was also a trustee of the Bible Christian chapel and thus had another motive for giving Henry a helping hand. Henry's four children were not baptised in the Parish Church, so Henry and Rebecca were presumably Methodists.

After Candy's son John was taken to the workhouse in 1848, she went to live with her daughter, Jane, in Victoria Street, St Columb. Jane, former parish apprentice in housewifery aged 9, married William Polkinhorn, blacksmith. They had four children, but then he died. Jane and her two sons spent some time in the workhouse but by 1851 Jane had found work as a general servant and her two sons, now 16 and 13, were working as farm labourers and living with her. Her mother, Candy, now 84 years old, is stated by the census enumerator to be a 'farm servant'. Henry is still contributing to his mother's keep at the rate of 8d. a week.

Candy Brewer was nearly 90 when she died. Although never strong enough to work to support herself entirely, having first when married and also in widowhood been partially supported by the overseers, partly by her son Henry, she still outlived her husband by 20 years, reached the grand old age of 89 and was not an inmate of the workhouse when she died.

James Gill and family proved a more intractable and costly problem than the Brewer family and we do not know the whole story. It starts mildly enough with a peck of wheat, a few months later a house rent paid, the start of regular weekly payments of 2s.6d. in 1828, and a pair of shoes, then in 1829 the weekly payments increased to 3s. In 1830 comes the first hint of trouble: 'May 1830, For going to St Columb with James Gill, 2s.6d.', and again in July. The journey to St Columb was to see a magistrate. The weekly payments continue, then: 'Oct 1833, Expenses on the case of James Gill and family as a Bill £54.6s.5½d.'

This was a huge amount. The overseer dealing with the Gill family was James Brabyn, but his payments for the poor for the whole month were only £61. The second overseer that year was William Hawken. Compare this bill of £54 with Hawken's expenditure of £55 for the whole 12 months (though that was usually higher). The average expenditure per overseer a year was £110. By any standards £54 for the Gill family was a colossal sum to spend on one case. Expenditure on this Gill family continued but no explanation appears in any documents that have been found. And there were other members of the Gill family who required a lot of assistance as well.

The strange thing is that in spite of the fact that no fewer than 12 members of the Gill family are listed as in need of help in the 1830 poor accounts, yet by 1841 there are only two young families of that name in the census returns, one on Bear's Downs, the other at Rumford. Also, it has proved impossible to identify all the Gills who were helped, even though a number of them featured in the St Ervan registers from the early days.

One pauper lived to be 91 years old. When the parish overseers' accounts opened in 1826 William Benney was 72 years old and received 5s. a week for himself and family, though later it settled down to

3s.6d. a week. In addition, clothing was provided for him and his children, also furze and coals and mutton.

William Benney's career is easy to follow because he stayed in one place, but the Gill family illustrates the fact that the lower classes were not static, or confined to their parish of birth. They were very mobile, moving to different cottages in one parish or moving from parish to parish within an area. It can be more difficult to construct the family tree of the labouring branch of a family than of one of the families who farmed the big farms. To track down the labourer one has to chase around in several parishes, which they moved in and out of again at frequent and short intervals to find work.

Information about wages and prices comes from the accounts of the St Ervan Overseers of the Poor, which survive from 1827 until the union of parishes in 1837, and from the account ledger kept by Richard Brewer, miller and grocer, from 1832 to 1845.

A labourer employed casually earned 1s. or 1s.3d. a day, according to the season. Frank Ould and Thomas Parsons worked frequent but not consecutive days for Thomas Stribley on Penrose Farm at the turn of the eighteenth/nineteenth century. In August they received 1s.6d. for a day 'cutting barley', or 'mowing barley', and the next day 1s.3d. for 'reaping barley'. A day-labourer's week could go like this:

Aug 18 – to cutting barley,
Aug 19 – to turning dung and reaping,
Aug 20 – reaping,
Aug 25 – reaping,
Aug 26 – mowing barley,
Aug 31 – binding barley,
Sep 3 – bicking the wheat,
Sep 9 – threshing wheat,
Sep 15 – picking barley,
Sep 16, 17, 23 and 24 – threshing,
Sep 30 and 31 – threshing barley,
Oct 7 and 8 – to driving dressing.

For some days he was paid 1s.6d., for others 1s.3d.

What we do not know from farmer Stribley's account book is whether Thomas Parsons found work with another farmer on the other days. In November he worked six days for Mr Stribley, four of which were spent 'hedging', that is repairing the stone and earth walls. Hedging, drawing or carrying stones (there was a quarry at Penrose), carrying dressing or dung, or threshing, were jobs that could be carried on throughout the year. Other jobs were seasonal; setting potatoes in April and drawing them in November, setting coalplants in May, turning the wheat in March, cutting furze (gorse, used as fuel) in May, carrying earth over, or hacking the earth in May and June, mowing grass in June, mowing barley in August and September. The same man did all these jobs and a host of others besides, including spinning ropes and making goose cages. The agricultural labourer became skilled at many jobs.

Richard Brewer's land provided regular full-time employment to two labourers, but also occasional work for a number of others. He gave occasional work to the poor. In 1833 Sarah Benny worked three days at 6d. a day to reduce a bill for meat and flour of 4s.7½d., and Martha Cowle frequently worked a day to keep her purchases of beef and other food going. They also worked to pay the rent of potato ground.

Richard Brewer employed field labourers by the day. For example, John Coul worked for him on seven days in March 1833 and for odd days through April, May and into June – one day only. Let us hope John Coul was working for more than one employer.

In March and April 1835 Matthew Rabey managed to keep his earnings for the day on the top line: 10 days in March, 5 days in April and 12 days in May were paid at the rate of 1s.8d. a day and one day of piecework, '20 yards spadeing on 15 April', earned him 2s.6d.

Richard Brewer employed men to do the heavy work of getting ley land ready for crop sowing. The summer of 1839 saw a great deal of this activity and again in 1840, both in ground at Rumford Mills and at Cluckey. He also needed extra labour to maintain the hedges, most of which were built of earth bound and capped by turf. Ditches were cleaned out, the sludge thrown on the top of the hedge, and breaks in the hedge repaired. Stone hedges needed repairs, or new hedges had to be built. Also, if the area where the hedge meets the ground is allowed to collect earth, it encourages weeds. That is when the Cornish shovel comes in useful, to dig out the weeds at the foot of the hedge using the sharp, slightly pointed blade to cut through them before lifting them away. Thomas Spear did some such work for Richard Brewer in February 1842: '2½ days Aging in the Millmore... 6s.0d', i.e. 2½ days hedging in the Mill Moor field.

Women were employed occasionally, picking up stones, weeding in the hay and harvest fields. They worked occasional days in summer, helped with root crops in autumn, and worked in the barns in winter. They were paid 8d. a day for working from 8a.m. to 5p.m. Children were paid 6d. for the occasional day of stone picking.

Richard Brewer, who was generous to his labourers, paid pauper women 6d. a day (not 8d.). Perhaps this reflected their inability to do a proper day's work, through age or poor health, the reason for them receiving poor relief in the first place.

Men in regular employment, earning 10s. a week and a rent-free cottage, fuel and potato ground were, with corn at 20s. a bushel for wheat, 10s. a bushel for barley, better off than the daily labourers at higher daily rates. A casual labourer would have to be guaranteed a six-day week at 1s.8d. a day to reach the 10s. wage, without any of the benefits.

This was subsistence living. Their earnings provided essentials, food, fuel, clothing, rent. Anything beyond this, such as schooling, was a luxury.

The staple diet was barley at 10–12s. a Cornish bushel (3 Imperial, or 24 gallons). Wheat was almost twice as expensive. St Ervan was a land of sheep pasture as well as tillage. In the 1830s Richard Brewer sold mutton for about 6d. a pound. Beef was slightly cheaper. Bacon cost around 7d. a pound, containing, of course, much more fat than one would buy now. Many kept and killed their own pig. To employ another to do it would cost a day's wage. Potatoes were 8s. a Cornish bushel, turnips were sold by the yard at 4s. a yard. Flour cost just over £1 a Cornish bushel.

They could buy cheaper food, such as a pig's head, heng and tripe (1s.3d.), hame, or a bullock's heels and bites (9d.).

For fuel they bought coal at about 7d. a Cornish bushel, which could be easily supplemented by slow-burning turves at about 2s. a load, and the quick-flaring furze at 7–8s. per 100 faggots or bundles. Furze fire had to be treated carefully. In 1803 a fire started by furze in the kitchen gutted Trethewey, Gregory Tom's farmhouse. A stack of these prickly bundles was built on a piece of ground, and turves were piled into a rick. The overseers of the poor paid a rent of 1s.6d. a year to stand the rick of turves for the parish poor house, plus a rick of 500 faggots of furze.

Clothing was a principal item, boots and shoes being the most costly articles. For work in all weathers, in mud and on rough ground, men needed a new pair every 12 months costing, in 1830, 9s. Women's were cheaper, 5s.3d. A man's coat cost 14–15s., including the tailor's bill, a waistcoat 2s.1½d. and a shirt 3s. Trousers for a boy were 2s.8d. A woman's gown cost 5s., a shift 1s.9d., a petticoat 2s.8d. and a bed gown 2s.4d. To clothe a poor child cost the Vestry 18s.8d. A blanket was essential and cost 6s.6d., a sheet 2s.7d. Calculate the number of days a man earning 10s. a week, or a woman 8d. a day, had to work to earn enough to pay for these.

The 1834 Poor Law Amendment Act introduced the first major administrative changes since 1601. By 1838 16 parishes – St Breock, St Columb Major, St Columb Minor, Colan, Crantock, Cubert, St Ervan, St Eval, St Enoder, St Issey, Little Petherick, St Merryn, St Mawgan, St Newlyn East, Padstow and St Wenn – had combined into St Columb Union and the Workhouse had been built in the town of St Columb Major. However, for a time the majority of those receiving financial support were able to continue to live in their parish.

The transitional five months were administered by:

Overseers	John Sandry, 26-year-old farmer, Rumford
	John Hawken, 49-year-old farmer, Treginegar
Assessors	Philip Hawke, 44-year-old farmer, Trevengenow
	Thomas Sandry, 73-year-old landowner and owner of houses in Rumford
Constables	Joseph Hawken junr, 24-year-old farmer, Penrose
	Peter Sandry, 28-year-old black-smith, Rumford
Waywardens	Richard Williams, 60-year-old farmer, Trenouth
	James Brabyn, 30-year-old farmer, Treginegar
Churchwardens	George Biddick, 45-year-old farmer, Treravel
	James Key, 54-year-old farmer, Trewinnick.

Outdoor relief was almost entirely abolished. People unable to support themselves were accepted into Union workhouses after being subjected to the 'workhouse test'.

The Act established three central Poor Law Commissioners and under them an independently financed Guardian of the Poor was elected in each parish. On 30 June 1837 'paupers from St Ervan parish... were examined'. The 1841 census lists no St Ervan paupers in the Union workhouse. One candidate, William Benny, was maintained in his native parish by the device of the 'parishioners' leasing part of the old parish poor house on Bogee land from John Paynter Esq., who had bought it from them in 1840. Mr Paynter farmed the land around. By William Benny's death in June 1845, aged 91, the old parish poor house was no doubt ready to merge again into the earth on which it had stood.

There were classes of poor. The most deserving were 'aged and wholly disabled', then came 'aged and infirm', 'partially disabled', 'able widows and families', 'orphan children' and finally 'other children', the awards ranging from the top 2s.6d.–3s.6d. to the bottom, 3d.–1s.6d. 'in kind only'. These payments were still at the same level as those which had been made in St Ervan during the previous ten years.

The first Guardian representing St Ervan was George Biddick, 41-year-old father of nine children, farmer at Treravel. His elder children were old enough to work on the farm and he employed two men besides, which left him free to attend the weekly Board meetings at St Columb, five miles from his home. Also, St Columb was his market town, the Union Board meetings were held on market day, so he could combine both activities. George Biddick had served as an official of one kind or another for at least the past ten years in the St Ervan Vestry so was familiar with local government and the maintenance of the poor. Although the system of administration changed with the amalgamation of parishes into Unions, and the terms in which the poor received their relief changed considerably, the men running the affairs of the parish were the same as before.

Each year, 'on or about the 25th day of March at a meeting of the Inhabitants of the Parish in Vestry Assembled' under the chairmanship of the same Revd William Molesworth, rector, the same rotation of farmers were elected waywardens, overseers, churchwardens, and one was now elected Guardian to attend the weekly meetings of the St Columb Union Board.

The main business left to the parish Vestry consisted of examining and allowing the waywardens' accounts. In 1841 the meeting had to adjourn for four days. It met again at the Churchtown Inn with James Hawken as chairman 'to audit the waywardens accounts'. Perhaps it was this that gave rise to the resolution at the following Vestry meeting, where it was 'unanimously agreed to appoint Mr James Rowe to the three offices of assistant Overseer, Waywarden and Assessor with a salary of five pounds a year.' George Biddick was chairman at this meeting and farmers Jonathan Bennett of Trewinnick and James Hawken of Treginegar Mill signed the agreement.

James Rowe came from St Columb parish in about 1839 to farm Trembleath barton farm. In 1851 his household consisted of himself and his wife Mary, Mary's widowed mother, Fanny Hoblyn, owner of leasehold houses and lands, and their seven children. Living-in servants were 18-year-old Louisa Tippett, who had the 'care of the children', house servant Mary Ann Bennett and two farm workers.

Immediately on arriving in the parish James Rowe was chairman of the Vestry annual meeting. One of his first acts, in March 1840, was to get the Vestry to agree he had been overcharged poor rate by £1.1s.10½d.! The first population census recording each household in some detail was taken in June 1841, just two years after he arrived. He was the enumerator, as he was in 1851 and 1861, by which time he was also registrar of births and deaths. The farming of Trembleath's 212 acres was left to his brother, Peter. James was never chairman again but continued to serve the parish in other ways. In 1843 his £5 salary was raised to five guineas 'for keeping the parish accounts and other services.'

Highways continued to preoccupy the overseers of the parish. In March 1845 the parish meeting dealt with: 'an objection having been made against that part of Treginegar Lane which leads from Little Veal's gate to Lewidden.'

At the next meeting it was resolved: 'that ten shillings be paid to the parish by Mr John Hawken (Waywarden)... being the amount spent for the repair of the above Lane.'

John Hawken was the tenant of the whole of Treginegar property except Treginegar Mill. Was he trying to wriggle out of his obligations?

On 19 December 1851 a special meeting was held at St Ervan Churchtown for the purpose of deciding about the repairs of the road leading from Bear's Downs to Trewinnick Lane

It was resolved that if the Proprietors of the Lands adjoining the Road leading from Bear's Downs to Trewinnick Common [passing Eddystone Farm] will provide and cart material, necessary for putting the road in repair, the Parish will round the road and break and spread the Stone.

In 1856 it was resolved: 'that if the Proprietors of Trewinnick will draw the stones in Trewinnick Lane the Parish will agree to form the Road and Level the Stones.'

The vacancy for waywarden occurred with the retirement of Robert Higman after ten years in the job, during which time the salary had doubled to £2. Then the 1862 Highway Act came into force, which empowered Quarter Sessions to set up Highway Boards to administer highways for a combination of parishes. They were abolished again 30 years later, but meanwhile St Ervan parish had to send someone to Padstow each year to pay the rate for the maintenance of highways to the Treasurer of the Highways Board. The journey cost the parish 3s.6d., and their contribution amounted to £65 altogether paid in October and February.

St Ervan farmers did not accept the imposition of the new Highways Board without putting up a fight, and left the Board in no doubt about their objections. At a special meeting of the parishioners held at the house of Mr John Hawken (the Inn at Churchtown):

... for the purpose of taking into consideration an order of the Highway Board relative to making a new Road through Trewinnick Green. Mr Gregory Tom junr in the Chair.
Resolved unanimously:
From evidence adduced at this meeting the testimony of some embracing a period of more than fifty years it appears that there never was a road either made or repaired by the parish, over the uninclosed Common called Trewinnick Green the property of Mr Hart Key and others and that this meeting earnestly protests against the orders of the Highway Board to make such a road at the cost of the parish. And further that this meeting pledges itself to use every legal means to prevent such a road from being a road to be kept by the parish until it has first been made by the parties liable (and for whose special use it is intended) in accordance with the provisions of the several Highways Acts – that a copy of this resolution be sent to the Surveyor with a request that he will submit the same to the Highway Board at their next meeting.

James Rowe had work to do.

In 1869 a Parliamentary Commission investigated

the conditions of women and children in agriculture. An Assistant Commissioner held sessions in St Columb Major to hear evidence from officials from all the parishes in the St Columb Union, which included St Ervan. From these we learn that:

A man living in a cottage on the farm and employed all the year round received 10 shillings a week with corn (harvest included), a cottage rent free, about 30 yards of garden, potato ground free, sometimes a cow to milk, he keeps a pig and the manure goes to the garden.

The Parliamentary Commissioner in 1869 was told of small farmers who claimed they could not afford to spare their children's labour for the sake of education. In St Ervan parish, however, the census returns of 1851 indicate that a high proportion of farmers and of labourers sent their children to school. On that census there were two 10-year olds, five 11-year olds and five 12-year olds who declared as their occupation 'agricultural labourer'. There seems to be no obvious distinction between small farmers and labourers. The children of John Sandry, living in Rumford, farming 40 acres (two sons aged 12 and 9 and his daughter aged 6), were not 'scholars', but Mary Brenton, widow, living on Bear's Downs, sent her 9-year-old daughter to school, though her 10-year-old son had to work with her on her 16 acres.

According to the 1861 census, six 'farmers' with school-age children sent their children to school, eight did not, the eight including men such as Thomas Spear, who farmed 130 acres at Trewinnick, but also including Robert Giles (20 acres at Little Trembleath – his 11-year-old son, John Henry, was working as a 'servant' in Joseph Strongman's household at Trevengenow), Nicholas Parsons at Homelong and Matthew Rabey with 18 acres at Osbornes. These small acreages were in the poor land in the south, but then John Binny, farming 105 acres at Penrose, and Joseph Hawken, of the well-to-do Hawken family, did not send their children to school either. As we shall see in a later chapter, it may all have had as much to do with the relationship between farmer and parson as with economic considerations whether or not children in this parish attended school.

The opportunities for education in the parish were unsatisfactory before the Board Schools were established by the 1870 Education Act, but the worst excesses of abuse of child labour experienced in some industrial areas were not evident here, or at least were not acknowledged by the census enumerator or in evidence given to the Parliamentary Commissioner.

In the nineteenth century nearly half the population was under 20 years of age. The bulk of the population was made up of labouring families with young children.

According to G. Collins, clerk to the St Columb Union, their cottage accommodation was indifferent. Some had two bedrooms but many only one. There were sufficient cottages of cob and thatch for the labouring families, on the whole conveniently situated for the labourer to reach his work each day. They had space for good-sized gardens to grow vegetables and keep a pig. Access to fresh water was usually no problem throughout the parish and fuel in the form of furze or turf was plentiful.

The only comment referring to privies for the poor concerns the lack of any satisfactory provision.

Mr J. Hawken, giving evidence for St Ervan parish, told the commissioner there were 15 'one-up-one-down' cottages at Rumford. The total of inhabited dwellings in the village at that time was 21. As almost all the families had more than three persons over 13 years of age, it must have been difficult, if not impossible, to sleep the sexes separately. Throughout the nineteenth century census statistics show that the average occupancy of a house was five persons, declining only slightly with the decrease of the population generally.

Overcrowding was considered to encourage immorality. In St Ervan an average of 5 per cent of baptisms were of illegitimate babies.

In this chapter we have seen how the poor, that is all those who either from sickness, disability or extreme old age, were unable to work to keep themselves, were supported by the community in which they lived.

In the following chapters we will look at the lives and work of the farming community from whose incomes this support was provided.

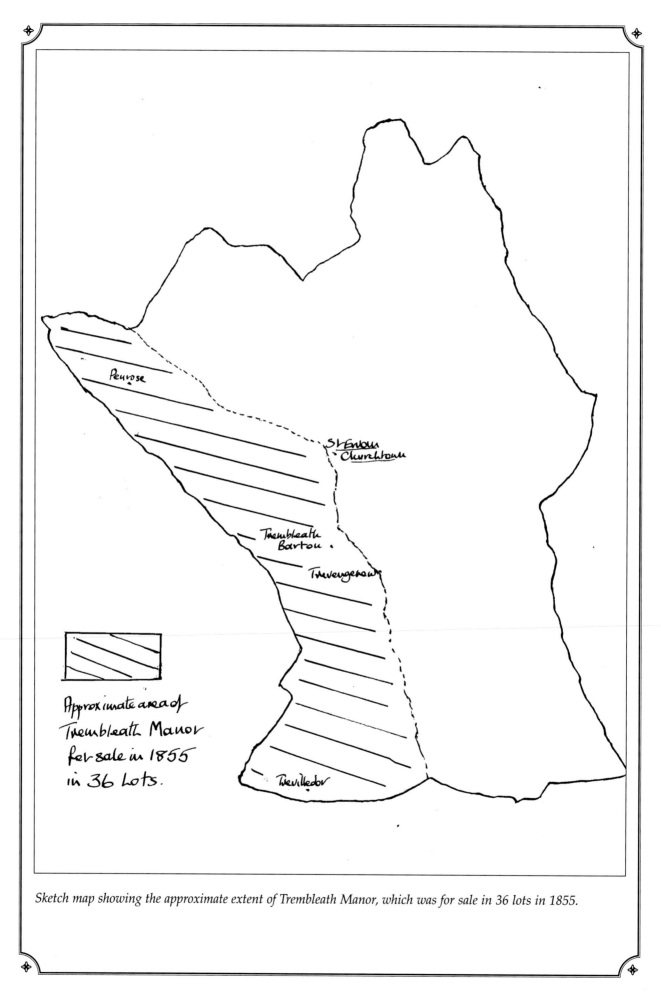

Penrose

St Ervan
Churchtown

Trembleath
Barton .

Trevengenow

Trevilledor

Approximate area of
Trembleath Manor
for sale in 1855
in 36 Lots.

Sketch map showing the approximate extent of Trembleath Manor, which was for sale in 36 lots in 1855.

✦ CHAPTER 6 ✦

Farming in the Nineteenth Century

The parish of St Ervan lies between the barren moorlands of the spine of Cornwall and within a few miles of the north coast, reaching almost up to the Camel estuary and Padstow. The warm, wet west and south-west winds drive in off the Atlantic and drop their rain on the moorlands. A great part of this is carried off their impervious granite by innumerable small surface streams. One of these small streams rises in the sandy beds on the downs in the south of the St Ervan parish and coarses swiftly down north and west, through the lower, more fertile part. The river flows near St Ervan Church and under the Lewidden bridge. Further on it meets and joins another river, which runs along the western bound of Trembleath, before together they flow into the sea at Porthcothan Bay. Another river rises in the north-east of the parish and runs north out into the Camel estuary at Harlyn Bay. The parish has always been well watered.

There was great variability of quality of soil, but generally the most fertile soils were on the slates, on the west side at Penrose and the northern part of Trembleath manor in the centre. It was fairly rich across the northern half, which rose to 200ft above sea level, the south-facing slopes running into the calcareous series. It became less rich down the eastern side, the lightest soils and most extensive covering of furze being across the southern part, or 'barren downs'. The rent values of the mid-nineteenth century reflect these varying qualities, and the mixture of farming, both arable and pastoral.

Fertility is determined by climate even more than by geology and St Ervan enjoys mild temperatures and high humidity. Its proximity to the Atlantic coast makes it subject to fierce storms, a distinct disadvantage, though it benefits from the frequent rainfall which accompanies the violent gales. The slaty soil has been found highly productive of barley and wheat in the past, but it lacks one important element, lime. The proximity of the parish to the coast is therefore very important.

Before the age of artificial fertilisers the abundant harvests of wheat and barley could only be produced by adding sea sand to the acid soil. The sand in the Camel estuary on Cornwall's north coast is composed not so much of quartz grains, but of up to 60 per cent of comminuted sea shells, and thus has a high lime content. In the early-nineteenth century a writer recorded that in the Camel estuary:

... nearly twenty barges are constantly employed here, in dredging sand at low water, for manure. The bars of the sand yield an inexhaustible supply; they have been pillaged for ages, but they still remain undiminished. The sea is continually supplying the deficiencies which the barges and the current occasion. And from the manner in which the sands accumulate on most parts of that coast, it seems probable, that had it not been for these causes, Padstow Creek would long since have ceased to be a harbour for ships of any considerable tonnage.

Sea sand was carried inland by pack animal and cart along the sanding roads, to be mixed with the dung produced on the farm. The vendor of Trenouth and Penalewes Farms in 1845 announced proudly in the Conditions of Survey for a 14-year lease that they were 'within two miles of sea sand of best quality'.

In July 1817 the following item appears in the farm accounts of Thomas Stribley, of Penrose Farm: 'reparing the sanding road... 2s.0d.'.

This follows immediately after: 'to highwais one day... 1s. 6d.', which indicates that the sanding road, as well as highways or roads in the parish, was considered important enough to be the responsibility of the parish vestry, and that each farmer had to make his contribution towards the upkeep of both for the general benefit. The sand was spread on the land in April: 'one day sanding... 1s.6d.'.

In 1855 Francis Cross, a major landowner in St Ervan, put the large Trembleath estate up for sale. The importance of sea-shell sand to the productivity of the land is demonstrated by the priority given to its availability in the Sale Prospectus. Heading the list of advantages generally enjoyed by the estate was proximity to:

Porthcothan Beach, where any quantity of Sea Sand (pulverised shell) and often large quantities of Sea Weed can be obtained gratis, and by which the agriculture of the district is mainly supported...

Trembleath manor included not only Trembleath barton farm but covered the whole of the western side of the parish, from Penrose and Churchtown at the northern end down to the southern part of the estate lying at the foot of Bear's Downs. Here the soils were lighter. Farmers had concentrated on the heavier wheat-growing land, but Francis Cross points out that the lighter soils could also be put to good use:

The Bulk of the Land is exceedingly fertile, and the samples of Wheat and Barley that it produces, are of first rate quality; and the lighter soils might be vastly improved by a proper system of Green Cropping and Folding; which ought to be adopted throughout.

Polsue, 20 years later, wrote of the parish generally:

There are several carefully managed estates in this parish; the grazing lands, however, which are generally of good quality, might be very much improved by cultivation.

The fact that sea sand was of first importance is shown again by the good husbandry clauses in leases. In 1845, when George Biddick leased Trenouth for a term of 14 years from George Wightman, it was on condition that he:

... upon every fresh breach for Tillage shall carry 8 Butt or Cartloads of good Salt Sea Sand or 100 Bushels of well burnt Lime... on every acre broken for Tillage... and shall mix the same with at least 80 Butt or Cart Loads of good Dung Earth and other Manure according to the rules of good husbandry.

Trenouth lay within two miles of the best-quality sea sand of the Camel estuary, and burnt lime was not to be found anywhere within such a convenient distance, so George Biddick's choice was made.

Sea sand was considered so important that when in 1845 John Hawken took out a seven-year lease on Brabyn's Tenement (146 acres in Treginegar), the first husbandry condition to which he had to agree stipulated very precisely the use and quantities of sea sand. The lessee:

... shall bring into and upon every acre of said demised premises which he shall intend to till and before tilling the same. Eighty double Winchester Bushels of well burnt lime or in lieu thereof twelve cart loads of good Salt sea sand and so proportionably for a less quantity of ground than an acre and well mix the same with twelve cart loads of good rich compost and proper and well rotten dung and manure the ground therewith according to the most approved rules of good husbandry.

Sea sand is still used by St Ervan farmers today.

Having produced his crops, the next concern of the farmer was to get them to market. The Trembleath Sale Particulars of 1855 next emphasise the proximity of markets:

The Port of Padstow from whence large quantities of Corn are annually exported, and the Market Towns of St Columb and Wadebridge are within easy distances of the Estate. The Cornwall Railway too, which will shortly be completed, passes within a few miles of the property.

As early as 1787 William Henwood leased Treglinnick on a 14-year term. Yet as late as the middle of the nineteenth century, land in St Ervan was still being leased on the three lives system. This was the old custom of granting leases for lives to the tenants for a term of 99 years determinable on the death of the longest living of three people named by the tenant. Usually the landlord agreed to the buying-in of a replacement life on the death of one, to add to the two remaining. On being granted the original lease, the tenant would make a down payment, a 'fine' or 'consideration', of from 14 to 18 years' rent of the land, and thereafter a small annual rent, often a nominal amount, known as the 'conventionary' or 'reserved' rent, and would also be obliged to give 'suit and service to the manor court'. To buy in a new life, the tenant would have to pay the equivalent of three years' rent for one life, or seven years for two lives.

The disadvantages of this system were that the tenant had uncertain security. Often he took out an insurance against an inconveniently early death of one of his 'lives', and in order to finance the consideration he often borrowed or took out a mortgage. All these expenses left the tenant with insufficient capital to invest in the long-term fertility of the land, so at the end of the term the landlord got back a dilapidated farm. Hence the change to leases for prescribed terms and the imposition of good husbandry clauses.

In the 1855 sale of Trembleath manor some of the smaller holdings were still being tenanted on the 99 years and three lives system. They were all the small tenements at the southern end of the estate, at the foot of the downs and running up to the parish boundary on the ridge, Trevilledor, Middle Trembleath, Little Trembleath, Iron Gate, etc., each containing 20 or 30 acres and subject:

... to the residue of a Term of 99 years, granted by Lease bearing date 25th March, 1824 and now determinable [for example] with the lives of James Ball aged 68 and William Ball aged 40 years, under the yearly rent of £6.0s.0d., a Tithe Rent Charge of 2¾d., and a Heriot on the death of each life of 5s.

These small tenements were less fertile, a mixture of arable, coarse pasture and furze (gorse), so rents were lower than for the richer land at Trembleath Barton or for the rich land in parts of Penrose, which were let for anything from £1 to £4 per acre per year.

An advertisement in the *West Briton* of the Sale of Reversion records that up until 1841 the different farms making up Treginegar were tenanted on the three lives system, the lives being the lessee, 30 years old, his sister Catherine, 20 years, and his son John, four years. John's was the remaining life in 1841. In 1845, when the 146-acre Brabyn's Tenement was leased to John Hawken on a seven-year lease, his rent

These old barns at Trewinnick still have a use.

Hand mows or 'sharps' at Treburrick, St Ervan. Seven or eight sharps stood in a circle, with two or three upside down on top like a little hat. They were left to mature before adding to the mow or rick.

Old outbuildings at Trevengenow farm and a corner of a more modern smithy (on the right).

was reduced for the first two years to allow the new tenant time to get the land into good order.

The Conditions of Survey for the 14-year lease of Trenouth in 1845 described it as 195 acres of 'very good land' but the rent required from George Biddick, the tenant who took the lease, £150 for 195 acres, reveals that it undoubtedly still contained as much of the 'moory lands, sometimes partly in Tillage but of no great value per acre' and the 'coarse land' of the 1733 Survey. The 1845 Tithe Award describes most of the fields as arable, but also describes a large number of fields as 'pasture'. At Trethewey, Gregory Tom's annual rent was £36 for 66 acres, which had been set in 1834 and continued at the same level into the twentieth century. Mr Tom raised sheep for their fleeces, which he sold to a wool factory. The tenant at Bogee Farm paid £115 for 290 acres, which included a large area of Bogee Common still covered in furze. All farms showed a mixture of types of land. The 1841 Sale Advertisement for Treburrick described it as containing 141 acres of 'good Arable, Meadow and Pasture Land'.

All farms had pockets of swampy land waiting for more modern drainage methods. The furze was not limited to the downs in the south. It spread in a discontinuous line up through the Trembleath estate (as indicated by field names, Higher Furze Park, Lower Furze Park, both noted as 'Waste' on the Tithe Map) and as far north as Trenouth on the east. Apart from its use as fuel – the clome ovens were fired by it – the existence of furze was partly the reason for so many bees being kept, indicated by the number of fields called 'Bee Park' – 13. Trenouth had no 'Bee Park' field, but had a stone wall containing bee boles, niches which sheltered the straw bee skeps during the wet and windy winters.

St Ervan parish covered 3,180 acres. In the nineteenth century 2,280 acres were 'arable', 125 acres 'pasture', 200 acres furze land, and 350 acres common. With the availability of sea sand and careful management these arable lands could be made very productive, wheat, barley and turnips being the principal crops.

As the century progressed, as tenure of land moved from the three lives system to shorter leases of 14 or even seven years, and no doubt given a boost by the bad harvest of 1840, the leases of property in St Ervan which survive show a strong emphasis on approved methods of good husbandry. These followed a standard formula:

Taker shall not break up or till any part of said premises with more than two crops of Corn or Grain successively during said term (except a Crop of Turnips between the Wheat and Spring Tillages) the first only of which... shall be of wheat... and only then will let said premises lie fallow and out of tillage the three next succeeding years at least and upon every fresh breach for Tillage shall carry 8 Butt or Cart loads of good Salt Sea Sand or 100 Bushels of well burnt Lime... on every acre broken for Tillage... and shall mix the same with at least 80 Butt or Cart loads of good Dung Earth and other Manure according to the rules of good husbandry –

Taker shall be allowed to break a lay field and till

Trethewey farmhouse, c.1946. The old wash-house is still attached to the side of the house and the 16-pane window lower left has been renewed.

Turnips and after the Turnips, barley, and See the same out –

Taker shall not carry off from said premises any Hay Straw –Taker shall provide sow and harrow or brush in 5lbs of good Red Clover 21lbs of good White Clover 1lb of good Trefoil Seed and 10 gallons of good Eaver Seed in every Acre... that shall be tilled with Barley or Oats –

Taker shall not grow more Potatoes on said Premises than shall be necessary for use of himself and his work people with manure arising therefrom –

Taker shall not cut any part for Hay twice in any one year nor two years successively – nor cut for Clover after cutting same for Hay.

And so it continued, with measures to keep the protective hedges in good condition, important on land so near the Atlantic coast. It was essential that with so much swampy ground the tenant should agree to scour and cleanse the drains and ditches 'so as to carry off the surface water from the land' and with the difficulty of growing trees in a salt-wind-blasted climate, the landlord would require his tenant not to 'cut lop or prune any Trees Saplings or Shrubs... growing on said premises.'

Their intention was to keep the land in good condition, but as difficult seasons followed each other during the late-nineteenth century these clauses became restrictive and deterred initiatives to improve farming methods.

The main pastoral farming was of sheep for wool. At Treginegar there is mention of sheep, and at Trethewey the fleeces of sheep were the farm's principal product. 'Mr Tom's Wool Book' was begun in 1823 by Gregory Tom senr and continued by Gregory Tom junr after his father's death in 1862, and continued until 1893 when Gregory junr, still a bachelor, was 84 years old. It details the number of fleeces and their weights in pounds, usually around 50lbs. The fleeces often include a few 'lambs'. From the total weight is subtracted 'breakages', and added are

'tails' or 'tailings'. Prices fluctuated, but 1838 was a good year, Mr Tom selling his 1,210 fleeces for £49.17s.10d., to the wool factory firm of J. Allanson & Son of Talskiddy in St Columb Major parish. In most years he earned around £20, the number of fleeces sold per year averaging 600.

In 1853, after Gregory junr, aged 42, had taken over, there was a big jump in the sales – 2,112 fleeces earned him £80. An income of £80 was maintained for a few years, but the average from then on was £60, and a decline shows as Gregory Tom junr approaches 84 years and the book ends. He was a bachelor and had no heir to continue his work. Living with him were two sisters who were widowed early, Richard Brewer's widow, Jane, with her two sons and a daughter. The elder son left on marriage to farm at St Eval and the younger farmed Trethewey with little enthusiasm or success.

Gregory Tom's other widowed sister, Mary Martyn, carefully copied out, in 1840, recipes 'For Curing the Fellon in Sheep', 'For Preventing the Rot in Sheep', 'Pills for Curing the Rot in Sheep', 'For Curing the Scab or Scouring in Sheep', 'To prevent the fly from attacking the sheep':

For Curing the Fellon in Sheep
Take 3 pounds of Salt; one pound of Nitre, and ½ pint Spirits of turpentine; stir them well together and add ½ pint of tar. Stir the mixture again to prevent the spirits from separating from the water; then add 4 ozs of roll tobaco, opened; a large handful of bannel broom, and a handful of wormwood. Pour on these ingredients 3 gallons of pond-water; then boil the mixture over a slow fire, for about two hours, until the quantity is reduced to two gallons; then strain and bottle it for use.

To administer the above
Bleed the sheep until it becomes faint, then pour it the sixth part of a pint of the drench. Should it appear, in about an hour, that the animal is not better, bleed it again, and give the same quantity of the liquid as before.

Pills for Curing the Rot in Sheep
Take 5 grains of colomel; 5 grains of comphor, and 5 grains of opium; mix them well together, and make the whole into 14 pills which will be done by the druggist. One of these pills is to be given to each sheep for 14 successive days. If the pills are too strong for a sheep, the animal will leave its food and be taken with a scouring, when this is the case, no more pills must be given until the scouring ceases. If the pills be not suffi-ciently powerful for a sheep, the disease will be found to increase, when a pill and a half must be given each day. Whilst taking the pills, the sheep must be kept from water, and be housed by night.

Mary Martyn refers to sheep as 'these valuable animals'. A farm sale at Eddystone a year later gives us some prices.

Lot 1 – 2 Ewes sold	at 22/1 Each	
Lot 2 – 2 Do.	at 25/3 Do.	
Lot 3 – 2 Do.	at 25/3 Do.	
Lot 4 – 2 Oxen	£23.4.0.	
Lot 5 – Cow in Calf	8.13.0	
Lot 6 – Heifer in Calf	6.0.0	
Lot 7 – Horse bought in at £7		
Lot 8 – Pig	1.12.0	

Two years later, Nicholas Rundell, who had bought the first three Lots above, held a sale:

Lot 1 – 3 Ewes	22s. Each
Lot 2 – 4 Do.	20s. Each
Lot 3 – 3 Do.	21s. Do.
Lot 4 – 5 Withers	21s.6d.
[Lot 5 is missing on the MS]	
Lot 6 – 6 Lambs	10s.
Lot 7 – 2 Oxen	£20
Lot 8 – 2 Steers	£17.1s.
Lot 9 – Cow	£5.8s.
Lot 10	Horse bought in at £5.12s.0d.

The method of payment is interesting: 50 per cent down, and the rest four months later 'on giving Approved Security'.

On the farms in the east and south of the parish sheep were predominant. At Penrose in 1805 a farm sale shows some proportion of sheep to other animals, even on the generally richer soils of that area, illustrating yet again the variability of quality of land within the bounds of each farm.

The rest of the parish consisted of 200 acres of furze land and 350 acres of common downland.

'Coarse pasture and Furze' extended to the foot of the downs. Both furze from the 'furze lands' and turves from the common were important sources of fuel. The furze made a quick, brisk fire and the ash left enough heat in a clome oven to bake bread. Furze was cut in May, its awkward, prickly branches bundled into 'faggots' and piled into a loose stack or rick.

On the common, turves were cut, taken down to the house, and piled into ricks. These provided a smouldering heat, and the cottages smelled perpetually of smoke as a result.

The pattern of very small fields in St Ervan was ancient. The land was divided by hedges into 'closes' or 'inclosures' long before Enclosure Acts enforced it in the rest of Britain, simply because crops would have been flattened and livestock distressed if unprotected against the Atlantic gales. However, in the southern part of the parish there remained Trewinnick Common, a large open space of just over 100 acres owned in common by 14 smallholders who held rights of pasture and turbary. (Turbary was the right to cut turves which could be used as fuel.)

On 15 June 1839, under the General Enclosure Act of 1801, three Commissioners, yeomen from neigh-bouring parishes, made an Award, apportioning the common to the individual commoners and posting the printed notice of their decisions on the doors of the Parish Church and both the Methodist chapel and the Bible Christian chapel in Rumford.

Public meetings were held. The Commissioners:

... perambulated and set out and marked out the boundaries of the said open and common pasture lands and heard adjudged and determined all classes of every sort and having viewed and valued the same lands...

... held a final meeting on 19 April 1839 attended by those with an interest.

It was agreed to use the existing Poor Rate as a measure by which to divide and allot the common land, which measured 99 acres, 3 roods and 35 poles. This meant that for every £2.13s.4d. a person paid in Poor Rate on land and houses he owned he was allotted a one-acre strip of the common, and for every 4d. paid he got one yard of land (160 yards to an acre). (In the original document the following abbreviations are used: A = acre, R = rood, P = pole. There were 40 poles to a rood and 4 roods to an acre.)

For example, in return for forsaking all his former pasture, turbary and other rights on Trewinnick Common:

William Strongman, Farmer, in right of a certain dwelling House and lands by name of Eddystone in the occupation of Samuel Clemoe was allotted Plot A, measuring 4A 2R 1P plus a share of the Wastril (part W) measuring 3A 12 Poles.

Richard Brewer, Miller, of Rumford Mills was allotted section H, 4A 3R 4P plus Section V next the Wastril.

Thomas Key, Labourer who had a 'Dwelling House, Meadow and Garden' [New House Tenement alongside Trevengenow Farm], received 1R 19P in Section Q plus a share in the wastril marked W.

Peter Sandry, blacksmith, by right of a 'Dwelling House or Messuage &c.' acquired a small plot of 3 roods plus a share of the wastril. Almost a century later this right was invoked to prevent the RAF at St Mawgan airfield fencing off a water pump.

The sections of land allotted were long, narrow strips from south to north across the length of the common, and with them went responsibilities for the new proprietors. Each was to erect, by 25 December 1841, a 'good and substantial hedge' on the west side of their section and to keep it in good repair at his own expense. Each hedge (stone walls filled with earth) had to be 'five feet in the bottom, four feet and half in height and to finish with two feet and half at the top.' William Strongman and Michael Strongman converted their plots into arable fields. And judging from the amount of 'Burning and Sciding, and Beting' by Richard Brewer's day-labourers, he was

47

Trewinnick farmhouses. The house on the right dates from the seventeenth century with later additions, the house on the left was built by Jonathan Bennett in 1827.

well on the way to clearing the ground for cultivation in his plot:

Aug 27, 1839 Paid John Strongman
for Beting £5.16.6
" " Paid for Burning and Sciding £1.3.6
Oct 12, " Settled with John Brewer
for Beting £1.3.6
Settled with John Robins for Beting
and Burning and Skiding £1.7.6
£9.17.6

In a normal year Richard Brewer paid out no more than £3 for such work.

'Beat' meant turf, so 'beting' referred to the paring of turf, which was done by hand with a mattock. Where rough furze-growing land was being cleared, the stubbed-out roots of furze and pared turf were raked into heaps and burned, and the ashes spread over ('scading') the ground, sometimes mixed with sea sand or animal manure. This enriching mixture was ploughed into the ground to make it ready for cropping. The same method was used to prepare land which had been ley for a long period.

The Tithe Survey shows that many properties had gardens, orchards or plantations. Fruit trees of many kinds were grown. In 1910 Henry Tom wrote to his cousin, Gregory Brewer, who was the tenant at Trethewey at the time: 'Trethewey used to be noted for miles around for the fine fruit grown there.'

There were hop gardens at Trenouth and the rectory, and the glebe land, according to the 1821 terrier, contained a flower garden, a kitchen garden and one other. Every farm had a mowhay, an enclosed sheltered place in or near the farmyard where the 'mow' or rick was placed, on a raised platform to allow air to circulate beneath, and with a roof over.

Reading through a number of deeds and leases, one inevitably encounters over and over again the landowner's insistence on retaining all rights to the trees and to the minerals which might be found on the property at some time in the future. For example, when Peter Sandry leased as small a piece of land as three acres he had to allow the landowner, Robert Trefusis of Trefusis in south Cornwall, access to 'all Tyn Toll Tyn Tyn Works Copper works Mynes Minerals and Metals.' Thomas Tremain of Padstow did the same when leasing Great Treginegar's 146 acres to John Hawken in 1845 (brother to James Hawken, who was leasing and occupying Treginegar Mills since 1841).

Here there was a surprise in store. In 1847, at the bottom of a short slope, about 100 yards from the Treginegar corn mill, a copper lode was cut at a depth of only 8 fathoms. On this a level was driven for 40 fathoms, pumping being effected by an 18ft-diameter water-wheel erected on the adjacent river. *The Mining Journal* of 3 April 1847 reported:

WHEAL TREMAINE (St Ervan) – At a meeting of shareholders, held on Monday last, at the offices of Messrs WRIGHT and BONNER (solicitors to the company), London-street, Fenchurch-street, the accounts for the past two months were audited and the reports of the agents read, which were considered highly satisfactory, and the prospects extremely flattering. The proximity to the mine of a good river of water enhances the value of the property as there is a sufficient supply to work a powerful water-wheel which has just been erected and is expected to be at work this week – this will render the expense of a steam-engine unnecessary, and enable the mine to be proved to a considerable depth at a very moderate outlay. The prospects are represented as very encouraging, a copper lode having been cut at 8 fms depth only, and driven on to the extent of about 40 fms, from which a considerable quantity of good ore has already been raised.

Only two miners appear in St Ervan records; Charles Seccombe, who married Elizabeth, daughter of miller Thomas Rawling, and John Grigor, from St Merryn.

By July 1851 the affairs of Wheal Tremaine were being investigated in the Stannary Court (Cornish tinners' court). Wages for clearing the mine had not been paid and men petitioned for compensation. It all ended unsatisfactorily for the plaintiffs. Part of the problem was that the 'Adventurers' (men who invested in the mine) never let their identity be known.

Two other people claimed compensation but in vain, the proceeds from the sale of the machinery and tools being insufficient to cover these additional costs. Thomas Tremain, the landowner after whom the mine was named, claimed £16 for five years' rent due:

... for and in respect of sixty-four Yards of Land which have been destroyed and rendered unfit for Tillage by the Adventurers... the said sum of one shilling per annum per yard being the amount reserved and covenanted to be paid by the said Adventurers in and by the original grant or Lease of the said Mine.

Equally vain was the claim by James Hawken on behalf of his father, John, whose farm he managed. John Hawken was a tenant of John Tremain and was bound by his lease 'to keep and leave the Hedges in good and perfect repair.' The mine workings had destroyed 5½ yards of hedging below a field called the Cow Close Hill, 14 yards of hedging in a field called Cow Close Hill, at 6s. per yard, and two quoins between Cow Close Hill and Middle Park Hill costing 10s., making a total of £6.7s.

The right of access to waters and watercourses was reserved to the tenant working the land. Even as late as 1825, when the very small piece of land next to Trevengenow farmhouse called New House Tenement was leased, it was 'together with waters and watercourses...'.

Water was obviously essential for livestock. Lot 37 in the 1855 Trembleath sale, Rye Park (69 acres), was to be sold:

... subject to the right of watering Cattle and Horses in [field] number 296, as is now exercised by the Lessees of Lot 18 [which was over a mile away in the middle of Penrose] and such right is to be permanently attached to such last mentioned premises.

On the face of it a strange agreement. Lot 18 was Spry's Tenement in Penrose, which did not even belong to the same manor. Field No. 296 on the sale map was at the end of a lane, near modern Trevilledor, in the middle of fields of coarse pasture

and furze right at the southern end of the parish on the boundary with St Mawgan. It was here in the 1976 drought that a retired farm labourer remembered a well which he claimed had never dried out. The farmer dug down a couple of inches, uncovered the spring, and his cattle never again lacked pure water in quantity.

A less traditional retention of rights was exercised at Treginegar, of clay and quarries of stone, for this was in the slate district where healing, or roofing slates were used for the farmhouses, and ragstone, irregular-shaped tiles of slate, were used in roofing of outbuildings, and ordinary stone for buildings and hedges. Thomas Roberts's farm accounts show him running a profitable business in healing stone.

With such varied activities the farmer's working year was bound to encompass a wide variety of work. The farm accounts, even though these show only the work done by paid labourers and not that done by the farmer himself, bear this out.

In addition to the seasonal activities, breaking in ground after ley, burning off the stubble, or arrish, spreading the dung, fetching and spreading the sea sand, sowing and harvesting wheat (some for straw reeds) and barley, and some oats, planting and harvesting roots – turnips, mangels and potatoes – sowing and harvesting trefoils, rye grass (eaver), haymaking, cutting furze in May, cutting turves and stacking them to dry for fuel, in addition to all these, there were the routine jobs which could be tackled all through the year; threshing wheat (most of the year, January to October in Stribley's accounts) and hedging (which seemed to go on through the year), at any time when seasonal pressures were eased.

Then there were the livestock to care for, to feed and to breed. Fleeces were sold, other sheep as mutton for consumption in the parish (the main meat eaten in the nineteenth century), working oxen and horses, and cows mainly for milk.

Every farmer brewed his own ale and some made cider.

And there was hunting and shooting for relaxation from their toils. In 1781, when Sir William Molesworth of Pencarrow in neighbouring Little Petherick parish leased land at Penrose to Henry Roberts, he reserved to himself: 'Free Liberty to hawke, hunt fish and fowle with his... retinue in or upon the said demised Premises doing thereby no wilful Damage...'

In the 1845 lease the landowner of Treginegar retained the right of access to 'rabbits and wildfowl'. In 1855 the Trembleath sale document proclaimed:

Perhaps there is no district in Cornwall that can boast of better Partridge Shooting; Hares too are in abundance, and the district is good also, both for Hunting and Coursing.

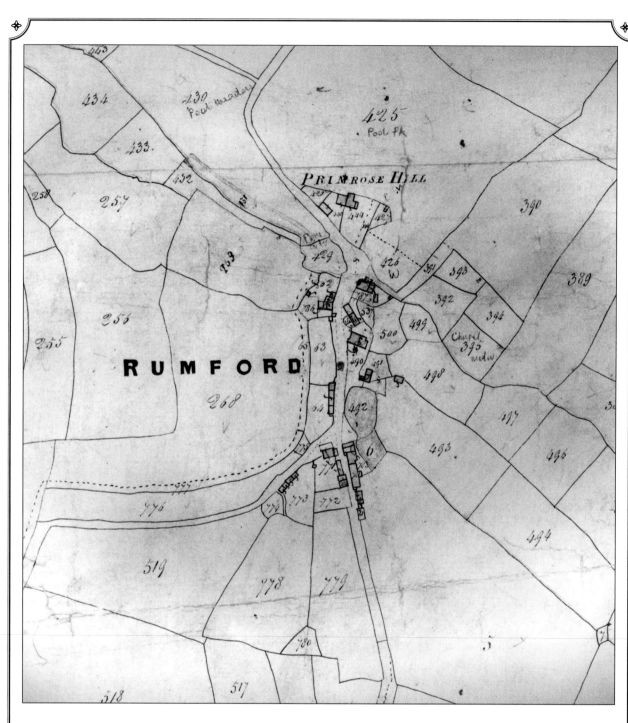

Rumford on the 1842 Tithe Map.

CHAPTER 7

Mills, Malthouses and Water-Powered Threshing Machines

Essential to any farming community was the mill. St Ervan had three in the nineteenth century, all on the same river, which rises on Trewinnick Downs at the end of Well Lane and runs first through the wastrel, to which several Trewinnick commoners shared the right following the 1839 Enclosure. It flows north past Music Water, continues north through meagre woodland which separates Trewinnick land first from Bogee property, then from Trenouth's fields, before turning westward to cross the road at Rumford. At this point it served the grist mills of Trewinnick manor at Rumford and was refreshed by a new spring rising in Couches Tenement. The Tithe Map shows a mill pool and mill weir above the millhouse. Both have long since disappeared, one covered by the yard of W.H. Old & Sons, the other behind a row of cottages.

Shortly after the bridge at the bottom of Rumford village, the river began to serve the grist mills at Millingworth. A leat was cut above the river and the water powered the water-wheel from above, before rejoining the natural course of the river. Millingworth ('new mills') was Trembleath's manorial mill.

The waters from three springs near the church gave fresh power to the river as it flowed on west-ward through the narrow valley to serve, with the aid of another leat, Treginegar Mills between Churchtown and Penrose.

Two of the rivers form part of the boundaries of the parish. One separates St Ervan and St Merryn, the other, a tributary river, parts St Ervan from St Eval, before they join together at the north-western tip of the parish to run finally into Porthcothan Bay.

The livelihood of the miller was assured by the reservation of certain rights to him as tenant. The landlord had the right to enter the premises to inspect the state of repair, but he could not interfere with the watercourses or inhibit traditional trade, i.e. the condition imposed on all lessees to use the mill belonging to the manor of which their land belonged. In 1834 Richard Brewer, yeoman, leased 'Millingworth Mills and Premises' from Francis Cross Esq. on the lives of his three youngest children:

... together with all waters and watercourses Leats and by Leats wanes, Multures of Griesters with all Griest and Griesters of the free customary and Conventionary Tenants as many as do appertain or belong to the said Mill or of right have been used and accustomed to grind their Corn or Griest there...

Mill and malthouse went together. The malthouse rented by the Sandry family was located beside the millpool at Rumford. The mill at Millingworth had a malthouse alongside. The innkeeper at Penrose Lowertown was also a maltster.

Water powered the winding gear for the mine at Treginegar when it first opened, and earlier it was used to power a threshing machine at Trembleath. This feature had a high place in the sale literature in 1855: 'A most desirable and very fertile MESSUAGE TENEMENT, or FARM, with a water-power Threshing Machine... called TREMBLEATH BARTON...'

At Trethewey a water-wheel manufactured by Otin of Wadebridge in 1839 powered a threshing machine. At Treburrick there was another water-powered threshing machine, the water being fed from a millpond in a leat along the side of a field and across the top of a low wall before dropping onto the wheel. The wall had a dual purpose. Below the gulley were square niches cut into the stonework for hens to nest.

Other farms had their winding gear for threshing in a building attached to the side of the barn, called a roundhouse. It was usually hexagonal with an open side and a six-pointed roof supported by a pretty pattern of cross beams. The winding gear in the centre was pulled round and round by a horse. This drove the shaft which passed through the wall into the barn to operate the machinery inside. Treleigh, Treravel, Treglinnick, Trewinnick, Treginnegar and Glebe Farms all had their round-houses, and there was an open round at Penrose. The men put the sacks of grain up over the beams to keep them off the ground away from rats. Richard Brewer (1779–1853), leader of the Bible Christians, was one of three millers in the parish. He operated the Trewinnick manorial mill in Rumford village. He came from a long-established St Ervan family of farmers, and in 1803 he married Ebbett Spear, daughter of Malachi Spear, who leased land on the east side of the parish in Trewinnick manor, which included the manorial mill at Rumford. The prop-erty is described in a sale advertisement in the *West Briton* on 5 June 1812:

Lot 4: A Tenement and Premises, called or known by the name of Rumford Mill Tenement, comprising a capital pair of New built Grist Mills, Dwelling house, Barn, Stable, and other Out buildings, about 8 Acres of fertile Meadow Land, in the occupation of Malachi Spear, on a

The old corn mill, Millingworth, and cottages at Underhill, taken in 1976. The centre-hung casement windows were from the eighteenth century and the 16-pane sash windows were from the early-nineteenth century.

Mill Cottage, Rumford. The thatch roof was removed c.1931. This picture was taken in the 1960s when the cottage was due to be modernised. Phyllis Alberta 'Bertie' Cowling lived here with her grandparents, William and Emma Rabey. After they died their son, William, allowed Bertie to stay on until she married and moved in with her parents-in-law, Richard and Lillian Gregor, at Trevilledor.

The old malthouse and cottages, Trewinnick Lane, Rumford, after refurbishment in 1958.

Roundhouse at Glebe Farm in the 1970s.

Roundhouse at Trenouth in the 1970s.

Old and new barns at Trewinnick, in the twentieth century.

lease for 99 years determinable on the Deaths of Three Persons, aged about 43, 37 and 34, under the yearly reserved Rent of £4 10s. and an Heriot of £2 on the death of each life.

Malachi was a wealthy man. When he died in 1820 he left goods to the value of £600, besides leasehold property in Rumford. To his daughter, Ebbett, he left a house and a garden in Rumford, 'which Gregory Gill has now in his possession for a carpenter's shop.' Gregory Gill was a millwright who probably played a part in the building of the 'new grist mills' in 1812. (There is another intertwining of kinships here – Gregory Gill's mother was Mary Spear of Padstow, who also called her youngest daughter Ebbett.) Malachi bequeathed the leasehold of the manorial mills to his son, Edward Spear, who died in 1827 aged 55. The leasehold passed to Edward's sister, Ebbett, wife of Richard Brewer, and her eldest son, John Brewer. With a family of eight children aged between nine and 24 years, Richard Brewer must have been rather pleased at this additional security for his family. From 1814 the Brewer family was living at Churchtown and Richard was the miller. He was working the Millingworth mills, the manorial mills of Trembleath. After Edward Spear's death in 1827 they moved to Rumford.

Two years later there was a sad occurrence at the mill in Rumford. Although Richard Brewer was not

working the mill himself – a man called Perry did that – he must have felt closely associated with the events. The story was dramatic enough for the report in the *Falmouth Packet* to be reproduced in the *Royal Cornwall Gazette* and, for an even wider readership, in the *London Morning Chronicle*. This is the version which appeared in the *Royal Cornwall Gazette*:

DEATH BY POISON. – On Wednesday last, a lad named John Snell, son of a small farmer... was sent by his father with some corn to a mill kept by a person called Perry in the same parish. Being compelled to wait longer than usual, in having the corn ground, he was invited by the miller to take dinner with the family, which consisted of Perry, a servant man, and a house-keeper. A large pasty was produced for the repast, of which all present partook. Shortly after, young Snell left for home, but on the road he was taken ill being affected with sickness, pain in the stomach and bowels, and all the usual and alarming symptoms felt by persons who have taken poison. With difficulty he reached home, where his mother conceiving his illness to be a violent attack of a stomach complaint to which he was subject, gave him some tea and put him to bed. His illness however continued to increase, and in a few hours he expired.

His father rushed to the mill and found Perry, the miller, alone in the house, suffering similar symptoms. The housekeeper was found and given emetics, but the servant-man did not appear until the next morning, having suffered a night of agony. However, all three adults eventually recovered. An inquest found that, the mill being greatly infested by rats, Perry had procured arsenic to destroy them. He had mixed it with flour and placed it in various parts of the premises. Some must have got into the flour from which the pasties were made.

John Snell's father was farming six or seven acres, parts of two small tenements on the downs, Kestle's Tenement and Barn Ground, which belonged to Trewinnick manor, so he had to take his corn to the mill at Rumford. This tragedy took place the day before Christmas Eve. The formalities of the inquest were quickly completed and John Snell was buried on Boxing Day. In the parish register: 'Buried 26 December 1829 John Snell aged 12 years.'

Curious to know what other children the Snells had, I searched the baptism register and found: 'Baptised 26 December 1829 Susan, daughter of John and Ann Snell, Bear's Downs, Farmer.' So, on the same day that John, aged 12, was buried, his baby sister, Susan, was baptised. Even allowing for the greater familiarity with death at an early age, the sudden death of John would have made the baptism of his baby sister seem that much more urgent. The practical consideration of a farmer who, having just lost his son, his labourer, and living two miles from the church, needing to make best use of his time,

Penrose village in 1976.

probably also played a part. In 1834 John and Ann Snell had another child. They named him John.

Richard Brewer had roots in the parish going back several generations right to the earliest surviving records. He was also literally at the centre of everyday life for those parishioners who used Rumford village rather than Penrose. Besides being the miller, he was a grocer. His Account Book, 1832–45, reveals that he was at the centre of a complex trading operation.

More than 100 individuals, mostly from the parish but several from further afield, had accounts with him. They bought mutton and lamb, beef or pork. They bought small amounts, say 3lbs. at a time, the better-off buying 10–40lbs. Occasionally he sold large quantities to William Hawken, the butcher at

The mill at Trembleath Barton possibly provided the housing for the water-powered threshing machine.

Churchtown. Prices fluctuated from season to season, but there was little difference between the 1833 prices and those of 1845, when the account ledger finishes. 'Backen' (bacon) varied between 4½–8d. per pound in 1833 and 7d. in 1845.

Richard Brewer bought sheep and lambs from people in the parish, from Biddick, Williams, Clemoe, Bennett and Spear. He also reared sheep and lambs himself and sold the skins to the wool dealer in St Columb Major.

People bought wheat and barley from him, flour and bran and 'shops' and 'coarse grait', the poor-quality stuff which made up animal feed. He bought wheat from other farmers, besides growing some himself. He sold malt and hops.

Peter Sandry (1784–1831) owned Couches Tenement, on which stood the large malthouse. It is said he cornered the malting market by buying up inns in the neighbourhood, but in 1829 misfortune struck. A fire broke out: 'which entirely consumed the building, and a cottage adjoining, together with upwards of 500 bushels of malt... No part of the property was insured.'

It was fortunate that no stray sparks caught the thatched roofs of nearby cottages. Peter Sandry applied to the Quarter Sessions Court for a reduction in taxation on the lost and damaged goods – 1,242 bushels of malt were damaged to some degree. At current prices these could have sold for very nearly £1,000. Peter Sandry did not rebuild the malthouse but converted the damaged building into dwellings. From this account ledger it seems that Richard Brewer had taken over the malting business on this side of the parish.

For malting he needed coal, which he bought by the bushel, 12 bushels at a time, 'from the Vesel at 6½d. per bushel'. This meant that he had to fetch his coal from where it was landed by boat at Porthcothan or at Little Petherick in the Camel estuary. In the course of a year he bought more than 100 bushels of coal, the price averaging out at 7d. per bushel. He sold it in small quantities to people in the parish at a good profit.

Accounts were not settled monthly or even at the end of the year. There were two customs, one for the poor and one for the rich, which seemed to work well. The poor would run up a bill of, say, 1s.6d. for 3lbs. of mutton, and pay it off at 6d. a time, occasionally by doing a day's work, for which they received 6d. Seldom did the poor clear the total amount outstanding before making further purchases.

At the other end of the social and economic scale was Philip Hawke, farming 150 acres. He bought something every month, 10–40lbs. of mutton at a time, and potatoes or turnips by the bushel. Occasionally he bought a whole sheep. Philip would run up an account averaging £3.5s. per year, whereas a pauper such as Rebekah Hawke spent only 9s. over a whole year. She had only herself and a daughter to

feed; Philip had six or more adults in his house. On the other hand, Philip was a farmer and his purchases were surplus only to his own food production. He could wait 12 months before settling his account; pauper Rebekah Hawke paid off little by little every fortnight. She was dependent on the Vestry for her income, which naturally exerted restraint on her budget.

Richard Brewer had five house tenants, too: Jenny Hicks, who lived at Churchtown, mother of Brewer's apprentice Thomas, John Coul, Thomas Spear, John James and Ann Harris at Rumford, who needed occasional assistance from the poor rates. Cottage rents in the parish averaged £2.10s. paid half yearly in March and September. These tenants never seemed to pay off the whole amount. By 1 April 1839 John James signed his name against an entry in the account ledger that he had paid £4 rent up to the September 1838 half year and still owed a further £12.4s.3d. This rent might have been for land as well as the cottage, but there must have been some special reason for Richard Brewer to allow him to build up such a colossal debt. Most of his customers were reminded of the state of their account when £3 or £4 was owing, and the poorer agricultural labourer, who earned no more than 10s. per six-day week, never got into debt with Richard Brewer for more than half a week's wages. As a Bible Christian leader, Richard would have encouraged discipline in the payment of accounts.

Richard was a farmer as well as a miller. The account book records the yields of corn, wheat and barley that grew in his different fields in each year. Though it is not a continuous or complete record, it does give an idea of the scatter of land held by an individual. He records when his cow 'went to the Bull' or that his 'Sow went to the Boor Mar 21 the seckent time.'

The letting of pieces of his land as potato ground was recorded in detail. In 1841 he lists 30 names, all from the parish, who rented potato ground, anything from 5 yards to 60 yards at 1s. per yard. The 1841 list includes the curate, the Revd Polwhele, who took 60 yards. Nearly everyone on the list had land of his own, but perhaps Richard Brewer's potato ground was especially good for that crop. In 1843 15 names are listed as renting potato ground in Rumford More. Each year a different field was used. How the different lettings were defined on the ground is not revealed to us, but Thomas Key had three yards 'by the Gate'. Dung was important for the success of the potato crop, especially when the field used was at Cluckey, on the rising ground to the common. One year John James supplied his own dung and got his ground more cheaply: 'John James – 5½ yards with his own dung – 2s.10½d.'

As well as grinding corn, Richard Brewer had a threshing machine powered by the water-wheel. He threshed corn for the farmers, and also bought corn from them for resale. In the Day Account for 28 October 1842 he has two entries:

For thrashing H. Brewer's Corn:
Wheat   *6s.0d.*
Barley   *2s.6d.*
Received of H. Brewer:
Bushel and half Barley   *13s.1½d.*

Finally, Richard Brewer was a money-lender. He frequently lent small sums of 1s. and often lent £1, and very occasionally larger sums, £5 and even £10. Six years' interest on one loan of £5 amounted to £1.

On 26 October 1833 Richard enters in his accounts: 'Pead John Strongman For working to the rods [roads] 10s.7 ½d.'

This was the year that Richard Brewer was elected constable by the Vestry and it was the constable's function to see to the maintenance of the parish roads. It seems from the amount of wages paid that a week's work by one man was all that was required in 1833 to bring the parish roads up to the desired standard.

The following year Richard Brewer was overseer to the poor, one of the two Vestry officials whose function it was to distribute the rate collected to maintain the poor of the parish. In 1855, as waywarden, he collected the Way Rate from 45 parishioners, a total of £50. He listed the names and the amount he collected from each.

It was unusual for the miller or any craftsman to be an official of the Vestry. Richard's entitlement was due to his land holdings. The Tithe Map (1842) shows Richard, in addition to being a miller and grocer, farming 20 acres at Churchtown and a further 9 acres of Trembleath land. The land at Rumford Mills had included pasture rights on Trewinnick Common and, when the common was enclosed in 1839, Richard was allotted his own long, narrow strip, about 5 acres in all. Often work done was not immediately paid for. It is possible that all the 'beting, burning and scading' that was done in August and October 1839 on the 'ground belonging to Rumford Mills' referred to the breaking in of this new patch of enclosed common.

The ledger finishes in 1845, the year that Richard junr died of typhus. By 1851 Richard senr, now 72, had retired to the smaller mill at Millingworth. He

had set up his surviving sons in good businesses. John (the eldest) looked after the mills at Rumford, assisted by William, Thomas (the carpenter) looked after the grocery and Edward was working the land at Churchtown owned by his father. John also took office in the Vestry in some years.

So why was Richard Brewer senr in Bodmin gaol? The story is that he invested heavily in modern machinery for milling corn at a time when it was being centralised by big companies taking advantage of the development of the railways and the shipping of large quantities of grain from abroad. This put many small millers out of business. The new machinery for the mill at Millingworth had cost him a fortune and, as he did not get extra business to cover the costs, he went bankrupt. Shortly afterwards he entered the prison and on 20 September 1853 he died 'by a Visitation of God'. He was a Sheriff's Ward and was buried at Bodmin, the burial register giving his place of residence at the time of death as 'Bodmin Jail'.

The lease of Millingworth mills was assigned to Thomas Whitford, bankers. They continued to be worked by various millers until the early 1880s, when it was the only one in St Ervan still functioning. By this time it was being worked by Richard Brewer, grandson of bankrupt Richard, who had returned to the parish after a few years as a miller in Luxulyan.

Other families associated with milling were the Higmans and Rawlings. The family of Robert Higman, farmer at Penrose, were Methodists. One son, 17-year-old Robert, worked as a servant for Richard Brewer senr at Rumford. Ten years later he married Richard's daughter, Rachel. Another son, Joseph, was a wagoner living with Richard Brewer senr at Churchtown Mill in 1851. He worked his way up and by 1871 was a journeyman miller, living with his family at Penrose, and perhaps working at the mill over the river near Lowertown, Trethewell Mill in St Eval parish.

Thomas Rawling was an agricultural labourer living at Trewinnick Lane in 1841, and a miller at Treginegar Mills in 1851, with his 21-year-old son Thomas as his 'miller's boy'. By 1861 the 'miller's boy' had become a 'master miller'.

Milling ran in families. The miller came up from the ranks of the agricultural labourer and learned his trade on the job.

This typical stone-built house on the left as you leave Penrose to go to Rumford is Lindisfarne as it was in 1960s.

An ox having new shoes, or cues, early-twentieth century. The animal would fight hard against this process so is securely lashed. Can anyone identify any of the men? One of the men in the centre might be Jim Parsons.

CHAPTER 8

Craftsmen, the Parish Middle Class

If we think of the tenant farmers working the large farms of 150 acres as our parish upper class, then it was the craftsmen – the miller, the blacksmith, the carpenter, the mason and shoemaker – who were the parish middle class. These were the people to whom everyone else had to have recourse at one time or another. They were the ones who were paid in cash, and often they had their own smallholding as well to support their family's food needs. Unlike the labourer, they had a measure of independence.

The interdependence of farmer, miller and black-smith is obvious. The blacksmith was essential to repair tools and machinery, and such domestic items as pans. There were two blacksmiths in the parish, the Penrose side being served by a smith at Churchtown until the 1840s, after which one smith worked from the village of Penrose, another in Rumford village.

The smithy at Churchtown seems to have been a launching pad for young smiths in their twenties. Peter Sandry started his family there, as did Jonathan Dawe and Edward Spear.

From 1851 there was a smithy in Penrose village manned by master blacksmith George Dryden. He came from near Bodmin but had married a St Merryn stonemason's daughter, Jane Brenton. Jane's father died in 1857 aged 75. By this time he had evidently settled his sons, for he paid them off with a shilling each, and left all his money, up to £100, plus the lease of two houses in St Merryn, to his daughter and to his son-in-law, George Dryden, should he outlive Jane. If once he had been able to write out his account, by the time he came to make his will he had lost the skill and signed it with a mark.

At Rumford, the smithy had been in the hands of the Sandry family for generations. We can trace this St Ervan branch back to the marriage of Peter Sandry and Blanch Gill on 11 Sep 1695. Peter Sandry (1702–83) was the first we know to have been a blacksmith. In 1747 he leased a 'Dwelling House and Blacksmith's Shop... within the Village and Town of Rumford... and one little Plott of Land adjoining thereto' for 99 years determinable on three lives. He signed the indenture as 'blacksmith', the beginning of several generations of Sandry blacksmiths in Rumford. It was their twelfth child, Peter, baptised in 1750, who took the blacksmith business on from his father.

The blacksmith's mastery of fire had set him aside from other people from ancient times and this craft still had a high status in the twentieth century. From

an account Peter Sandry sent out to Mr William Roberts in 1790 for work done and materials supplied between February 1788 and July 1790, we see the wide range of work a blacksmith did and the diversity of services he performed for the local farmers. The blacksmith repaired all the tools used by the farmer. For example, 'laying a coulter' or 'laying a sheer' were parts of a plough being renewed by welding a new piece of metal onto the worn parts. The two layers of metal had to be fired to exactly the right temperature then, as they cooled, beaten together precisely.

Mr Roberts was still using oxen, which needed new shoes from time to time. 'Octr 1790 – Cuying 4 Oxen – 4d.' We have no details of how they fitted new shoes at that time, but a more modern photograph (opposite) shows that it could be a tricky operation and that the oxen did not enjoy it. At other times the smith sold '2 shoes and 2 removers 10d.' and 'a Pound of Nails – 6d.'

Peter Sandry (1750–1824) had seven children, only two surviving to adulthood – John, born in 1782, and Peter, born in 1784. John left St Ervan and worked as a blacksmith at Lane, near Newquay, at Truro and at Perran Foundry in Mylor parish on the south coast, where he had Sandry relations. Here he learned to weld cast iron. The tremendous heat required was obtained from silica sand, from a mine dump or burrow, together with lime. The secret was to select the right quality of silica sand.

John died in 1823, leaving a widow and sons aged 14 and 12. She took them back to St Ervan, where her parents-in-law, in their seventies, were still living, and where her brother-in-law, Peter, was running the family business. Peter married Philippa, daughter of a St Columb coach-builder, Thomas Cornish, but there were no children.

Peter (1784–1831) inherited part of Couches Tenement from his grandfather in 1824 and soon had the whole of Couches Tenement and land on which the smith's shop and the malthouse were situated. Proof of his skill in business was Rumford House, the substantial and solid home he built for himself in 1828, a spacious stone-built house which dominated the village street from the top of the north-facing hill.

In April 1831 he died aged 47. His varied business activities had enabled him to leave nearly £1,500 in his will, a far larger sum than the largest farmer in the parish. His memorial in the churchyard is the first of several to the Sandry family in the south-west corner, where he has a table monument, a slate ledger laid on

It was the blacksmith's task to sharpen or repair the coulters of these ploughs.

wheels, fitted with second safety valve under lock and key, steam pressure gauge waterproof cover and appendages £230
One large size '6' double blast Machine 4'6" wide No. 13,455 with wood wheels, tin elevators, patent shockers, patent trussed frame, waterproof cover and appendages £150

Elevators for sacking chaff £5
Double shaft (extra) £1.10.
£386.10.
Delivered at Liskeard £14.10
By Cash Aug 2nd 1876 £372.0.0
for Clayton & Shuttleworth

[signed] John Hearn

five rows of red brick. The slate is of good quality, silvery grey and elaborately etched.

Peter Sandry's will shows his concern, though he had no children himself, to pass to future Sandrys the fortune he had built up, namely his two fatherless nephews, Peter, now 22, and John, now 21. Peter (born 1809) was married to Nancy Key and they had an 18-month-old son, also Peter, and lived in the old family home, the little cottage next to the smith's shop where he worked. John (born 1810) was still a bachelor and living in Rumford House, keeping his uncle's widow company. Their uncle's will left his blacksmith's business to the older brother, Peter. Then, looking further into the future, he left a substantial bequest to his great-nephew, Peter, which included Rumford House.

In the meantime, however, while Peter and his parents continued to live in the small cottage next to the blacksmith's shop, his uncle John (born 1810) remained in residence in Rumford House with his great-aunt Philippa. He was joined there by a wife, Caroline Key (sister to Peter's wife, Nancy), and their six children.

When Peter married Nancy Lobb of St Merryn in January 1854, he claimed his great-uncle's bequest, Rumford House. Ironically, John and his six small children (there would be two more) had to move out to a cob cottage at Iron Gate, while his nephew Peter and his wife lived in solitary splendour, childless, in the spacious stone-built house. Peter senr (born 1809) carried on blacksmithing, while Peter junr, at Rumford House, farmed the 85 acres made up of Couches Tenement and Rosa Parks, which had been acquired on lease in the 1850s.

Though a farmer rather than a blacksmith, it is said every Sandry is born with a hammer in his hand, and that this talent was passed from his father to Peter junr is shown by his interest in the early steam-driven threshing machines. In 1876 he bought a Clayton & Shuttleworth threshing machine for £386.10s. The invoice reads:

June 1876. For Cornwall Show One 8 horses power...
side cylinder Steam Engine No. 15,157 with wood-

Ten years later the threshing machine was fitted with a new firebox, by Claytons, at Rumford, for the sum of £45.

It was not the first steam threshing machine in the area. On the 1861 census John Hawke states as his occupation 'engine driver to a threshing machine', and again in 1871. Even earlier than that, James Old, who died on 3 June 1840, left to his son James £30 and 'my right in the threshing machine which he has now in use'. After all, it was first in Cornwall, on the farm of Sir Christopher Hawkins of Trewithen, that a simple but highly effective high-pressure engine and boiler, made by the great Cornish inventor Richard Trevithick, was used for threshing corn. It was successful and much cheaper to run than the horses it replaced.

Peter Sandry had two or three sets of threshing machine, working between Mawgan Porth and Padstow. The team of men would have meals at the farm where they were working but would sleep at home, travelling by bicycle. They would leave home at 6a.m. to light the boiler fire to get steam up by 8a.m. On Monday mornings the boiler would be lit by 6a.m., having gone cold over Sunday. The machine was hired by the day and 15 men would go with it to the farm, where the farmer would kill a pig, everyone sitting around the kitchen table to eat.

It was Peter Sandry's nephew, Thomas Hawken Sandry, born in 1899 the youngest of the ten children of Charles Sandry and Jane (née Hawken), who continued the steam threshing machine business.

As always, the Sandry family was active in more than one type of business. Concrete block manufacture had been started at Rumford in 1923, with a small wood-frame machine patented by Bangors Concrete Construction Co. Ltd of East Grinstead, who built the first six council-houses at Dolgey Post, near Rumford. In 1962 the business was taken seriously in hand and 4,000 sq.ft. of floor was laid and a Liner electrically-driven mixer and a multi-block vibrating machine installed, with a capacity of 1,600 blocks per day. In 1964 the floor was extended and a block loader purchased. In that year a total of 174,344 blocks were made. The following year another

208,016 blocks were made. A 20-ton silo was purchased.

Alongside was the haulage business, horse-drawn vehicles carrying sea sand to go on the land and clay-work sand for builders. Tom Sandry, or T.H. as he was usually known, finished with the haulage business in 1924 when lorries came in, and drove the threshing gear, claiming to have the biggest round in England. He drove the traction engine he hired out to Rowlands Fun Fair in summer to haul their caravans from venue to venue. In 1925 he bought a second set, and hired men to drive them. At the same time he began working up a fleet of lorries. He bought old First World War 5–6 ton solid-tyre American trucks. It took him nearly three days to get them back from Slough travelling at 12mph. In 1930 he bought lorries with pneumatic tyres and glass windscreens which reached 30mph, although they still had only a 2-ton carrying capacity. Tom did all the ordering, clerical work and servicing for a fleet of 12 lorries. In 1935 he became the proud owner of a fleet of 24 Morris Commercials. Thus it did not matter which vehicle broke down, any of his drivers could repair it and the necessary spare part was always in stock. These were employed on quarry operations, hauling road-making materials, sand and

Left to right, back row: *James Hambly Old, John Lobb (born Mylor 1870 – he and his sister, Mary, orphaned young, were adopted by Peter and Nancy Sandry at Rumford)*; front row: *James Charles Lobb, Annie Hambly Lobb (née Old), Myrtle Doreen Olivey (née Lobb)*.

ballast as well as agricultural produce over an area of about 50 miles from St Ervan. Gradients of 1 in 5 are encountered in every direction, and one hill of 1 in 3 had to be negotiated almost daily by some of the vehicles. One of the regular contracts was to collect sea sand from the coast for delivery to farms, where it was used for treating grass and corn land, such journeys involving hauls over portions of sandy beach, inland via hilly and tortuous lanes and finally across the actual fields.

T.H. Sandry lost a couple of these vehicles to Dunkirk in the Second World War. Others were used to haul aggregate from Trevose Quarry to make concrete for the construction of wartime aerodromes. The firm employed 25 men and right through the Second World War 70–80 tons a day were hauled to one or other of the three airfields, St Mawgan, St Eval and St Merryn.

In 1923 Kelly's Trade Directory described T.H. Sandry as 'agricultural machine owner, Rumford'. By the 1939 Directory he had become 'haulage contractor, agriculture machine proprietor, motor garage proprietor, quarry owner.'

In 1978 Tom wrote a letter to the *Cornish Guardian* defending the Cornish shovel. This has a heart-shaped plate and a 5-ft, slightly curved handle. By using the knee as a fulcrum and with a forward thrust stimulated by the weight of the body, the long handle makes for perfect leverage with very little strain on the arm and shoulder muscles. The men who drove his fleet of lorries in the '30s loaded by hand. His drivers could 'load five tons of soft beach sand in twenty minutes using a large type Cornish shovel'. When Tom retired his son Peter carried on the business of block making, followed by his son Richard. The firm no longer makes the blocks but still has a haulage business (though the vehicles have changed) and there is still a Sandry living in Rumford House.

The son of a shoemaker, grandson of a farmer, in 1880 20-year-old William Henry Old established W.H. Old & Son, blacksmiths, in the main street of Rumford. Later he moved to bigger premises next the Bible Christian chapel. His memoir writer called him 'a smith and a genius... He is as true as the British steel he uses in his trade.' Just like the Sandry family, the Old family business involved a lot of other activities. Kelly's Trade Directories of 1893 and 1897 describe W.H. Old as 'blacksmith, engineer, machinist, implement maker, cycle and commission agent.'

William Henry had two daughters and four sons, born between 1882 and 1899. His eldest son, William Henry, worked with his father as a smith until he married, but died at the age of 30. His daughters, Ann Maria and Nellie Caroline, married brothers James and William Thomas Lobb and moved to Lanivet, near Bodmin. Sons Arthur (born 1888), Tom (born 1890) and Ernest George, known as George,

A threshing machine working in Quarry Park, Penrose, c.1890. Standing, top left: Frank Old, small boy Ernest James and on the right James Hawke. Standing down by the engine is 'boiler Jim' Hawke. The small boys include Jack, George and Henry Parkyn, and behind them is young Ernest Tippett. Sitting with hands on knees is the owner, John Hawke, and the men standing include William Old, Samuel Paynter and John James with a 3-gallon jar of ale. In the cart is a large barrel of water.

T.H. Sandry's steam traction engine and threshing machine in the 1920s. T.H. is in the middle.

T.H. Sandry standing in front of his new fleet of Morris Commercial lorries in 1935.

Tim Hore, mechanic, in the efficiently ordered workshop at T.H. Sandry's yard, which stocked all the spare parts that might be needed if one of the new fleet of Morris Commercials broke down.

T.H. Sandry's yard showing the lift moving the finished concrete blocks, in 1965.

T.H. Sandry proudly showing off his personal automobile in the 1930s.

remained in St Ervan. All three married but Tom had no children.

Arthur and Tom feature in their father's account ledger in 1914, when W.H. Old & Son helped Revd Johnson to have a church bell that he could ring. When Revd Johnson arrived to assist the elderly and ailing Revd Barton he found a church tower in ruins and the bells on the floor. With the skills and ingenuity of the Old family he secured one that he could ring. The accounts read:

Mar 26	½ day myself
	1½ hrs Arthur
	1½ hrs George
	pulling up trees for bells
28	Preparing to fix bell
31	½ day myself
	½ day George
	½ day Arthur
Apl 1	1 day myself
	1 day George
	½ day Arthur
3	1 day myself
	1 day Arthur
	30 lbs new ironwork

| Total | £2.2.6 |

Carrying and preparing and fixing trees to fix Bell in the Churchyard £1.14.0
30lbs new ironwork for same 8.6
£2.2.6

Paid June 9th 1914

They also repaired the old church sundial with new ironwork in the same shape as the old ironwork, they

Farm worker Reg Chapman showing the 'Cornish shovel', c.1920. This has a heart-shaped plate and a 5ft, slightly curved handle. By using the knee as a fulcrum and with a forward thrust stimulated by the weight of the body, the long handle makes for perfect leverage with very little strain on the arm and shoulder muscles.

'raised the cross with endless chain blocks and fixed it upright and straight.' They took the big bell out of the church tower, as well as the broken bell, and in the ruined tower fixed a galvanised ceiling at nave level and a door to the tower. Until then the tower had been open to the skies behind the congregation.

W.H. Old & Sons did essential work in the rectory for Revd Barton. They refixed the WC and repaired the earthenware pan and the water tank. They also repaired Miss Barton's bicycle. Revd Johnson was a keen gardener and it was W.H. Old & Sons who repaired and sharpened the rectory lawn mower.

By 1893 William Henry Old was already branching out, as Kelly's Directories show. The present structure of the forge was built in 1900, and although the interior has had extensive alterations over the years the basic structure remains as it was in the period of horse-drawn implements.

Tom Old, a carpenter, wheelwright and undertaker, built his workshop on the same site as the blacksmith's. There were many repair tasks where the skills of a carpenter were as necessary as those of the blacksmith, so Tom made a good team with his

father and younger brother Ernest (always called George). The business adapted to the changing requirements of their customers, Tom the carpenter working with the company, now managed by George, and building up to agricultural implement agents, blacksmiths, cycle agents and dispenser of cattle medicines. Machinery repairs continued to be the main activity during the year, with extra demand for repairs during the hay and corn harvest. The firm sold new implements and machines, including balers and combine harvesters. By the 1960s the carpenter's workshop had been demolished to allow more direct access to the yard and a new implement shed put up to accommodate those machines too large to enter the old forge building for repair.

The firm's account ledger for the years 1913, 1914 and 1915 is a wonderful document. The firm supplied anything from paraffin oil (for a machine or for the Wesleyan chapel) to nuts, bolts, screws and the many other small items needed to repair machinery, as well as repairing anything and everything made of metal. In August 1913 Mr Roberts of Trevone paid for:

Bolt repd and new nut
Casting of Binder repd
1 new bolt for same
1 new clip for sheaf spring and
1 new bolt

... all for 6s.8d. In 1914 he bought a larger item: 'New Hornsby No. 7 Force-Feed Drill – £17.10s.'

Horses were shod, a dung fork repaired and given a new handle, biddicks were sharpened, coulters laid (sharpened) and furrow guides for ploughs repaired, wagon wheels bound with 56lbs. of new iron, a wheel for a straw binder repaired, new ironwork for the front gate at Four Turnings (37lbs), and a corn drill repaired and put in working order, with every detail of each repair recorded and every bolt or screw listed. Any piece of farm or domestic equipment that needed a skilled eye, a steady hand and physical strength could be handled by W.H. Old & Son. In June 1913 the firm repaired the St Columb District Council's steamroller. Every detail is listed on four long pages of the ledger. The engine was stripped and the whole steamroller must have been taken completely apart and put back together again, all for a total cost of £52.12s.2d. Customers came from far and wide, one, Mr Arthur Carkeek, contractor, from as far away as Redruth.

Nothing was discarded if it could be recycled – an old double whip was made into a good single whip, or repaired. When a coulter was 'layered', the new piece of metal was heated together with the old, and welded while cooling very slowly to keep the correct tension. Even the broken crankshaft of a traction engine was repaired by the firm. A new piece of metal had to be aligned with absolute precision and

Rumford village from the north, early 1920s. The Wesleyan chapel is on the left, the low building attached to the house is the former W.H. Old smithy, near the top is Ladysmith, built by Tom Old in 1907, then their yard (not visible) *and the Bible Christian chapel at the top. Rumford House is top right.*

welded in, a highly skilled operation. W.H. Old & Son could do it. Today a V-shaped piece would be welded in with an electric welder. Likewise, today a broken harrow tine would be unscrewed and taken out and a new one screwed in. In the old days W.H. Old & Sons repaired them.

The family was strongly Methodist. In 1882 Arthur Old married Margaret Alice Northcott, the daughter of another Methodist family, of Roscullion in Little Petherick across the parish bound from Trethewey, and Arthur carried on the farm there. They had sons and Arthur, his family and his father-in-law played an active part in Rumford Wesleyan chapel affairs. At the time of writing grandson T. Henry Old and his wife still live in a bungalow near the old farmhouse.

During the Second World War W.H. Old & Sons installed Klister Startomatic diesel engines, with generators attached. They had a light switch to turn the engine on and off. Afterwards Old's men would go round all the farms in the area servicing them.

Ernest George died young. He was only 47 when he caught pneumonia through not changing out of wet clothes. Tom lived 20 years longer, but as he had no children the business was carried on by his nephew, William Henry Old, known to everyone as Larry. Larry's cousin (a first cousin though he was 20 years older), William 'Garfield' Lobb, came into the family business with him. Garfield showed a mechanical bent early in life and as a schoolboy enjoyed building models with Meccano. Later he displayed working models at garden shows. He and his brother also had an interest in cars and aeroplanes.

In 2006 Garfield has died and further changes have been made, but the firm is still run by an Old, Larry, who has been joined by his son, Richard. The firm of W.H. Old & Son (Rumford) Ltd now adver-

tises itself as horticultural and motor engineers, vehicle repairs and servicing, MOT testing station, tyres, batteries, hand-tools, horticultural machinery sales and service, agents for various tools, for chain saws, mowers, hedge trimmers and shredders.

One thing they still do, unusual in modern times, is that local farmers can take their sheep-shearing cutters and combs to Larry Old to sharpen. Otherwise they would have to send them away to Listers, who are the only people who will do this. Larry Old glues large sheets of emery paper to metal disks which are rotated at speed to sharpen the blades. Ever changing, ever improvising, ever adapting to the times, Olds are still serving local people and those further afield.

There is still an agricultural contracting business in St Ervan, the Powell family at Four Turnings, Rumford. Charlie Powell's maternal grandfather, James Henry Parsons (born 1866), started his working life as a farm labourer. In the 1901 census he gave his occupation as engine driver to a steam threshing machine. In 1904 he rode his pushbike to Falmouth and drove the engine home. It was owned by a company in which his grandmother had a share, as did Thomas Northcott. In about 1914 Jim Parsons bought out the other shareholders and became an agricultural machine owner. He died at Kola, Four Turnings, in 1946. His son, Charles Henry, continued working as a wheelwright. His daughter, Mary 'Emma', married Albert Powell. Albert had been out to Canada, found it too cold and swiftly returned. He was less interested in the business, but his wife carried it forward, to be joined by their son Charlie (born 1920). At the time of writing Charlie runs it with his two sons, Ivan and Harry, and grandson Mark. Once again, the combined talents of a family keep the business going.

W.H. Old (founder of W.H. Old & Son), wife Ann Maria and six children, c.1910. Left to right, back row: *Annie or Nellie, Arthur, Willie, Tom, Nellie or Annie;* front row: *W.H. Old, Ernest 'George', Ann Maria.*

Jim Parsons started with one threshing machine only. In the 1960s the business had three combine harvesters, a spreader, two pick-up balers, two threshing machines and a spraying machine. Today they have a fleet insurance policy covering 16 different vehicles – tractors, combine harvesters, vans and cars – with all the implements – drill, baler, sand spreader and plough – included in the tractor insurance. The modern farmer, instead of employing several labourers, contracts C.H. Powell & Sons to do their ploughing, drilling, hedge trimming, dung spreading, foraging, silage, harvesting, combining (corn) and round baling.

Traditional skills are remembered. Charlie Powell claims to be the last man in the area to have worked with oxen. His grandfather is remembered in a letter to a local newspaper in the 1950s by John Henry Lobb of Penrose, who wrote:

I distinctly remember a fine team of oxen being worked (rolling) in the early eighties by Mr James Parsons (a Cornish bandsman for over 60 years) for Mr James Paynter in a field I now occupy.

Right: *Wm. Henry Old bill head, 1913, for goods supplied to wheelwright Harry Parsons.*

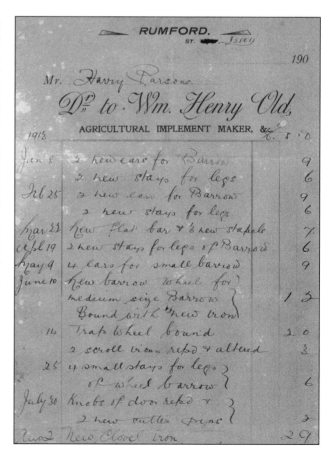

Four generations of the Old family. Left to right, back row: *Arthur Old, wife Margaret Alice Old (née Northcott);* third row: *Fanny Northcott, husband Thomas Northcott;* second row: *Thomas Henry Old, wife Emily Doreen Old (née Kestell);* children in front: *Wendy Eileen Old, David John Old.*

'Rolling' was the smoothing of the arable land after it had been ploughed, the roller being hauled by oxen.

These old-established but enterprising families started businesses using traditional skills and have succeeded in maintaining them as family businesses in a rural parish by being willing to change and adapt to what today's customers need.

The mason, carpenter, shoemaker, tailor and grocer also had sources of income independent of the land.

Each of the two main villages, Penrose and Rumford, was entirely self-supporting, each having carpenters, masons, shoemakers, dressmakers and a grocer.

The middle of the nineteenth century finds Thomas Brewer, son of miller Richard, his cousin Henry Brewer, and Henry Lobb (whose second wife was a dame-schoolmistress) well established as carpenters, all living at Rumford.

In 1854 Henry Lobb died. His bequests to his wife included: 'all the Household furniture, working tools and timber.' Only one of his three sons remained in the parish, Thomas, the youngest, who became a shoemaker at Penrose.

Thomas Brewer, son of the miller, who helped build the Bible Christian chapel at Penrose in 1861 and was a trustee of the Bible Christian chapel at Rumford and no doubt helped in its building; his cousin, Henry Brewer, who came from a pauper family of ten children but, probably with Thomas's assistance, worked his way up the ladder as a carpenter and even leased some fields; and Henry Lobb, sufficiently well off to leave nearly £100; all three were economically well above the level of the landless agricultural labourer yet not as well-heeled as the farmer. Therefore I am including them in the middle class of the parish.

William Dawe, born into an agricultural labouring family in Penrose, was apprenticed to a cabinet maker. He called himself variously carpenter, cabinet maker and master carpenter.

There were fewer masons. Thomas James, mason, lived at Bogee Downs, and Thomas Tallick, who repaired the millstones at Trewinnick Mills for Richard Brewer in 1840, lived at Bogee. He probably also helped build the Bible Christian chapel at Rumford in 1844.

In 1861, when the new chapel was built at Penrose, James Tippett, master stonemason, aged 26,

Left to right, back row: *Richard Gregor, Bill Found, Arthur Old, William Rabey, Arthur Strongman (holding banner with Tom Old), Mr Northcott;* third row: *Reg Chapman, ?, Raymond Brewer?, ?, ?, ?, Philippa Hawke, W.H. Old (holding hand of Garfield Lobb);* second row and front row: *no names known.*

Rumford Sunday-school anniversary, June 1914, in a field at Rumford. Left to right, standing: Bill Found, Charles Eyers, Tom Old, Arthur Strongman, William Thomas Lobb, John Henry Lobb, Arthur Old, Annie Maria Strongman, ?, ?, ?, ?; sitting: William Henry Old, Ernest 'George' Old, ?, Dorothy Strongman?, Nellie Old, ?, Miss Emma Old, Mrs Fanny Found.

Garfield Lobb (born 1916) with his mother Nell (née Old). She died when he was only eight years old.

Modern advertisement for W.H. Old & Son (Rumford) Ltd.

and his brother William, journeyman mason, aged 19, were the masons who built the walls we see today. Both lived at Penrose, sons of James Tippett, shoemaker. James became a leader among the Penrose Methodists. From baptism certificates kept by Leonard Masters we know that at least two of William's children were baptised in the chapel, Mary Annie (mother of Leonard) in December 1879 and Ernest in October 1888.

Another William Tippett was making boots and shoes at Penrose in 1833 when his first and only child was baptised. In 1873, when an old man of 66, he was still making boots and shoes.

William Old was a shoemaker for a lifetime at Penrose. His grandfather, James Old, was a yeoman farmer at Treleigh, but his father, James, was an agricultural labourer. He worked himself up to become master cordwainer with his eldest son John as apprentice under him at Penrose. Another son,

Jim Parsons with his first traction engine, a 6hp Marshall, at work in 1928. The boys are, from left to right: *George Trenouth, Rex Trenouth, Charlie Powell, Dennis Trenerry, Dennis Kestell.*

Jim Parsons's threshing machine at work on a farm in Padstow, c.1920.

Rumford village in 1960s, showing Endsleigh House (left), Mill Cottage and the Rabey's shop (centre) and the petrol pumps of W.H. Old & Son (right). The monkey-puzzle tree in the garden of Ladysmith has long since gone.

The yard of W.H. Old & Son in the 1960s. The new shed is on the right, the old one on the left is still in use.

Kola, at Four Turnings in 2005, built by Jim Parsons in 1920.

W.H. Old & Son on Open Day, 1984. Modern workshops have been erected alongside the century-old one which is still in use. Richard Old has joined his father, Larry, in the business.

Samuel, served as a shoemaker for a short time before returning to St Eval, his parish of birth.

John Strongman, son of an agricultural labourer who had died a pauper in the workhouse, learned his trade under fellow Bible Christian William Pope at Rumford and by the time he was 31 was a master shoemaker with an apprentice, his eldest son, William. His second son, Paul, also learned the trade. The ninth of John's ten children, Alfred, began as a 'shoe closer' at the age of 11.

Often the shoemaker started working life as an agricultural labourer, the work available for those who were in no position to do anything else. Francis Rabey, son of agricultural labourer Matthew Rabey, was an 18-year-old apprentice in 1861 and a cordwainer by 1871. Craftsmen were versatile. By 1897 he had added shopkeeping to his shoemaking. His son carried on the trade into the twentieth century.

Among the purchasers of shoes was the overseer to the poor. New shoes for a man cost 9s.3d., almost the weekly wage of a labourer, and for a child 5s. William Benney, an adult pauper, was bought new shoes once a year. For a woman shoes cost 5s.3d. or 5s.6d. Even if each person had only one pair of new shoes a year, it can be seen that there would be enough work for five men in 1861, even for the seven shoemakers in 1871.

Dressmakers were numerous, but there was only one tailor, Charles Old, who had his workshop above the Lowertown Inn, Penrose. A relative, William Old, joined him later.

Young widow Maria Ball earned enough as a shirtmaker to raise her two small boys, though she probably had additional help from her own family, the Higmans. Several women were dressmakers, for example, 50-year-old spinster Loveday Edyvean, as-yet-unmarried daughters such as Jane Strongman, daughter of John, shoemaker, and even 14-year-old Cordelia Pope, daughter of small farmer William, or wives of farmers, such as Margaret Hawke, wife of Robert. It was the kind of work that almost any woman could turn her hand to. Some, like Mary Ann Hawken, wife of the wayward William, became very expert, as seen in the family photographs taken about 1895 after they moved to London.

The Vestry would call on the tailor and dress-makers to make clothes for the paupers. For example, in 1828 it is recorded:

C.H. Powell & Sons threshing with their Ransome's machine, c.1960. Standing lower left, posing for the camera, is Charlie Powell, who worked the boiler, and Henry Warne, who carried the bales away. On the right, standing, with hand on cap and holding the pike with which he pitched the sheaves, is Hugh Biddick. Below him, with back to the camera, is John Crews, feeding the machine.

Teenager Ivan Powell driving a Fordson Major diesel tractor, with a Banford BL57 baler. The baler had its own engine on top, a twin-cylinder Enfield diesel. There was no guard on the pick-up – it could be lethal! The year 1958 was a very wet season and binders could not harvest the corn, so farmers bought little combines and combined as soon as it was dry enough. The balers then had to rush round to bale it.

Charlie Powell's Oliver 90 tractor, his first, bought in August 1945, and his threshing set at Jack and Edith Cowling's Glebe Farm in 1954. He still had the tractor working in 2004. Note the wartime hangars on St Merryn airfield on horizon.

Penrose chapel in 1965.

To a coat for William Benny	10s. 3d.
To a waistcoat	2s.1½d.
To Shift for Sally Benny	1s.4d.
To making the above said garments	5s.6d.

After two years William Benny had another coat: 'For making William Benny's coat – 3s.6d.', and after three years again: 'For William Benny's clothes... 10s.10½d. The Taylor for Making do... 3s.8d.' Again, his coat lasted three years.

In 1830 calico cost 8d. a yard, print 10½d. a yard, blanketing 16d. a yard. A blanket cost 6s., and 'for making the blanket 6d.', 6d. being the cost of a

Farm worker Leonard Masters at Penrose. He was very knowledgeable about anything to do with farming and a keen amateur archaeologist, supplying old farm tools he found on the ground to Padstow Museum.

At a Rally in August 2000 C.H. Powell & Sons won first prize for best turned out threshing machine and tractor. Left to right, at back: great-grandchildren Richard Blake and Charlotte Blake; front: grandson Mark Powell, son Ivan Powell, Charlie Powell and John Boyle presenting the cup.

Charlie Powell baling at Trevilledor Farm in September 2002.

BIBLE CHRISTIAN CONNEXION.—BAPTISMAL CERTIFICATE.

No.	Child's Christian Name.	Parents'		Father's Rank or Profession.	Date and Place of Baptism.	By whom Baptized.
		Full Names.	Residence.			
	Ernest	William & Mary Jane Tippett	Penrose St. Ervan	Mason	Bible Christian Chapel Oct 14th Penrose	W.F. Ellis

I certify that the above is a true copy of an entry in the Baptismal Register Book, No. _____ for the *Padstow* Circuit.

Witness my hand this 24th day of *October* 18 88

William Francis Ell...

BIBLE CHRISTIAN CONNEXION.—BAPTISMAL CERTIFICATE.

No.	Child's Christian Name.	Parents'		Father's Rank or Profession.	Date and Place of Baptism.	By whom Baptized.
		Full Names.	Residence.			
881	Mary Annie	William & Mary Jane Tippett	Penrose St. Ervan Cornwall	Mason	December 15th 1879 Bible Christian Chapel Penrose	W. Brown

I certify that the above is a true copy of an entry in the Baptismal Register Book, No. 881 for the *Padstow* Circuit.

Witness my hand this 13th day of *January* 18 80

Walter Brown

William and Mary Jane Tippett of Penrose were keen Bible Christians. These are the baptism certificates of two of their children, Mary Annie in 1879, Ernest in 1888, at the Bible Christian chapel in Penrose which William had helped to build in 1861.

Harry Hawken, son of William and Mary Ann Hawken, in London, c.1895.

Ernie Hawken, youngest child of William and Mary Ann Hawken. In 1901 he was working as a saddler in Battersea. This suit was made by his mother.

woman's work for a day. Other materials included flannel, 10½d. a yard, cotton for shirts and fustian.

The tailor was the only trained worker in clothing. Charles Old's nephew was apprenticed to him, then became a journeyman, still under the rule and teaching of his uncle, before he could finally launch out on his own as a master tailor.

Shopkeeping or the grocery business was not usually a business on its own. Peter Sandry, who died in 1831, had been a grocer and draper in Rumford as well as blacksmith, maltster and farmer at one and the same time; Richard Brewer, miller, was also a grocer, then his son added it to his carpentry business. In Penrose Thomas Paynter, farmer, was also the grocer. From Richard Brewer's account book we know this business was operated on a cash basis. The grocer would buy from farmers and sell to others, wheat, flour, meat, etc. The mason, miller, carpenter, shoemaker, in having a source of income independent of the land, were free men and their

businesses were free of the burden of tithes.

This freedom allowed them a certain independence of thought from the overwhelming authority of the established church. The big farmer paid his tithes to the rector and was, to a limited extent, part of the rector's social class within the parish, but the craftsmen's work kept them constantly in touch with the ordinary people of the parish. Hence their emergence as the natural leaders in the development of the new and exciting evangelical movement of William O'Bryan, founder of the Bible Christians. While doing their duty by the Church of England, Richard Brewer, the Higmans and Rawlings, millers; Thomas Tallick, James and William Tippett, masons; Thomas Brewer, carpenter; William Pope, Francis Rabey, shoemakers; Charles Old, tailor; William Old, Peter Sandry, blacksmiths; were all strongly motivated by the new faith, by the new opportunity to express their spirituality outside the rigid formality of the Church of England liturgy.

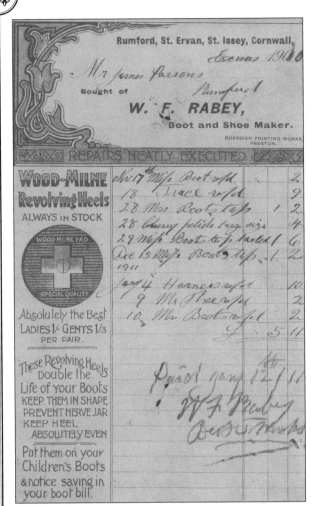

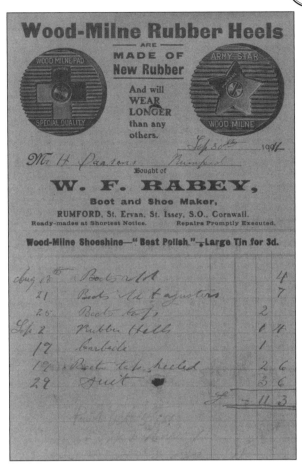

W.F. RABEY bill heads for goods supplied to Jim Parsons in 1910 (left) and 1911 (above).

Above: *Susan Jane Knight, eldest daughter of Mary Ann Hawken, c.1895 in London.*
Left: *A later photograph of Mrs Mary Ann Hawken in London. In 1901 she was working as a 'monthly nurse'.*

Revd Henry Nowell Barton MA, rector of St Ervan parish for 60 years, c.1900.

✦ CHAPTER 9 ✦

Revd Barton Surveys His New Parish

Revd William Molesworth, MA, JP, rector of St Breock and St Ervan since 1817, died on 28 March 1851. On 11 November 1853, having bought the advowson, Henry Nowell Barton, MA, instituted as rector at St Ervan, was the first resident rector of the parish for 50 years. During November the parish was looked after by John Dunn, vicar of St Eval. Revd Barton did not arrive until the second week of December. The reason for the delay can be found in his very first entry in the register of baptisms: '18 December 1853 Margaretta Eliza, daughter of Henry Nowell and Caroline Sarah Barton, residence, rectory, father's occupation, clerk.'

They had two older children, Katharine, 3, born at Paddington and John, a year old, born at Southampton. The Bartons and the parish of St Ervan were at the beginning of a long association. It would not always be amicable.

What kind of man was this who was to rule as rector and, in the absence of any socially superior person, as squire, or 'squarson', for 60 years in this

Miss Margaretta Barton (1855–1948), daughter of Revd H.N. Barton.

tiny parish of fewer than 450 souls, and what was the nature of the parish?

Revd Barton was a 'foreigner' not only to St Ervan but to rural Cornwall, so remote from London. He was born 30 years before in Bombay, East Indies. His 27-year-old wife, Caroline, came from Hertfordshire. Henry Nowell Barton had gained his MA at Pembroke College, Oxford, where he had been a tutor. He had served in Paddington, Middlesex, and in Southampton but nothing in his past experience had equipped him to serve in an agricultural parish in a remote corner of Britain, where men toiling in the fields had their roots in the same area, if not the same parish, for generation upon generation. He was to be isolated from the community he had come to serve by all his education and experience, by his cultural background and above all by his own personality and by those of his independent, individualistic and hardheaded Cornish parishioners.

The living of St Ervan was worth about £470 to the rector per annum. He had a large, though old, residence and 84 acres of glebe farm. Let us take an imaginary ride around the young rector's new parish to meet the people who paid the tithes, each according to his landholding, which formed his main income.

On Christmas day he performed the burial service for a member of a leading Wesleyan Methodist family, Malachi Spear, aged 76, who had been living at Outer Bogee with his daughter, Margaret. On 30 December the rector baptised William, the baby son of William and Anna Biddick, who farmed Trenouth. During January he is free to explore his little parish.

The largest manor in the parish is Trembleath, which, however, still benefits financially from an ancient agreement whereby 10s. a year is paid in lieu of tithes. The barton farm is the principal farm of Trembleath manor, about 150 acres, and is farmed by James Rowe. James, a principal citizen in the Vestry, is also census enumerator and registrar of births and deaths. He and his wife, Mary, have seven children. Living with them is James's widowed mother-in-law, Fanny Hele Hoblyn, 'owner of leasehold houses and lands'. It is a large and well-to-do household. Perhaps the children take the new rector to see the water-wheel that powers the threshing machine.

If, while conducting the service in the church on a Sunday, the rector allows his eye to be distracted by the scene through the altar window, perhaps he lets it stray further on across the valley to the edge of Rumford village and up over the south-facing slope

The Rowe family in the garden of Trembleath barton farmhouse. Left to right: ?, ?, ?, Richard Henry Rowe, Mary Jane Rowe.

View as seen through the altar window, before thicker glass was installed, across the fields to Treravel Farm.

of the hillside where he can see, in a sheltering clump of trees, the farmhouse at Treravel. This farm, 150 acres, and another big one, Trenouth, 190 acres of land to the east of the village, are both occupied by Biddicks, an important family in parish affairs and well worth a visit.

At Treravel lives George Biddick, his wife Ann and their five grown-up children. George has often taken the office of Guardian representing St Ervan parish on the St Columb Union Board since its formation in 1837. The rector has already met 25-year-old William Biddick, George's son, who farms Trenouth, and his wife Ann, when he baptised their son, William, on 30 December. They also have a three-

year-old daughter, Ann. Already William is following in George's footsteps, playing a full part in Vestry affairs. This year he is an overseer to the poor. Between them, father and son are contributing a major part of the parish rates and, through the tithes, a major part of the rector's income.

To reach Treleigh farmhouse further north the rector has to ride through the village and up the hill to Four Turnings, where the lane to the farm leads off between a cluster of small cottages. Here live widow Elizabeth Edyvean, who leases a few acres of land, and an agricultural labouring couple, John and Eleanor Vivian, in their sixties, whose newly married son and wife are lodging with them, and elderly widow Harriet Benny. Next is John Bettison and wife Mary and year-old daughter. They are said to be 'pious parents, who bring their children up under the influence of the Bible Christians.' One son will become a Bible Christian preacher.

Treleigh is a 150-acre farm, occupied by 51-year-old William Old. Treleigh farmhouse, though stone built, is soon to be replaced by the Paynter landowner with a grander house. William and his wife Mary have seven children under the age of 15. They are Wesleyan Methodists. One of their live-in farm labourers is 17-year-old Thomas Lobb, son of the carpenter Henry and his schoolmistress wife, Prudence.

The Tom family living in the stone and slated farmhouse at Trethewey are also Wesleyan Methodists. Gregory Tom senr is a wealthy man.

Cottages at Four Turnings, late 1800s. Note the washing drying on the bushes, the pig shed at the side of the road and the furze rick on the right.

Though he has retired from farming, he and his wife Elizabeth (née Hawke), sister to Philip at Trevengenow, continue to live in the farmhouse. Their son Gregory, 45, farms the 80 acres. Rearing sheep for wool is the main activity on these farms down the eastern flank of the parish. Gregory Tom has a good income from selling the fleeces to the wool-packing factory at Talskiddy. This year he is the parish Guardian of the Poor.

Revd Barton continues on to the north-east point of the parish to visit the eldest of the successful Hawken brothers, Joseph, and his wife Margery (née Dawe) at Treburrick, a large farm. One of their 11 children, James, lives with them with his wife Louisa (née Rowe), their three infant children and baby Jane. James is farming the 104 acres at Treburrick plus 50 acres of common land. Louisa Hawken is from the Roman Catholic family of Reterth in St Columb Major parish, and their four children were baptised by the Roman Catholic priest from Lanherne in St Mawgan, the former Arundell home given to the enclosed order of Carmelite nuns.

From Treburrick the new rector climbs steeply back up to the rocky plateau and follows the path which cuts across the fields straight down the hill again to Treglinnick, site of the first licensed Methodist meeting-house in the parish. This is a 100-acre farm, where Joseph Hawken's sister, Mary, for 40 years the widow of Nicholas Key, keeps house for her bachelor brother-in-law, 76-year-old Silvester Key.

Revd Barton returns to Churchtown in the valley, where he meets a daughter of Mary Key married to Edward Brewer, miller and Bible Christian, and their seven children.

On another day Revd Barton calls on Joseph Hawken's other sister, Ann, wife of James Key, who farms 90 acres at Trewinnick. They live in the old manor-house dating from the seventeenth century. Two of their seven children are still living with them, 32-year-old bachelor Nicholas, and 26-year-old Nancy with her two small children. The other part of Trewinnick property is farmed by a younger man, William Bennett, who acquired it on the death of his uncle, Jonathan, a few years earlier. He lives in the house his uncle built alongside the manor-house in 1827.

From a field above Trewinnick Revd Barton can take a path which cuts eastwards and down over the river, lined with trees, to Bogee (66 acres), farmed by Samuel Paynter of the St Issey branch of the family, which owns both Bogee and Treleigh. Samuel is a wealthy man aged 60. Most of the farmers visited so far have labourers and domestic servants living in the farmhouse with them, but at Bogee there is a separate cottage where agricultural labourer Henry Parsons and his wife Elizabeth live with their three small children.

From here the rector can take a path past the ruins of the former parish poor house and on past the field where the magnificent Longstone stands sentinel, to enter the lane which runs along the foot of Trewinnick Downs. He meets 23-year-old Margaret Spear, daughter of Malachi Spear, who was buried on Christmas Day.

Treburrick farmhouse soon after it was re-roofed by John Skinner.

A side view of Trewinnick farmhouses, showing old barns on the left and a very modern one behind.

View from Churchtown, the old mill in the valley, with Treglinnick on top of the hill.

Trevilledor farmhouse, the old half built in cob, the more modern half in stone.

In this part of the parish the rector can no longer follow straightforward tracks linking farmhouse to farmhouse, but must dart from cottage to cottage in order to visit the smallholders and agricultural labourers who live in the small clusters of dwellings scattered over the slopes of the downs at the 400ft mark above sea level.

At Music Water widow Mary Brenton makes a living off a 16-acre farm assisted by her two sons, 21-year-old John and 12-year-old William. Ten-year-old daughter Marianna goes to school. Mary's 19-year-old daughter Jane is married to Richard Chapman, who is farming to the west on Bear's Downs.

At the cottage of 43-year-old cobbler Samuel Arthur and his wife the rector finds lodgers, 40-year-old widower William Tregay and his two young children. When William's wife, Ann, died his children were looked after in the St Columb Union workhouse. They can now contribute to the family income so can live at home. John, 13, is an agricultural labourer, and 10-year-old Amelia is kept busy in the house. William never rises much above the poverty line and eventually his children will move away to find work.

Nearby, a smallholding of 8 acres plus 20 acres of the common land provide a living for 48-year-old Richard Pope and his wife Joan. Their son James is 14 and employed on the farm and no doubt 9-year-old Richard too, if only intermittently at peak seasons, since neither he nor his sister Jane attend school.

Matthew Rabey, born to an agricultural labourer on the downs 29 years ago, has married a St Merryn girl and their first child is now 2½ years old. He has already acquired 6½ acres and is someone who will work himself up the ladder. By 1861 he will be farming 18 acres at Osborne's, just to the east of Eddystone.

A large number of the parishioners work the small tenements of mostly coarse pasture and furze scattered across Bear's Downs. Mary Bettison, a 76-year-old pauper widow, works on the land whenever she can get work. Joseph Chapman leases 98 acres of 'enclosed common' at Middle Trembleath which he works with sons William and John. At Iron Gate widower Philip Strongman, 72, is farming 70 acres with the help of his youngest son, Joseph. At Hill Tenement Richard Veal has a 99-year lease on two

Miss Christine Sandry standing in front of the ruins of a labourer's cottage opposite Trevilledor.

plots of furze and coarse pasture lands, with a little arable, determinable now on his own life and that of his brother, David. At Trevilledor James and Grace Ball, in their sixties, lease 70 acres of common land, the lease determinable on the lives of three sons. One of these 'lives' died a year ago, at the age of 33, of typhus. (Typhus had taken 38-year-old Richard Brewer of Rumford in 1845.) James Ball has two cottages on his land. His son's widow, Maria (née Higman), lives in one with her two sons, Christopher 3, William 2, and daughter Anne Maria, 7 months old, born 5 months after her father's death.

Eddystone is in the process of changing owner-ship, so next Revd Barton calls at New Barn, where live young marrieds William and Maria Key with infant daughter Anna Maria. As son of James Key, who farms Trewinnick, and a Hawken mother, William has advantages over most agricultural labourers. Nearby is widower Richard Johns and a pauper widow who housekeeps for him. In Trewinnick Lane live John James, his wife Mary and their five children. Their eldest daughter, 14, has gone into service at Trevengenow.

In this southern part of the parish the rector has seen the semi-derelict cottages and uncovered grounder stones from cob cottages which have started to merge with the earth again. Harvests in the 1840s were poor, with the larger farmers employing fewer labourers. They had to find work elsewhere and several families had emigrated to America. The James family will also soon give up trying to wrest a living here and will move to more fertile land at Churchtown. Others will move further afield to towns and centres of the Industrial Revolution. John Morrish, 35, has come from Bodmin to farm Cluckey but will soon move on. Often these small cottages provide the first accommodation for young marrieds, such as John Higman and his wife Jane (née Brewer), or George Hawke and his wife Ann (née Higman).

From Cluckey a path cuts across boggy ground following the run of a fast river to Trevengenow, 120 acres, tenanted by Philip Hawke. He and his wife have six older children and two servants living with them.

Another day the rector goes into Rumford. Here 27 of the 29 houses are occupied. At least half the cottages (15, according to a government report in 1862) are only one room up, one room down. In these live 16 agricultural labourers with their families. Most have small children, for example James Benney, 38, and his wife with their six children, aged from 11 years down to two. Two cottages house paupers'

Rumford village in late 1800s, with the old sawpit on the left. Note the 16-pane sliding-sash windows in the cottage on the left.

widows with children. Even here the population decline is evident, with two houses uninhabited.

The largest and newest house is Rumford House, built by the late Peter Sandry in 1828. John Sandry lives here with his six children. John's older brother, bachelor Peter, is living with his parents, Peter and Nancy, and siblings Thomas (19), Grace (14), 11-year-old schoolgirl Margaret Ann and 8-year-old schoolboy William Henry, at the old family cottage opposite.

Revd Barton passes the Bible Christian chapel, built nearly ten years ago, and comes to the mill house, where the late Richard Brewer worked as miller and grocer for so many years, where his son Richard died of typhus in 1845, where his other son, William, worked till he moved to Little Petherick in 1852 to become the miller there, and where yet another son John is now the miller. John is a widower and lives with his three children, Philippa (15), John (13) and Richard (12).

Next to the mill is the grocer's shop, run formerly by the late Richard Brewer, then by his son, Richard, now by his brother, Thomas Brewer, carpenter and smallholder. Thomas lives with his wife Elizabeth, 18-year-old Maryann, 14-year-old John and a 10-year-old niece, Emma. His mother lives with them.

There are two other carpenters living in Rumford village. Henry Brewer, a cousin, lives with his wife Rebecca, a busy dressmaker, and their three children; 70-year-old Henry Lobb and wife Prudence, a dame-schoolmistress, in the end cottage of the little row at Primrose Hill across on the other side of Rumford Bridge.

There is one shoemaker in the village, 33-year-old John Strongman, his wife Amy and their five small children. John and his wife were 'converted' to the Bible Christian society in 1849. Their son Paul, whose schooling is to cause so much bitter argument between John Strongman and the rector, is five years old.

Their neighbour is William Pope, another Bible Christian, who taught John Strongman his trade and his Bible Christian faith. He is 55, married to a sister of Henry Brewer. Their 25-year-old daughter, Mary

Ann, lives with them. William will continue as a local preacher until his death.

Both William Pope, assessor this year, and Joseph Strongman, are active in the Vestry.

Thomas and John Brewer, John Strongman and William Pope are in the process of negotiating the new trusteeship of the Bible Christian chapel, which will have an indenture drawn up in May. Below the mill stands the Wesleyan chapel, built in 1830.

Penrose, the other village, is the more ancient of the two. It is smaller and a jumble of houses. The village is at the centre of farms whose fields are intermingled. Five farmers have houses in Penrose.

One is Thomas Paynter, his wife Kitty (daughter of Joseph Hawken of Treburrick), and their six children, including a delicate 5-year-old, Sarah.

The farmer owning the most land, 70 acres, is James Hawken senr, brother of Joseph at Treburrick. Aged 74, he is the second churchwarden this year.

A nephew, William, farms land at Penrose but considers himself primarily a butcher and deals in cattle. He is married to his cousin, Sarah, daughter of the late Joseph of Treburrick. They have four young children.

Joseph Hawken's youngest daughter, Fanny, also lives in Penrose, next door to her brother, Joseph. She is married to John Hawke, agricultural labourer, eldest son of Philip at Trevengenow.

The wealthiest man in Penrose, not simply a farmer but a landed proprietor whose family have owned houses and lands in Penrose for generations, is Stephen Binny, a widower for many years now. Stephen's 25-year-old son, John, is also a 'landed proprietor'. John married Jane Hawke in July. He had been living with his aunt Ann and recently inherited the residue of her will (£200). This was a good start for the married couple, but they are not blessed with good health. They live next door to the inn, where John's brother, Richard, is innkeeper of the Maltster's Arms, and a maltster.

John Niles farms 20 acres, which he holds on a short-term lease from the Trembleath estate. He pays around £50 in yearly rents (i.e. twice the total annual income of an agricultural labourer). His house is large. They have six young children, the older ones, at 13 and 11, are experienced workers on the farm.

Devout Methodist Robert Higman, 63, farms 33 acres on a short-term lease. His eldest son, William, is a local preacher. Nearby are shoemaker and dedicated Bible Christian William Tippett and his wife Maria. William farms several small fields. Though there are several Methodist families in Penrose, as yet there is no chapel.

There is one blacksmith in Penrose, a 'foreigner' from St Mabyn, George Dryden. His son, John, is his apprentice and his wife's father, widower William Brenton, retired mason, is living with them.

Two houses in Penrose are classed 'uninhabitable'.

Rumford House and Gwenny Hawke's cottage attached, 1965. Left to right: Gwen Hawke, Kay Sandry in pram, Richard Sandry and his grandmother, Mrs T.H. Sandry.

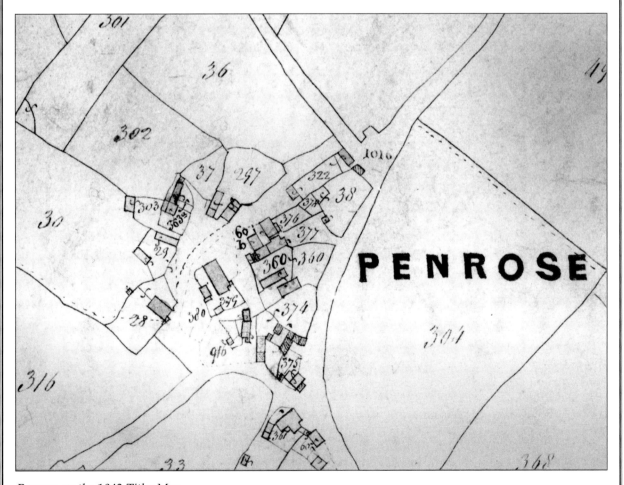

Penrose on the 1842 Tithe Map.

Agricultural labourers occupy the rest of the cottages. They include James Old, his wife Ann and their four sons. James, an older brother of William at Treleigh, is well connected but remains a labourer.

After visiting Lowertown to the south and Lewidden to the north, the rector makes his way over the river and across three fields up the steep and rocky hillside to the farm on the 225ft level, Treginegar. John Hawken is farming Brabyn's Tenement, 146 acres of Treginegar, one of the biggest and best farms in the parish.

Revd Barton returns to his rectory by dropping down the hill to pick up the path along the river again. Immediately after passing the shaft opening and heaps of spoil from the short-lived copper mine, closed two years since, he meets Thomas Rawling, miller, his wife Jane and their 23-year-old son Thomas at Treginegar Mill, a corn mill, and nearby John Grigor, 15-year-old son of John Grigor who, until two years before, was a miner in the copper mine which, after several periods of working for a few months at a time only, has left nothing but its scars on the hillside beside the mill. A short ride along the narrow river valley will bring him back to Churchtown.

Trembleath's manorial mill, Millingworth, stands on Treravel land on the north side of the river. It is temporarily occupied by a young member of the Biddick family of Treravel, Richard, and his new wife, following the bankruptcy and death in Bodmin gaol of miller Richard Brewer. The 99-year lease of the grist mills and malthouses is determinable on two lives still, Edward Brewer, 31, and Richard Higman, 31, the son and son-in-law of the late Richard Brewer.

One 'life', Edward Brewer, lives in a house facing the church. He occupies 20 acres between Churchtown and Rumford village, on a year to year basis, at an annual rent of £42. He and his wife Mary, (née Key), Methodists, have seven children and are expecting the eighth, who will be taken to the Parish Church to be baptised, just as all the others were.

Thomas Spear farms 78 acres from Churchtown with the help of two labourers. He is a cousin to Edward Brewer and a more active Methodist. In May Thomas will sign the new indenture for the Bible Christian chapel in Rumford as a trustee.

One cottage at Churchtown is occupied by William Bennett, a 33-year-old groom who works for the rector, his wife Susan and three infants. Susan is a daughter of Philip Strongman, whom the rector has met already at Bear's Downs.

Next door to the rectory is the 'Old Inn'. It is 'an excellent and well-accustomed Inn, with stables and all convenient Outbuildings and about three acres of garden and meadow land.' This tenement is occupied by James Key and his wife's brother, Samuel Hawken, for an annual rent of £10. Samuel and his wife Sarah have a new baby son. Samuel is also sometimes a butcher and alternates between the two

occupations. Nancy Hawken, Samuel's widowed mother, lives with them. His youngest brother, Joseph, is serving as groom to Revd Hugh Molesworth, formerly curate at St Ervan and now rector at Little Petherick.

Even following this route, the new rector has not met all his parishioners. Several smallholders and agricultural labourers live in cottages at a distance from any cluster or grouping. One of these is John Bennetts, 40-year-old agricultural labourer, his wife Jane and their eight children, all under 14, who live out at West Parks, between Trembleath farmhouse and Lowertown, Penrose.

As the new rector has surveyed his parish he has passed 13 cottages uninhabited and in various stages of crumbling dilapidation. Within a short time many of the smaller cob cottages scattered in the fields will be in complete ruin and no longer feature even as 'uninhabited house' on the census enumerator's returns.

On his tour he has found a wholly agricultural community. Of the 84 families, the heads of 29 call themselves farmers, their farms being anything from 5 to 200 acres, with 69 men and boys working as agricultural labourers. The families are all interlinked through marriage. Those not born in the parish of St Ervan have, with very few exceptions, including the rector and schoolteacher, come from an adjoining parish.

Henry Nowell Barton is 30 years old. Though half the population at that time is aged 20 or under, all the big farmers, those farming 100 acres or more and who will dominate the Vestry meetings, are considerably older than him. The majority of his flock are the agricultural labourers starting their families in the cob cottages on the downs, men earning 10–15s. per week if they are lucky, against the rector's living of £380 per annum; men whose cottages were rented for £15s. or £1.10s. a year against the rector's house, which had a rental value of £18; men who know intimately each other's families and their histories. Barton's family, his educational background, his place of upbringing, his apparent arrogance, his aloofness, his style of living, nothing could be more alien to his new parishioners, men whose skills are entirely practical and based on long generations of experience of the soil and climate; men who might be able to read familiar passages in the Bible, but who, with few exceptions, because of lack of opportunity to practise the skill, will never write and who will pen a cross in place of a signature.

Their spiritual experience is different, too. There has been strong Methodist influence here for the past 50 years, and it has gained momentum with the reception given to the Bible Christian preacher, Elizabeth Dart, in 1818 by the late Richard Brewer. Richard's sons continue the enthusiasm for his work, especially Thomas the carpenter, supported by such men as William Pope, a small farmer, John

Farmworker Henry Bennetts (one of the 14 children of John and Jane at West Parks) and his wife Elizabeth (née Hawke) were already established at Treleigh by the 1891 census. This was taken c.1890, before the birth of their youngest child, Harry. Left to right, back row: Jane, with hand on her mother's shoulder, Henry Bennetts; front row: Minnie, Elizabeth 'Bessie', with baby John on her lap, Emily.

A close-up showing the structure of a cob cottage. The lower part is built like a Cornish stone hedge, on which a cob wall is raised.

The L-shaped barn at Glebe Farm before it was converted.

Strongman, shoemaker, and Robert Higman, small farmer.

These are men from the middle stratum of society, the craftsmen and agricultural labourers who have moved up the land occupancy scale. Several of the bigger farmers are involved, notably Gregory Tom, a Wesleyan. Methodism was very much a movement of the people, who produced such leaders and preachers from their own ranks as Richard Brewer, William Pope and William Higman. Of James Rundle senr it was said:

Brother Rundle was no pulpit Preacher; yet it might be said he was a preacher of righteousness, both by his conversation and example. He was a man of faith, and it was of that kind which is lively and active... and was anxious that all the world might know Christ crucified; and though he had not a talent for preaching yet he has been made instrumental in the salvation of some, whom we hope are now in heaven, and of others who are still on their journey.

Revd Barton, MA, with all his learning, could not touch these men.

Before he turns into his rectory, as he pauses to look at his church, the new rector can see the repairs Hugh Molesworth and his father have made to the fabric of the church. This is still in sufficiently good condition not to need his immediate attention.

Revd Barton, however, considers the condition of the rectory, now well over 100 years old, below the standard required for his family. He builds a spacious new one. At the same time the barn below

The former rectory in 2005.

Glebe farmhouse was rebuilt by Revd Barton in the mid-nineteenth century using stone from the old rectory, which he replaced with a new one.

A nineteenth-century barn at Glebe Farm, since demolished.

the rectory is rebuilt and extended, with a new roundhouse for the horse-driven whim for threshing. A new stone farmhouse is built, using stone from the old rectory, to make a completely independent farm and farmyard, 'Glebe Farm'.

On his tour of the parish the new rector met many old people who were still working on the land, but was undoubtedly made aware of the number of very young children working and not receiving any kind of education. His next task was to provide a school for the parish. Since curate Hugh Henry Molesworth had left in 1847 the numbers attending any school had dropped back to 50 per cent of the potential. There was an urgent need to put education on a proper footing. On 5 May 1856 the new school was completed and opened, a good start.

✦ CHAPTER 10 ✦

The New School, Rector Barton and Nonconformists

The new school building, opened on 5 May 1856, had cost £456 altogether, of which the National Society had contributed £38. The school could accommodate 100 pupils and had furnished lodgings, rent free, for a schoolmaster in the attached six-roomed house. The first master was young George Holborow. He received a salary of £25 a year and free accommodation. A year later his wife, Anna, gave birth to their first child, George William.

The figures for 1860 show how wildly optimistic the rector had been in providing places for 100 pupils. On the books were 10 boys and 30 girls paying 'pence', one penny per week, but average attendance was only 8 boys and 17 girls, a total of 25. The census shows that a greater number than this were listed as 'scholars', that is, they claimed to attend school. 'Scholars' totalled 59 out of a potential 105 in the age group. They included the children of half the farmers and a third of the farm labourers. Not all of these would have attended the new school in St Ervan. Farmers often sent their children to schools beyond the parish bounds, for example to private schools in Wadebridge. For the children living at Penrose it was a shorter walk to St Eval school.

In some cases the rector's inability to establish a good relationship with his Nonconformist parishioners displayed itself in open conflict. One example is that of Paul Strongman, a boy of eight or nine when the school opened. Paul's memoir in the *Bible Christian Magazine* tells the story, admittedly from a biased viewpoint. Bible Christian preacher H. Rundle wrote:

His early educational advantages were limited, and were rendered the more so by the methods of instruction employed and the nature of the teaching imparted in his youth under the voluntary system. He was the victim of a grave injustice. His father, a sturdy nonconformist, objected to the Church of England teaching that was enforced in the school, and because he would not submit Paul was ostracised and virtually expelled.

The memory of that incident, with the disadvantages it involved, would arouse his righteous ire to the very last.

Paul was one of those noisier and more eccentric individuals which the Bible Christians often attracted, so he and his father were the wrong people for the rector to cross swords with. By the time he was in his thirties, Paul:

... occupied a prominent position and took a leading part in the religious life of the neighbourhood. As circuit steward, Sunday School superintendent, class leader, local preacher, etc., he filled many posts and played many parts; and he did the whole well. In physique he was a noticeable man...

Paul Strongman must have been a constant thorn in the rector's side.

St Ervan School, ready for sale by auction in 1973.

After only six years, in 1862, St Ervan School closed. There appears not to have been sufficient financial support within the parish. The possible reason for this reluctance comes in a reply sent to the National Society questionnaire by the rector:

Committee: Revd H.N. Barton is sole manager, the others only farmers unable to read or write, having refused to act or have anything to do with the school.
Signed H.N. Barton, 1 Feb 1860.

Five years after the school opened only one of the original committee was still active. Philip Hawke had moved to a smaller farm in St Columb Major parish. James Hawken senr had died at the end of 1857. (These two had been churchwardens together for many years.) George Biddick remained but he was nearly 70, though this did not prevent him being very active in Vestry affairs. The rector had failed to persuade other farmers to succeed Philip Hawke and James Hawken on the committee.

The farmers may well have seemed illiterate to the rector, with his MA degree, but they often showed that they were not men to be pushed around by the authorities. A younger generation was taking over in the Vestry now. Several had Methodist associations, e.g. churchwarden James Hawke was married to Philippa, granddaughter of a Bible Christian leader. Well-known Bible Christian William Pope was an overseer. The Methodists, especially the Bible Christians, were a strong, popular and independent body of people.

John Binny, farming 105 acres at Penrose and assessor in the Vestry of 1850, did not send his children to the rector's school. He belonged to the well-to-do Binny family of Penrose and St Eval, and it was on one of his fields, Well Park (bought for a nominal £5), that in June 1861 the new Bible Christian chapel was being built. Now the rector would suffer competition from three Methodist chapels in his small parish; the Wesleyan by the bridge in Rumford, the Bible Christian chapel just above Rumford Mill (which had been granted a new trust indenture in 1854 shortly after the rector's arrival), and now, just a mile from the church and in a prominent position at the side of the highway, there was all the fussing and rejoicing among the parishioners at the Penrose side of the parish at having their own place of worship. The foundation service was held on 24 May 1861, and John Hawke, engine driver to a thrashing machine, and William Dawe, carpenter, of Penrose attested to the receipt of the conveyance of the land from John Binny on 27 June 1861. The masons were the young Tippett brothers, James, who lived in the cottage next door and became a leader in chapel, and William, an apprentice who lodged with Thomas Sandry Lobb, the cordwainer son of Prudy. The carpentry was done by Thomas Brewer, second son of the late Richard Brewer.

James Tippett was a trustee, as were Thomas's elder brother, John Brewer, the miller at Rumford, and his brother, William Brewer, the miller at Little Petherick. The other three, James Strongman, William Tucker Chapman and William Bennett, came from the neighbouring parishes of St Wenn, St Breock and St Merryn. All had family connections in St Ervan.

The Bible Christians still asserted their independence from the Wesleyans. The deeds of both Rumford and Penrose Bible Christian chapels stipulated that the trustees would permit such persons appointed by the annual conference of the people called Bible Christians to use the chapel... 'and no other without the consent of the Pastor of the Circuit.'

The opening services were held on 17 and 18 November 1861. Samuel Ley Thorne, grandson of James Thorne, the pioneer leader of the Bible Christians with William O'Bryan, was minister of the St Ervan Circuit 1860–62 and reported the events at Penrose for the *Bible Christian Magazine*:

With the care of the Divine Hand upon our undertaking, the chapel was opened Sabbath, November 17, 1861, and following Monday... The sermons on both days were earnest, spiritual and eloquent. The congregations were crowded and the offerings to God's cause, including the tea, the provisions for which, as at the foundation tea, being given, £4.6s.

On the next Wednesday, after the regular preaching, the sittings were all let and paid for one quarter in

Madeline Binny, daughter of Bill Brewer's sister Annie, died of heart failure aged 26.

Ethel James (born c.1886) (left) married Will Millett (centre left), and Will's sister (centre right) married Ethel's brother, Fred James (born c.1884) (right), in August 1915. The Jameses were children of John James, farmer, and Louisa of St Merryn, and left Penrose and St Ervan in about 1896. Will Millett was baptised in Penrose Bible Christian chapel.

Mrs Jane Rosevear (née James), widowed young, who lived all her life in St Ervan. Her son trained as a shoemaker, then moved away to the china clay district around St Austell.

advance. From this source of income there will be enough to pay twice as much as the interest on the money borrowed. The chapel is crowded constantly, the singing is excellent, and a small church formed.

On the local government front the rector seems to have decided to let the parish go its own way. After 1857 he no longer chaired the Vestry meetings. In 1858 the Vestry, with James Rowe as chairman, held its annual meeting on the Easter Monday in the vestry of the church once again. In 1860 James Hawken (son of John at Treginegar) succeeded William Biddick of Trenouth as chairman and took the meeting over the road to a more comfortable place, the Old Inn, where his cousin's widow, Nancy Hawken, was innkeeper. She ran it with the assistance of a married son, John.

John's conduct of the inn business displeased the rector, who made an attempt to curtail his activities. The *West Briton* of 31 August 1866 carried the following brief report:

John Hawken, keeper of the Old Inn at St Ervan, was charged with having his house open at 9.30 am on Sunday morning the 19th instant, but the summons was dismissed.

The magistrates were local men to whom any reputation for bad conduct of an innkeeper would have been only too well known, so was this the rector being spiteful?

In the following years the rector, with all his intellectual advantages, failed to make any headway against the simple conviction of his less educated Bible Christian parishioners. In the autumn of 1874 he called to see Paul Strongman's father, John, during his last illness and tried to persuade him that 'he could not know his sins forgiven'. John Strongman replied with as much energy as he could: 'I believe in the Lord Jesus Christ'. His memoir in the 1875 *Bible Christian Magazine* records that the day before John died he said 'feelingly':

> There is a fountain filled with blood,
> Drawn from Immanuel's veins,
> And sinners, plunged beneath that flood,
> Lose all their guilty stains.

John Strongman died on Sunday, 13 September 1874. The rector performed the burial ceremony the following Wednesday.

The memoir for John gives a vivid glimpse of the spiritual condition of the parish in the 1870s. In 1873, the memoir reports: 'the lord graciously favoured our church at Rumford with a large outpouring of his Spirit. Three of the converts were our dear brother's children.'

John Strongman had participated in a revival at Rumford and his wife reported that:

> ... he ever afterwards appeared like a different man; more

intensely in earnest in serving the Lord, more fervent in prayer, more deeply concerned about the salvation of souls... Feelingly he sang, fervently he prayed, and loudly he shouted, in the revival services. The evening the revival commenced he walked the aisle of the chapel, and with a loud voice said

> Who can resolve the doubt
> That tears my anxious breast?
> Shall I be with the damned cast out,
> Or numbered with the blest?
> I must from God be driven,
> Or with my Saviour dwell;
> Must come at His command to Heaven,
> Or else – depart to Hell.

The effect was great, causing sinners even to tremble. One evening in the prayer-meeting, when a powerful influence filled the place, I remember seeing him walking in the chapel aisle with a smiling face and hearing him shout several times with extraordinary emphasis and feeling 'Hallelujah!'.

The keen involvement in religious activity of the Strongman family did not end with John's death. Of John Strongman's ten children four were still at home; the indomitable Paul (35) who, with Alfred (15), had followed their father at shoemaking, Reuben (23), a blacksmith working with Peter Sandry senr, and Mary (12). Paul:

> ... having experienced the re-creating power of the Gospel, henceforth zealously employed his faculties and exercised his energies in the services of the church of his choice.

Shortly after this, in 1877, Bishop Benson of Truro stated that Methodism had kept religion alive in Cornwall at a time 'when the church had almost lost the sacred flame.'

The 1860s saw the deaths of several of St Ervan's more well-to-do old men. In 1862 Gregory Tom senr, yeoman, died aged 85; in 1863 Silvester Key, farmer, died aged 86; in 1864 Samuel Paynter, yeoman, died aged 70, and William Houghton, miller (he had bought Millingworth Mill), died aged 72. It is interesting to compare what these wealthy men of the parish left at the end of their lives, sums from £300 to £450, with the rector's annual income of £380.

Rector Barton built himself a grand new rectory in 1856. In 1859 a member of the Paynter family built a new farmhouse at Treleigh in granite, containing entrance hall, dining-room, drawing-room, six bedrooms, boxroom, kitchen, dairy and usual domestic offices. Its size and solidity are impressive for a farmhouse even today. Also, about 1870, James Hawken, auctioneer and farmer, built a new farmhouse at Pentruse entirely separate from the main farmhouse at Trenouth.

Clifford Strongman (1925–99) of Penrose.

Farmers in this purely agricultural area had the advantage of proximity to Padstow, three to four miles away, a port which shipped their produce to larger markets than the local St Columb one. The mixed farming they practised, because of the variability of the land they farmed, meant they could keep their heads above water when the markets for a particular produce were depressed, though their capacity for employing labour decreased.

In April 1869, when the Government Commissioner looking into employment of children, young persons and women in agriculture, held a meeting at St Columb, he enquired about the cottages, wages and education and learned that conditions for labouring families were not good. Gregory Tom junr, who had come into Trethewey on his father's death, represented St Ervan at the St Columb District meeting.

The reports and speakers at the meeting were very critical. Means of education were limited and the district was badly off for schools. In one report this was blamed on the indifference of parents. There was a class of small farmers who could not afford to spare their children's labour for the sake of education and dissenters did not send their children to the school. One report considered that grants in aid should be allowed in rural districts even where the teacher was uncertified.

Mr J. Hawken stated that in St Ervan: 'the school established under the Government regulations is now closed.' He thought there was great need of a better system of aid for education. At this meeting the resolution 'that children should not be employed constantly in agriculture under 10 years' was carried, perhaps because it would affect so few. However, in spite of their former criticism of the state of schooling in the area, they could not accept the resolution that 'certificates of ability must be obtained before children begin work'!

Economic pressures and religious differences caused prejudice against Church- or Government-aided schools. The rector of St Ervan would need a much more conciliatory personality to overcome such a volume of resistance. The 1871 census showed there were 48 'scholars' in St Ervan parish, down from 59 in 1861, but 26 of these lived at the Penrose side of the parish and probably attended St Eval School. The school in St Ervan was still closed.

National events were now to decide the future of schooling in the parish. W.E. Forster's Education Act of 1870 provided that the country be divided into districts, each managed by a Board, that is a local authority, and that elementary schools should be set up in areas where school provision for children aged 5–14 was insufficient. They were to be secular and non-denominational, but were permitted to provide religious instruction if they wished. The Boards could build new schools or absorb existing ones. In St Ervan Churchtown stood the rector's school

building, just 20 years old, which had never been much used; indeed there had been no school for some years past. The only surviving manager of the old school was the rector; he had played no part in the Vestry annual meetings for the past 15 years and appears to have taken no part in the setting up of the new School Board.

James Hawken at Pentruse, 46, practising as an auctioneer, was in an excellent position to know the land and people of the parish intimately. His father, John, and his uncles had all played a prominent part in the running of parish affairs and now it was his turn. The first entry in the St Ervan School Board minute-book records:

At a meeting of the Ratepayers of the parish of St Ervan held in the Vestry room of the parish and thence adjourned to the school room this 17th day of November 1874 such meeting being convened by Mr George B. Collins, returning officer, for the purpose of passing a resolution that it is expedient that a school Board is formed for this parish.

It is proposed and resolved that Mr James Hawken be Chairman of this Meeting.

It is proposed by Mr Rowe and seconded by Mr Thomas Tremain that it is expedient that a School Board be formed for this Parish, and carried unanimously.
James Hawken Chairman

On 1 January 1875 14 principal ratepayers met in the schoolroom and nominated the following as:

... fit and proper members for the school Board...

Hawken James	*Pentruse*	*Auctioneer and surveyor*
Rowe Peter	*Trembleath*	*Farmer*
Sandry John senr	*Trewinnick*	*Yeoman*
Tom Gregory	*Trethewey*	*Yeoman*
Tremain Thomas	*Treginegar*	*Farmer*

and at the first meeting of the Board on 28 January 1875 James Hawken was elected the first Chairman.

The activity surrounding the reopening of a school in premises built by his initiative were not witnessed by Revd Barton. He left in April 1875 for two years, leaving curate W.H.H. Sidney in charge. Before leaving he sent notice to the Board of his consent for the schoolhouse and premises to be given up to the new School Board. The Board's solicitor, Mr George B. Collins of St Columb, prepared a lease for securing for a term the schoolhouse and premises from the National Society. Revd Barton must have facilitated this transfer, in spite of the National Society's strong objection to transfer any of their schools to local Boards; and Bishop Phillpotts would only give his signature on condition that a rent of £4 per annum was devoted to a Sunday school. The archdeacon's request to St Ervan School Board for £4 was refused, since £1 rent had been agreed by Revd Barton and they had no intention of paying more. The transfer was effected in February.

Much work had to be done on the 20-year old building. James Tippett, mason, was employed to work on the roofs, etc.; Thomas Brewer, carpenter, to repair the woodwork and William Daw to repair the glass. The sanitary inspector insisted on the well being properly covered, and Mr Charles Hawke of St Columb was engaged to repair the pump. Fences had to be repaired, watercourses to be paved and the school yard levelled.

In June the Board felt ready to open the school and advertised for a schoolmistress. There was no response. They advertised again. Miss Dunstan replied and was engaged. She arrived in September and promptly gave notice. They persuaded her to stay. Now at last they could think about the reopening.

Books and other articles had to be purchased along with furniture for the schoolmistress's house. Coal had to be bought for the schoolroom and for Miss Dunstan. The pupils were to pay weekly on a scale decided by the schoolmistress, and each was provided with copybooks and other requisites at the expense of the School Board. The account at the end of the year shows that materials, repairs, labour, furniture, etc., came to a total of £61.2s.6d. even before the teacher's salary was found, a vast amount for a small parish, much of which had to come from the rates. Needless to say, the largest sum went to the solicitor, Mr G.B. Collins, £11 for 'forming of school board' and a further £15 fee 'for arranging the transfer of the school premises from the National Society to the St Ervan School Board.' Further, in December 1876 the overseers paid £90 to the Treasurer of the Board, in March they were asked to collect from the ratepayers £12, in May £30, in July £22, in October £15 and in January £40. In subsequent years the precepts averaged £80. The Government grant supplied a further £25.5s. per annum and the pupils' 'pence' about £20, making a total sum well below expenditure. The managers did not squander the money. In fact, they took every opportunity to cut costs. Mrs John Key's bill for lodging Miss Dunstan while the schoolmistress's house was got ready was knocked down from 21s. to 11s.

Thomas Tremain resigned at the end of 1877, his place being taken by another Hawken, another James Hawken, of Penrose, a 50-year-old farmer in the process of squandering his inheritance from his uncle James, who had died 20 years before. Soon after, chairman James Hawken had his 18-year-old son, Edred, voted in as clerk to the Board, a job he himself had fulfilled in an honorary capacity, at a salary of £2 per quarter.

The path would not be smooth. Before 12 months had run, it was discovered that Miss Dunstan's certificate did not:

... constitute her a certified teacher for the purpose of Article 17 New Code and that therefore the Board should discharge her and get a duly certificated teacher in her place [letter from the Department of Education].

The Board had to comply if it wished to continue receiving Government aid.

An advertisement for a certificated mistress gained no response, but a second advertisement for a master, offering a salary of £50 plus half the Government grant (which depended on the attendance and proficiency of the scholars, so it was fair to reward the teacher by results) brought several applications. Mr T.W. Sandry (no known connection to the local Sandrys) was appointed. School reopened after two months' closure.

Buildings and grounds occupied the attentions of the Board continuously, especially as the condition of the building was another factor on which the Government grant depended. Paths and fences were repaired by James Tippett, coal and furze were delivered, the schoolyard had again to be put in order, the school was whitewashed and the 'offices' (toilets) cleaned out, school desks were fixed and altered to suit the requirements of the inspector, and it was agreed that Thomas Brewer should construct a gallery for the younger children 'similar to one in St Eval school'.

We can smile at one item:

Sep 1878: resolved – that a coalhouse be built 8 feet by 15 feet without, with a lean-to roof against the south window of the School House to block a portion of the window to prevent the boys from seeing the girls' privy, and that James Tippett (mason) be ordered to send an estimate for said coalhouse.

James Tippett's estimate of £6.19s. was accepted. The Board insured the school premises in the sum of £300 in the West of England Insurance Office.

Still they could not rest. A month after Mr T.W. Sandry had been appointed, the Board received news from the Department of Education that they should check with his former employer in South Wales 'as to the circumstances under which Mr Sandry left his former school.' Mr Sandry was alleged to have borrowed money and not returned it. He claimed it was a misunderstanding. The Board made no further investigation and declared themselves 'fully satisfied with Mr Sandry's statement... he is a very able teacher', and rescinded their suspension.

A year after Mr Sandry's appointment the school was visited by Her Majesty's Inspector, who reported:

The children are very orderly, attentive and obedient, and thus a good foundation for future progress has been made. Their attainments, however, are very low for their age, though considering the want of previous instruction, nothing else could be expected...

There followed criticism of the 'dilapidated furniture'and the lack of reading books, and the threat of withdrawal of the grant if there was no improvement among the infants. The following June the inspector reported:

The children are very orderly, attentive and obedient, they work honestly and with perseverance. Their attainments show some progress since last year but improvement is still needed. The scholars have not yet been taught to use their intelligence, they merely remember what they have learned by rote. This weakness is shown in the classwork especially geography has been taught with very little success. The singing is remarkably good. The infants are much less proficient than they were, though they too may improve. The sewing is quite as good as can be expected. A map of the British Isles is much wanted... The girls should be provided with an inner door or a heavy curtain.

This report speaks volumes for the lives and outlook of these children in a Victorian Cornish rural parish. It was an uphill struggle but progress was being made. Then, in 1879, Mr Sandry 'absconded leaving his wife and small children behind.'

Meantime, the domination of the Board had passed out of Hawken hands. In November 1877 Edred William Hawken, clerk to the Board, had given notice to resign, and his father James did not stand for re-election. Edred was ill and in 1881, aged 22, he died. James's eldest child was Alfred, aged 23, then an undergraduate at Oxford University, and his two daughters, Martha and Emma, were 21 and 18. In September James and his wife Joice had another son and called him Edred William.

The rector, Henry Nowell Barton, now 53 years old, returned from his two years' leave of absence from the parish in April 1877 and was an outside observer of the beginning of Mr Sandry's tenure in the schoolroom. When the elections to the new Board came up in January 1878 the rector was elected to the Board, then elected chairman and clerk. Vice-chairman was 58-year-old Peter Rowe, who farmed over 200 acres at Trembleath and was the census enumerator. New members were Peter Sandry, 47-year-old farmer of 80 acres living at Rumford House (no children), and Philip Hawke, a bachelor farmer. Thomas Tremain, who had resigned while James Hawken was chairman, now returned.

The Tremains were comparative newcomers to St Ervan. Thomas Tremain, a Padstow merchant, had bought the freehold of Treginegar from Sir William Molesworth and leased it for seven years to John Hawken, and again for a further seven-year term. After this a kinsman, John Tremain, farmed the 280 acres. By 1871 another kinsman, another John Tremain, was farming 140 acres at Treglinnick. The Tremains had now become the principal landowning family in the parish. Thomas Tremain also owned the freehold of lands at Penrose occupied by John Binny, and it was Tom Tremain who built the present house at Lewidden by the boundary stream with St Merryn parish. Treglinnick, however, did not remain long in their hands. In 1872 it was one of the first properties to be purchased by John M. Williams Esq., of Carhayes near Newquay, who would soon own one quarter of the parish.

The rector's chairmanship of the School Board is initially characterised by brisk business and formal language. He wrote in the minutes that it was resolved 'that a Precept be issued for £40'. He immediately set about raising the 'pence' that the children must pay, the infants 'more than 2d. per week' and the top 'Standard IV 4d. per week' and he got a resolution passed 'that the list of books and apparatus &c. presented by Mr T.W. Sandry be ordered from the National Society.' Finally, a resolution was passed 'that the school be visited by the Diocesan Inspector.' Here we see the rector's motive in taking the helm of school management again.

Mr T.W. Sandry's successor was Mr John Tresidder, from the St Germoe Board School. He started work in October 1879, the beginning of a four-year period of stability for the school and its pupils. To assist Mr Tresidder with the teaching of the infants and sewing, Mrs M.A. Rowe was appointed at a salary of £8 per annum. She was the 30-year-old wife of Thomas Rowe, who was farming Trembleath with his father, Peter, and was the daughter of Richard Binny, innkeeper at Lowertown Penrose.

Several years earlier, while James Hawken was still chairman, it had been suggested that Mrs William Hawken should be asked to teach the children. Her reputation as a fine needlewoman and hard-working mother has come down through several generations of descendants to the present day, but so also has her husband's as a drunken idler. Whatever the reason, her name never again came forward once the rector took charge.

With the rector and Peter Rowe firmly in charge of the Board, and Mr Tresidder and Mrs Rowe apparently settled in the teaching posts, attention could be turned to absenteeism among the pupils, the level of which was endangering the grant. In October 1881 notices were issued to Eliza Varcoe and to Paul Strongman on account of non-attendance of their children. Eliza, herself an illegitimate child, no doubt needed her daughter's help to earn a living. Paul Strongman, our fervent Bible Christian, whose own schooling had been restricted by Revd Barton almost 30 years previously, was no doubt reluctant to put his children into a school now managed so closely by the rector.

Death was never far from these families. Paul and Elizabeth Strongman had seven children. In August 1882 the rector buried Jessica, aged 10, and in September 1883 he buried Reuben, aged 7. Their

Mary Ann, widow of William Hawken (1811–90), a superb seamstress, in London, c.1895.

sickliness might well have been a reason for their absence from school in 1881.

John Tresidder seemed to be settled at the school and even accepted, after two years, a reduction in salary from £5 to £4.11s.8d. per month. A year later his son was baptised in St Ervan Church, but before young William was one year old a cloud came over the horizon.

Peter Sandry, who had been a member of the Board for several years, was a wealthy man with no children of his own. In 1882 and 1883 he was also a parish overseer to the poor, and perhaps it was because of a desire to keep a check on Vestry expenditure that he gave notice that he would be raising the question of the schoolmaster's salary. At the Board meeting on 16 May 1883: 'It was resolved to give Notice to Mr J. Tresidder the School-Master that the Board wished him to give up charge of the school at the end of three months.'

If only we could listen in on the discussion which led to that decision! The standard of Mr Tresidder's teaching never seems to have been an issue, and he found another appointment within ten days. Perhaps the general economic situation was the cause of Peter Sandry's action. By this time the agricultural depression was biting deep and ratepayers were paying out a lot of money to educate a small number of children.

This photograph of the school, c.1891, was kept by Leonard Masters. His mother, Mary Annie (née Tippett, born 1879) is standing middle row at the right shoulder of head teacher Miss Winsor.

Several schoolmistresses came and went, with more or less success, but on 2 December 1889 Miss M.M. Winsor 'entered upon her duties' as mistress in charge of St Ervan Board School. Within a year the Government grant was nearly doubled, yet throughout her stay of ten years her salary of £35 per annum was never increased. Towards the end of that period her half-share of the Government grant had risen to £17. Her teaching and her management of the school must have been effective. In July 1893 it was further agreed 'that Miss Winsor should have an assistant for the infants at a salary of one shilling per week.' The first one was Miss Dora Rowe, daughter of Mrs A.M. Rowe, whose services had been necessary to assist a master (but had been thought unnecessary once a mistress was in charge, even though a mistress was engaged at a lower salary!).

By the end of the century the population had declined markedly, as had the number of pupils, from 51 to 37. Attendance was further reduced by persistent occasional absenteeism and even further by the reluctance of agricultural labourers to keep 13-year-old children at school when they could be helping to increase the family income, however meagrely. While Thomas Tremain was on the Board he had started a campaign against employment of school-age children and threatened prosecutions. In 1893:

A summons against Isaac Parkyn for the non-attendance of his children was heard at the Petty Sessions... with the result that his wife was cautioned and the Board had to pay 3/6 costs.

And again in 1897 Isaac was summoned: 'It was found that Isaac Parkyn's two children John and George had only made 53 attendances out of 60 each – the former 28, the latter 25.'

This time the prosecution cost the Board 6s. These costs probably deterred the Board from making further prosecutions.

Poor Isaac and Mary. What use was schooling to their sons, who would earn their livings by hard labour on the land?

On 9 September 1891 the Board resolved that 'Free education should be accepted by the Board and the Hon. Clerk should write to the Education Department accordingly.'

My curiosity as to the reasons behind the decisions to discharge any master or mistress remain unsatisfied by the rector's haphazard and incomplete recording of the meetings. No log-book survives for this period (1875–1902) and the rector did not continue James Hawken's practice of copying HMI's reports into the Board minute-book. We can, therefore, only speculate as to why, on 29 April 1899, when Miss Winsor had served as schoolmistress for nearly ten years, she was given three months' notice that her

services were no longer required. If the Board, made up of George Sandry, H. Rowe, Silvester Key and Richard Brewer, all farmers of standing and all with roots in the parish or neighbouring parishes, were really looking for the ideal teacher, why did they unanimously elect Mr Thomas W. Sandry as master in the place of Miss Winsor? It was exactly 20 years since Mr Sandry had absconded from St Ervan, leaving his wife and tiny children behind. The rector had been chairman of the School Board then and still was; though now elderly, surely he could not have forgotten?

Mr Sandry failed to arrive to take up his appointment!

His action only prolonged the difficulty the Board of this tiny school encountered in replacing a discharged mistress. They had to appoint a teacher at as economical a salary as possible, which made it uncompetitive in the market with larger schools. By October there was still no successor to Miss Winsor, and Mrs Paul Strongman and Annie Old (who had been working as an assistant) agreed 'to take the school in hand, at a salary of 7s.6d. each per week.' They worked from November until April and, from tales that have come down of the formidable Mrs Paul Strongman, there is no doubt that she took the school in hand very firmly, and no doubt either that some religious principles with a pronounced Bible Christian slant were inculcated into the pupils.

Eventually, in April, nine months after Miss Winsor's dismissal, Mrs Mackin became mistress of St Ervan School, but at the higher salary of £5 per month (£60 a year). After 18 months she, too, was given notice to leave.

In 1902 School Boards were abolished by A.J. Balfour's Education Act and the County Council became the local education authority. A new school management committee was elected, under a new chairman, George Sandry, who had been a member of the old Board since 1896. Vice-chairman was Richard Henry Rowe and the committee were William Binny, William Powell Old and William Henry Old. They began with a new mistress, Miss Cottrell, who had energy and enthusiasm. Only two months after she took charge, HMI reported:

Some of the children very backward for their age, but under the vigorous care of the present mistress the school is rapidly improving and showing a promising condition.

Miss Cottrell, in turn, expressed appreciation of the efforts of the managers: 'The new maps and a globe have arrived, and besides being a splendid help they very much improve the appearance of the schoolroom.'

And later: 'The partition extension [up to the ceiling] is finished. The match boarding has been done. The room is now very much warmer'.

However, all through September she had less success with the attendance levels: 'low attendance because of late harvest', 'weekly average 14 [out of 24]', 'great many picking up potatoes', but by November she could write: 'Attendance much better since the Board decided to summon parents who would not send their children to school.' However, neither she nor any future teacher would win the battle against the demands of the agricultural seasons and opportunities for children to earn a few extra pennies. 'April 6: 7 boys present out of 16. The others are planting potatoes.'

Miss Cottrell left and again several teachers came and went, with varying degrees of success.

At the end of 1903 the St Ervan Board School, with its 23 pupils, became a member of Group 5 (together with Padstow Boys' and Girls' Schools and St Merryn School) under the Bodmin and Wadebridge District Education Committee. The committee minutes, of necessity, are briefer and less informative. We have to rely on the teacher's story as recounted in the log-book, which has survived from 1902.

In January 1905 the new head teacher, Mrs E.M.M. Hall, wife of the headmaster of St Merryn School, records her dissatisfaction with the state of the school. On 20 January 1905 she writes:

I find the children are extremely careless and untidy with their books... almost every reading book in the school is written upon and the edges of leaves rolled up... I am cleaning the books in turn and have promised punishment to the offenders in future.

And on 23 January: 'Commenced all work in Standards on paper with ink this morning. Slates will not be used again.'

Further comments reveal the state into which the school had descended, not surprising with the constant changes of teacher.

Reading throughout the school is exceedingly poor, those who know the words fairly well have not the least idea of expression... I ought also to mention that grammar, if it has been taken at all must have been forgotten by the children, for they are unable to answer the most simple questions.

No wonder, when one earlier teacher had spent time giving 'Object lesson – the potato' to these children who spent spring and autumn seasons planting and picking potatoes.

Throughout all these changes there were frequent complaints about lack of materials, the condition of the schoolrooms, of the desks, and especially about the toilets, and frequently withdrawal of the grant was threatened. It was Mrs Hall's good fortune to report finally, on 6 March 1905: 'The new desks are in position today'. But that same year HM Inspector reported that:

The floor and wainscoting should receive attention before the dry rot spreads further... Proper lavatory facilities are wanting... and more frequent cleansing and disinfecting.

In spite of all the problems Mrs Hall was given a good report by His Majesty's Inspector in June 1906:

This diminutive School is conducted with painstaking care which meets with gratifying success: but it is impossible for one teacher to instruct children of such widely varying ages without assistance. Unless a competent Monitress at least can be found it would seem advisable to exclude the very young children who now form a not inappreciable proportion of the school.

Mrs Hall's problem was keeping the older boys in school:

September 21 1906: Parkyn, a boy of 13 has been working for one of the farmers. Bennetts a boy of nine was kept at home to pick up potatoes. I have reported the matter of illegal employment to Mr Yates [the clerk].

She also crossed swords with parents over other matters:

'
Oct 23 1906. On Friday afternoon last, Leslie Buscombe took off the hat of Fred Bennet (a boy much younger than himself) and threw it in the mud. On Monday morning I enquired into the matter and finding Buscombe to be the offender, decided to keep him in from play for the week as punishment. This morning I received the above note from the boys' parents: [the letter is pinned into the log-book]

Rumford
St Ervan
Mrs Hall,
If you decide to carry out your decision in keeping Leslie in all the week, I shall send him St Eval, next week
Francis Buscombe

In March 1907 Mrs Hall's husband died. She continued to teach at St Ervan but in August bade a touching farewell:

Aug 2nd 1907. I resign my position, as mistress of this school, owing to the illness of my parents, and deeply regret parting with my little scholars, who have tried to please both in their work and attendance.

E.M.M. Hall.

Her successor would be the formidable Miss Henrietta Drake, who deserves a chapter to herself.

CHAPTER 11

Miss Henrietta Elsie Adelaide Drake

Miss Henrietta Drake announced her arrival with the full force of her very strong personality. Her huge handwriting allowed only four or five words to a line, 4 November 1907, in extravagant flourishes sweeping over the page (see below).

This low number of pupils reflected the fall in population of the parish, now at its lowest ever – 256 in 1911 compared with the peak of 477 in 1841.

A selection of items from the log-book during Miss Drake's first three years gives a picture of the preoccupation of a schoolmistress, particularly of a tiny school, with the level of attendance (on which depended the grant) and her anxiety to show just cause for absences. Influenza, diphtheria, whooping cough, ringworm and mumps were among the illnesses that could close the school for days or weeks. The children often went down with heavy colds, coughs and general sickness, and rain and gales could deter children from arriving. It did not help that the school stove was inefficient and that complaints from both the parents and Miss Drake fell on deaf ears.

On 31 January 1908 Miss Drake recorded: 'Three children (Alfred, Lily and Dorothy Sowden) who have been attending St Eval school have attended this school this morning.'

This influx of three new pupils should have been a cause for rejoicing, but: 'Feb 3 – Alfred Sowden did not arrive until 10 this morning.'

However there were no absences for potato planting recorded that April.

In a parish with a Parish Church and three Methodist chapels there were frequent days out, not only for the harvest but also for Sunday-school anniversary teas. Still in 1908:

Jun 15 – Closed this afternoon for a Sunday School treat.
Jun 30 – Ditto.
Jly 3 – Owing to the Hay Harvest the attendance has fallen to 97.7% this week.

In spite of this, Miss Drake recorded on 22 July 1908: 'St Ervan is the first school in the County for attendance having made a percentage of 99.9 for the quarter.'

With Miss Drake in charge the children enjoyed frequent outings. On 24 July, following this good attendance record, a holiday was given:

I took the children to Harlyn Bay. It was a perfect day and I believe all thoroughly enjoyed it. Two children had never seen the sea before. The elder children went into the Museum [a prehistoric burial ground had been unearthed and the skeletons displayed in their stone coffins].'

Nevertheless, she had to write on 29 July: 'A picnic having been arranged by the parents of the children a holiday had to be given.'

The following year, on the same date, Miss Drake took the children to Constantine Bay herself.

The harvest was late that year. In September Alfred Sowden was absent for a week 'working in the harvest field'.

I have taken charge of this

School this morning

No. on registers 15

No. Present 15

H. E. Drake

St Ervan School in 1919. Left to right, back row: *Miss Henrietta Elsie Adelaide Drake (headmistress), May Thomas (later Mrs Powell), Gertrude Thomas (sister of May, later Mrs Curtis), Christine Sandry, Marjorie Powell (later Mrs Charles King), Eliza Turner, Ida Currow (later Mrs Hill);* third row: *Mary Hawke (later Mrs Reginald Chapman), Betty Brewer (later Mrs Mallett), Mary Powell (later Mrs Crews), William John Buscombe (known as Jack, not a pupil, lived at Underhill), Irene Buscombe (later Mrs John Deacon), Mary Salmon (later Mrs Harry Strongman), Madeline Binny, Dorothy Tippett (later Mrs Harry Bennett), Philippa Hawke (junior teacher, died aged 37);* second row: *Myrtle Powell, Edward Gregor, Raymond Brewer, Ronald Maitland Drake (known as 'Tanto', nephew of Miss Drake), Reginald Chapman, Jim Turner, William Rabey;* front row: *Howard Cowling, Rowe Binny (brother of Madeline), Russell Turner(?), Harry Rowe, Wilfred Turner, Alan Drake (brother of Tanto).*

All teachers were anxious to record the backwardness of children when first admitted to their school from elsewhere, no doubt in order to impress the inspector with the effectiveness of their own teaching upon this unpromising material.

1909 Apr 19. I have admitted 4 children this morning. They are all in a very backward state. One girl of 8 has only now been transferred from the 2nd to the 1st class infants.

More new children arrived during the year and by July 1910 she had '30 on the books, exactly double since I first came.' But still parents were keeping their children away whenever there was a chance of employment, particularly in summer. In 1911:

Jly 28 During the past two weeks attendance has suffered through the bad attendance of Lily and Dorothy Sowden, the former often being employed.
Aug 4 Lily Sowden employed again this week.
Aug 11 Lily Sowden employed all the week, Fred Bennet one day and Thomas, George and James Babb a half day, while Dorothy Sowden, Alice Northcott and

Thomas Sandry have been absent all the week helping their parents... so that the attendance for this week is very poor.

The number of Sunday-school treats was reduced following the amalgamation of the Wesleyan and Bible Christian Methodists in 1907; in 1911 only one half day off for such an occasion, in June, but other reasons could be found, such as: '1911 May 1. As several children wished to go to Padstow to join in the May Day festivities I assembled and dismissed them half an hour earlier than usual.'

In 1915 the churchyard extension was completed. There was a service and tea at Rumford, only three children arrived at school, so the managers allowed it to be closed. There would be a degree of pressure on all families to attend this occasion, to be reminded of their mortality, and 'chapel' families would attend as readily as 'church' families, since the Nonconformist burial-ground was not yet opened.

In 1911 Miss Drake took advantage of a brother and sister visiting the area to give the pupils the fun of presenting a concert. It was reported in the *Royal Cornwall Gazette,* 12 January 1911, that:

Children of St Ervan School gave a concert in the schoolroom in aid of the school piano fund. The children had been trained by the Headmistress Miss H.E. Drake.

An amusing sketch 'The proof of the pudding' was given by Mr Darrell Drake and Miss Effie Drake. A musical sketch 'Our Jumble Sale' was given by the senior boys and girls which was much appreciated.

Other children sang, gifts from the Christmas tree were handed out by Mr Darrell Drake as Father Christmas. Mr Tremaine of Treginegar was the stage manager, and there was a crowded audience.

Miss Drake was as patriotic as anyone. The *Royal Cornwall Gazette* reported on 3 May 1912 that in St Ervan:

St George's Day was observed by scholars and residents and at the school gate the flag was kept flying all day. The Headmistress pointed out to the scholars the necessity and value of patriotism and an address was given by Mr Darell Drake.

The children performed some flag and ribbon drills and dancing around the maypole was made the basis of further instruction. The children carrying flags and headed by Miss Drake paraded the village singing patriotic songs.

There was a similar report in the newspaper the following year.

The First World War period makes no great impression on the character of entries in the logbook, except as a reason for more excursions: '5 May 1915: A holiday was given in order that the children might see the soldiers... at Penrose.'

A total of 70 sat down to lunch at the end of a 'route march'. What an impact on this tiny village. In 1918:

18 September: We have been picking blackberries this afternoon to make jam for the soldiers.
24 September: Ditto.
25 September: Ditto – we managed to send away a nice quantity in splendid condition.

Was this series of patriotic jaunts the reason behind a parent's letter of complaint to the Committee that too many holidays were given? A visit of the Prince of Wales, Duke of Cornwall, to the Duchy afforded another outing.

2 June 1921. Empire Day: the older children – with the approval of the manager, Mr Gregor – and in the charge of the assistant Miss Hawke, marched as far as Winnards Perch to see the Prince of Wales pass on his way to Wadebridge. They carried a large Union Jack, the biggest boy mounted a sign-post with it. All wore the Empire Day flowers.

The damp of the school building, the ineffectiveness of the stove in heating the building, the uncertainty about the quality of the drinking water from the school well and the inefficient disposal of the soil from the school lavatories are all recurring themes in the minutes of the District Committee and, combined with the frequent wet weather in Cornwall's humid climate, the inadequacy of diet and clothing of the poorer children cumulated in a depression of their health. 'Bad feet' was not simply the reason for a day's absence from school, but a symptom of poverty and unhealthy living conditions.

Apart from the faulty stove, Miss Drake had continuing problems with the 'soil from the school offices' and where it should be deposited. A farmer agreed to have it dumped on his land, then the landowner demanded a rent. In 1920 the affair blew up again. On 10 and 11 October, Miss Drake despaired of getting results and took the decisive action of closing the school:

Reason: **The Dump**
The dump is a plot of land adjoining the school. It is the property of Mr Sandry of St Cadoc. On 13 September Mr Sandry called to see me and said that as the County Education Authority had not paid any rent from 1914 to the present time and as they had also built a tank without either his knowledge or permission he would not allow it to be used any longer.

Long discussions followed, promises were made, but Mr Sandry was an impatient man. Miss Drake appealed to the local school managers, Mr Lobb, Mr Binny and Mr Gregor, who all allegedly agreed that the school should be closed. 'Had they not done so the parents would have done. Only 12 were present on Monday.' The district clerk, however, disagreed with her action, and instructed that the school should dump all refuse on the premises for a time and stay open. Miss Drake was furious:

As there have been two very serious outbreaks of disease, Scarlet Fever and Diptheria, during this last few years I decided not to do so... However, I am now acting on instructions received from the County Secretary.

This brought forth a visit, on 20 October, from the county secretary himself, Mr Pascoe, together with the building inspector, the district clerk, and the chairman of managers, following which the problem was at last resolved. That was one explosion settled, but the sanitary arrangements were frequently condemned by inspectors and, from their reports and board and committee minutes, it seems they were never satisfactorily sorted out.

Miss Drake is remembered as a huge personality. She was an independent and forceful character. The unfortunate Mr Old, a local manager, had the bad luck to cross swords with her very early on: '21 Jan 1911: Resolved – Miss Drake be informed that every case of corporal punishment must be entered in the punishment book.'

On 20 May 19 the committee considered:

Miss Drake's conduct with regard to the punishment book and her remarks to Mr Old... and it was resolved that she be written to expressing the great dissatisfaction of the Managers and their strong disapproval of her conduct and that she be informed that in all Mr Old has done he had the concurrence of the Managers who will view any similar conduct very seriously.

I wish we could know her undoubtedly spirited reply!

She was neither systematic nor methodical and this is the main reason for her falling foul of His Majesty's Inspector in 1914, in the first report to be entered in the log-book by Miss Drake since her arrival in 1907. Mr R.H. Charles had commended her. 'The work shows improvement... the children read easily; their written work is done carefully and is very free from mistakes. They answer... readily and sensibly.'

Then he had the temerity to add criticisms:

... the work... does not provide sufficient advance above the middle of the school... NO syllabus of work has been drawn up and the teaching is not systematically recorded. The teaching of Needlework is not at present satisfactory... the instruction has apparently not included the actual making of any garments, and no girl in the school appears to have had any experience of making any.

Miss Drake was not a woman to let such criticism pass without a fierce riposte, which she wrote out at length in her enormous handwriting in the log-book, and copied to the rector. She defended her work hotly and gave a clear picture of the facts of life in her tiny rural school.

I have been mistress here for seven years and the above is the first report I have received. I have always been complimented on the work of the school by former inspectors and only in February last when Mr Bachedlor, HMI – the newly appointed inspector for this district – visited this school for the first time he congratulated both the children and myself on the work and said that he wished he could find such good work in every school he visited. I told him that I had never received a report on the work of the school and he assured me that when I did it would be a good one. I was naturally very disappointed when it arrived. I have always prepared a syllabus of work every year and I presented it both to Mr Charles and Mr Bachedlor when they visited the school but Mr Charles did not think it 'full' and 'definite' enough. As regards the Needlework I have refrained from making many garments as I get no

sale for them but the children have made paper garments. Mr Charles thought this practically useless and said that the garment must be made in the material.

Every child in the Upper Group has made socks and all have made dolls clothes. I have always tried to give satisfaction but it is no easy matter to manage a small country school like this where there are children of such varying ages and infants coming at all times of the year. The teacher of one large class in a town school can teach with far better results and I have long since ceased to expect to compare work with those. I taught in the largest boys' school in Hertfordshire before coming here where I had charge of only one class so I speak from experience.

She doesn't change. It was 1924 before the inspector could report that: 'a syllabus of work has now been drawn up... the teaching is on the whole effective.' Miss Drake once more defended her work, pointing out that she was teaching children aged between five and 14 in one room: 'I am very fond of my work of teaching but one cannot do the impossible nor can the children.'

Another schools' inspector, Mrs Heap, summed up the situation under Miss Drake in her report of 1931:

There is a serious lack of system and good method in the management of this small school. On the other hand there is a friendly spirit... the children are willing and anxious to learn. Moreover the Head Mistress has been singlehanded for over two years and has had as many as 32 on roll.

Even this level of awareness and sympathy for her situation was not enough to placate the injured pride of Miss Drake. She fought back: 'I get my fair share of scholarship successes and fail to see how that is so if the methods in arithmetic are all wrong for arithmetic is the chief subject.'

She continued in this vein, her huge handwriting flowing over several pages:

... and I say GOD knows I have been trying my best to keep the ship from sinking, if inspectors don't and are hard and cruel. I think too that most of the parents realise that I have tried to do my best for their children.

Her endeavours to keep control of her pupils are remembered by some as being a bit too severe, even sadistic on occasions. She held a thin bone cane – 1½in. wide, 12in. long – in her hand. One former pupil recalled how, one day, she lined up the whole school in the playground, girls as well as boys, to be caned for some misdemeanor but that when she was part way through the line the farmer opposite saw what was happening and went across to stop her. This man remembered it because he was next in line!

St Ervan School, c.1932. Left to right, back row: *Stewart Buscombe, Hilda Thomas (later Mrs Wright), Mavis Powell (later Mrs Kent), Alberta 'Bertie' Cowling (later Mrs Gregor), Margaret Hawke (later Mrs Salmon), Ronald Bunt; fourth row: Bill Salmon of Trewinnick, Tom Powell, Queenie Mounce(?), Mary Sandry (later Mrs Sandry), Doris Davey(?), ? Fox, Hilda Salmon (later Mrs Strongman), Dulcie Hawke (later Mrs Jones), Marion Ball (later Mrs Kemp); third row: Joan Mounce, Audrey Hawke, Doreen Mounce(?), Phyllis Hill(?), Una Hawke (later Mrs Jeffery), Ruby Stephens (later Mrs Hawke), Charlie Powell, Roy Mounce; second row: Mrs Robinson (headmistress), Cyril Buscombe, Dick Bray, ? Fox, Clifford Strongman, Bill Hooper, Graham Brewer, Ted Mounce, Joyce Mounce, Miss Betty Brewer (assistant teacher); front row, sitting: Jack Hooper, George Hill, Wilfred Davey, Dennis Hill, ? Hooper, Gilbert Hill, Donald Curgenven, Ervan Ball.*

Maybe that was when the boys took the cane, broke it into pieces, and threw them down the well.

She caned by the Biblical Seven, but she never caned on a major Saint's Day – so the pupils quickly learned which were the important days. One punishment for misbehaviour was to learn the stones of the new Jerusalem – he could still recite all these too. Others, while admitting that she was a strong disciplinarian, speak kindly of her.

By the end of the year 1931 Miss Henrietta Drake had dedicated 24 years of her life to her scholars at St Ervan. She had remained independent throughout, even eccentric on occasions, a larger-than-life character who was remembered with affection by most of her former pupils even 50 years later. One remembered reciting three verses of the Sermon on the Mount every day, and that she considered wine good for the stomach because of Biblical references. Another claimed that it was because of her training that he could memorise so well. She used to march the children back into the classroom by the books of the Bible, Genesis, Exodus, Leviticus... and he could still reel them off in sequence.

Miss Drake's final log-book entry was on 18 December 1931: 'I am with my little scholars for the last time today. I am feeling it very keenly.'

Inside the church, c.1955, before the tower was rebuilt.

St Ervan Church lit by oil-lamps, c.1905.

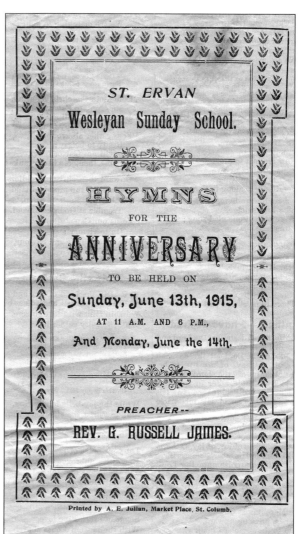

ST. ERVAN
Wesleyan Sunday School.

HYMNS

FOR THE

ANNIVERSARY

TO BE HELD ON

Sunday, June 13th, 1915,

AT 11 A.M. AND 6 P.M.,

And Monday, June the 14th.

PREACHER--

REV. G. RUSSELL JAMES.

Printed by A. E. Julian, Market Place, St. Columb.

Sunday-school anniversaries were celebrated over two days, with services morning and evening on Sunday and the tea treat on Monday.

Methodist Sunday School anniversary parade, c.1910. The two men standing in front are Tom Old and (holding the banner) Stanley Brewer.

✦ CHAPTER 12 ✦

Declining Congregations in Church and Chapel

In November 1853 Revd Henry Nowell Barton arrived in the parish of St Ervan with three small children, one a babe in arms. In his early years we know more about his work on the fabric of the church than of his struggles in ministering to his flock.

Since the 1840s little attention had been paid to the church building which, though nestling in the dell and sheltered by trees, could not escape the ravages of time nor the force of the north coastal wind and rain. Water penetrated the crumbling south-east coign of the tower, and caused further weakening of the structure where it meets the nave. Local legend has it that when St Issey church tower was struck by lightning and collapsed it caused panic in St Ervan. If so, it was a slow-fuse panic, as the St Issey event was 18 years earlier. Nevertheless, the people determined to bring the tower down before it crashed down.

Their first attempts, with a rope attached to a traction engine, failed, so they used dynamite. This brought down the upper part but also damaged the fabric of the lower stage, to the extent that architect Brakspear, in 1916, thought there must have been an earthquake! The remainder of the tower was left exposed to the elements. It remained in this ruined state for 70 years.

Revd Barton, however, spent money on the fabric of the church. The roofs were renewed in deal, arches were inserted across the chancel and transepts, and the north wall of the nave and west wall of the south transept were rebuilt, costing him £600. It is said he did much of the work with his own hands. Twentieth-century critics disapproved. Brakspear observed:

The church underwent a severe treatment at the hands of the restorer... all the old monuments were taken down and put away in the ruined tower and every vestige of ancient work except the bare walls was removed.

Having married off two of his three children in the 1880s the rector became more involved in church and parish affairs again, as well as in the management of the school. In 1883 he chaired the Vestry annual meeting. The minutes are formal and reveal no details. He continued as chairman until the 1894 Local Government Act removed control from the parishes to a wider authority.

A great deal of money had recently been spent on another place of worship in the parish. At the annual conference of the Bible Christians in 1884 it was reported that:

... the St Ervan Chapel [Rumford]... has been almost rebuilt, with new floor, new seats and rostrum at a cost of £95; £62.10s. has been added to the debt. This is more than it should be, and it is hoped a good effort will be made forthwith to reduce the amount by at least half.

The Wesleyan chapel was still flourishing alongside the younger Bible Christian chapel in Rumford. The list of pew rents – 6d. per quarter or 2s. per year – paid in 1891 to W.G. Old as Treasurer of the Wesleyan Methodist circuit for pews in the Wesleyan chapel in St Ervan, names several practising Methodist families: Gregory Tom, William Brewer, Francis Rabey, M.J. Rabey, Joseph Hawke, William Old, Fanny Rowe, Richard Brewer, Mrs Rowe, Henry Hawken, Peter Sandry, Mrs N. Sandry, Gregory Brewer, Thomas Northcott, William Rabey and Janey Brewer.

In answer to the Bishop of Truro's 1896 Primary Visitation queries, Revd Barton replied that 'the condition of Dissent in... [the] Parish' was 'Indifferent'. In fact, it was the Methodists as much as those attending the church who enabled the rector to reply that the general 'moral condition' in the parish was 'Good'. The Methodists, particularly, in their early days, the Bible Christians, were influential in converting men from the drunkenness which had been prevalent here as elsewhere.

Relations between the elderly rector and his dissenting parishioners remained strained. The burial register records: '3 April 1897 was buried Paul Strongman, aged 49.' In the column headed 'Ceremony performed by' the rector has written 'Paul Strongman [a 22-year-old son] Not a church Service.' Whatever the rector felt or thought about this strong-headed, redhaired, fiercely devout Bible Christian, others thought differently.

H. Rundle, writing in the *Bible Christian Magazine*, describes Paul Strongman thus:

His presence in the sanctuary as a listener was always a joy and a help to the man who had a sermon to preach or an important message to deliver. His attentive attitude, his very expressive face, and his hearty responses were an inspiration to many a preacher, whilst everybody could distinguish Paul Strongman's 'Amen'...

His religious life was delightfully real, and graciously sustained him to the end. He desired life, but did not

The Methodist chapel, Rumford, from the south, post-1907 rebuild. Formerly the Wesleyan chapel, it was rebuilt and enlarged in 1907 to take the congregations from the amalgamated Wesleyan and Bible Christian chapels in Rumford. The chimney of Paradise Cottage (formerly Chapel Cottage) is on the right. Here lived the chapel caretakers until it was sold in 1982.

Rumford Methodist chapel Harvest Festival, 27 September 1992.

The Wesleyan chapel, Rumford, in 1925, north side.

The Wesleyan chapel, Rumford, after the 1907 improvements. The oil-lamps gave out quite a bit of heat as well as light.

The interior of the United Methodist Chapel at Rumford (formerly the Bible Christian chapel) in the early 1900s.

Left: The Methodist Sunday-school room, Rumford, in the 1960s. Built in 1844 as a Bible Christian chapel, it was rebuilt in 1888.

The Methodist chapel, Rumford, at the laying of the foundation-stone, August 1907, for the rebuilding and enlargement of the chapel, which reopened in October 1907. The car lower right belonged to William Old of Treleigh. The large brass headlights were probably carbide lamps and the car had brakes on the front wheels only.

fear death, and when the silent messenger came to call him, he was ready.

It was a long tradition of the Bible Christians to have their funerals on a Sunday, the only day they did not work. There was a 'non-church burial service' in 1905, when 79-year-old Richard Buscombe died and Revd Barton refused to conduct the funeral on a Sunday. The services of a Nonconformist minister were therefore engaged and Buscombe's body was taken to the Bible Christian chapel at Rumford, where the first part of the service was conducted, then to the churchyard, where he was buried by his youngest son, Francis. The churchyard was the only burial-ground until 1919.

Revd Barton was a good churchman. In answer to another Visitation Query about which exhortation he used in the Holy Communion Service, he replied:

I read both exhortations – one in the morning and the other in the afternoon on the Sunday preceding the Celebration and have done so for 20 years – I never omit the longer exhortation at the time of celebration.

In the rest of the diocese the Bishop learned that these celebrations were seldom used.

After visiting St Ervan, the Bishop described Revd Barton and his wife as a 'nice old couple' and their daughter as a 'mild spinster', but that the rector seemed to have given up most of his study

and that the parish looked stagnant.

By the 1901 Visitations the rector was nearly 80 years old and a widower, and the general religious condition of the parish, he declared himself, had declined to a state of 'not satisfactory'. The Sunday morning congregation averaged only 12, and in the afternoon 30. The rector also estimated that one-third of the parish attended no place of worship at all, which means that the largest proportion, as in 1851, attended the Methodist chapels.

The Bible Christians were conscious of their own declining numbers and published a list of 'survivors' in their magazine of 1903, headed: 'Living Friends in Active Circuits. St Ervan (Rumford) is not without its living friends.'

The list begins with a photograph of the strong-featured, bearded face of Mr J. Bettison 'one of our oldest preachers'. He had worked for years as a general servant for auctioneer and farmer James Hawken and lived in a cottage at Pentruse. Now he was 75.

He has had a long and honourable record in the Circuit but his sun is setting. We wish his mantle could fall on some young man.
Mr W.H. Old, Local Preacher, is a smith and a genius. He is as true as the British steel he uses in his trade.
Mr H. Bennetts, Local Preacher, is a man with a sincere soul, and is a most willing worker. He has a high

ideal, and tries to climb up to it.

Mr J. Hawke, Local Preacher, is a quiet, unassuming man, but more thoughtful than the average man, and he is a good type of Christian.

Mr Rabey, Local Preacher, Mrs Strongman, Mrs Parsons, Local Preacher, Miss Old and Mr Sandry are among the list of living friends...

In Penrose: Mr and Mrs Tippett and daughter, Mr Courtis, Mr Old and Miss Old do good work. Mr F. Hellyer is a veteran local preacher... He has the prominent features of a man of strong character. Resolution and determination are evident even to the careless observer. His now aged face wears the calm and the peace of a man of deep spirituality and sincere faith.

There are no Brewers on this list. Both sons of their first leader, Richard Brewer, had died, though Thomas the carpenter lived to 93. Revd Barton had performed the ceremony this time, only a month after Paul Strongman's 'non-church' burial. Several of Richard Brewer's descendants had joined the Wesleyan Methodists. Soon the two Methodist congregations were to be re-joined.

The 'quiet unassuming' Bible Christian, James Hawke, worked enthusiastically towards the extension of the Wesleyan chapel in 1907 but died before the work was completed.

Death has visited this little Society and taken away one of our oldest members – Mr James Hawke. He walked with God in his daily life. He was very interested in the scheme, and a few days before his death he was carrying in stone to the masons at their work. The call came suddenly. He was ready and at the ripe age of 77 years, on July 18, he passed away. He was buried in St Ervan churchyard.

It is good to have this memorial to this attractive-sounding man. There is no headstone in the churchyard.

Though each of the two chapels had fewer in their congregations than they liked, when they amalgamated in 1907 an extension was needed to the Wesleyan chapel, which was the more substantial of the two buildings. Once again the people were asked to turn out their pockets.

Mr Will's tender of £294.10s. was accepted and, with £10 extra and the 5 per cent commission to the architect, W.I. Martyn Mears of Rock, near Wadebridge, the total needed for the extension and renovation of the Wesleyan chapel was £319.15s. Faced with this large bill, the Methodists obtained promises of contributions from several people, from which they could look forward to receiving £106.12s.8d. The local trustees, ministers Hodson-Smith and Lawson, together with Messrs J. Northcott of Trevibban, J. Lobb of Trevorgey, T. Northcott of Roscullion, G. Brewer of Trethewey and W.G. Old of Treburrick, who was treasurer, knew well the

people who promised money. There was no question of defaulting.

In addition, £20.12s.6d. was raised for the stone laying, and a collection at the ceremony itself raised another £61.8s.8d. In the North Cornwall Wesleyan First Mission journal, *Church Record*, it was recorded:

The Stone Laying of the New Church took place on Wednesday August 7th. A splendid luncheon at 1.30, presided over by Mr R. Trebilcock, was a great success. The Stone Laying took place at 3 pm, when several friends availed themselves of the opportunity of helping the cause. The Revd F. Woffenden gave a very beautiful and appropriate address. Tea was served at 5 pm and the evening meeting was held in the Bible Christian chapel, kindly lent to us for the occasion. Mr James Grose took the chair at 7 pm. Speeches were given by Revd W. Hodson-Smith, Revd F. Woffenden and others.

In October there were more celebrations:

On October 23rd, the friends in this village had a great day, the occasion being that of the opening of the new church... The transformation is wonderful, and we now have in this village a beautiful little church. We are thankful to God for all that was done in and through the old place we had, but we rejoice that to-day we have a church of which we can justly be proud.

The treasurer kept a record of all the costs, furnishings, the silver key, the paraffin oil for lighting the lamps and so on, and in April 1908 he wrote:

Final cost, including varnishing ceiling, rebuilding between windows on the side, re-pointing boundary walls, strengthening the Vestry floor £304.10.5d. all Settled on April 10th, 1908.

With what satisfaction and relief the treasurer must have written that last line!

Amalgamation and the building of an almost-new chapel brought new zest to the Methodist community in and around the parish. A descendant of W.G. Old recalls being told that 100 people walked down the lane past Music Water to the chapel at Rumford every Sunday evening.

The annual tea treat brought out the whole parish to a service on the Sunday evening, then, on the following day, they were led by a band with a banner held by two of the elders and followed by the children, twisting and turning in a serpentine walk, down through the village and up the lane to Treravel, where they gathered in front of the modern farmhouse for the photographer and the band played for Mrs Sandry. Then they went into the field behind the farmhouse for tea.

Everyone wore their best clothes and their most elaborate and smartest hats. Tea was laid out on long tables covered in white starched cloths and decorated

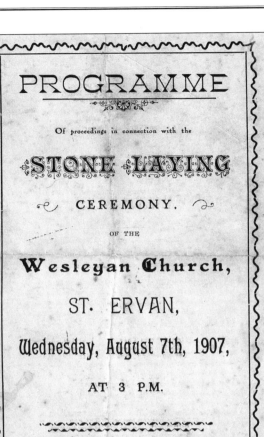

PROGRAMME

Of proceedings in connection with the

STONE·LAYING

CEREMONY.

OF THE

Wesleyan Church,

ST· ERVAN,

Wednesday, August 7th, 1907,

AT 3 P.M.

Chairman, Rev. W. Hodson Smith.

Wesleyan Sunday-school anniversary parade lined up beside the former Bible Christian chapel. A self-propelled traction engine is under cover in the yard of W.H. Old & Sons (behind the parade). The stack is shorter than on older machines, broadening at the top to let the expanding steam out faster.

Left and below: *Programme for the stone-laying ceremony of the Wesleyan Church, St Ervan, on 7 August 1907, as they started to rebuild and enlarge it.*

Hymn 1. O for a Thousand Tongues to sing.

O for a thousand tongues to sing,
My great Redeemer's praise,
My glories of my God and King,
The triumphs of His grace.

My gracious Master and my God,
Assist me to proclaim,
To spread thro' all the earth abroad,
The honours of Thy Name.

Jesus the name that charms our fears,
That bids our sorrows cease,
'Tis music in the sinner's ears,
'Tis life, and health. and peace.

He breaks the power of cancelled sin,
He sets the prisoner free,
His blood can make the foulest clean,
His blood availed for me.

Scripture. Rev. W. H. Lawson.

Prayer. Rev. W. Hodson Smith.

Hymn. 660.

This stone to Thee in faith we lay,
To Thee this temple, Lord, we build,
Thy power and goodness here display,
And be it with Thy presence filled.

Here when Thy people seek Thy face,
And dying sinners pray to live,
Hear Thou in Heav'n, Thy dwelling place
And when Thou hearest, Lord, forgive.

Here, when Thy messengers proclaim
The blessed gospel of Thy son,
Still, by the power of His great name,
Be mighty signs and wonders done.

Hosanna! to their heavenly King,
When children's voices raise that song,
Hosanna! let their angels sing,
And heav'n & earth the strain prolong.

STONES LAID BY—

I. MRS. W. HODSON SMITH.
II. MR. HAMBLY.
III. MR. T. T. STRONGMAN.
IV. MR. T. NORTHCOTT.
V. MISS J. NORTHCOTT.
VI. MR. J. LOBB FOR MYRTIE LOBB.
VII. MR. JOSEPH HAWKE.

IN MEMORIAM.

Mr. W. Rosevear in Memory of his Mother.
                    ,,   ,, Mr. Peter Rowe.
Mr. W. G. Old   ,,   ,, Mrs. T. Rowe.
Mrs. Gregory Brewer   ,, Mr. Gregory Tom

GROUP STONES.

Sunday School Stone laid by Mr. T. Northcott.

COLLECTION.

Address. Rev. Frederick Woofenden.

Doxology.

Benediction.

Rumford Methodist Sunday-school tea treat in 1913. The tea tables are decorated with vases of flowers and the little girl on the left is keeping a keen eye on the sweet stall. Tom Sandry is the young lad with a cap right at the back, the taller man is Revd Butt. Among the crowd are Mr and Mrs Jim Parsons, Mrs Curgenven, and Mrs W.G. Old. The small boy right in the middle is Charles Lobb. Front from left are: Harry Parsons, ? Nicholls, Dorothy Tippett, Miss Emma Brewer, looking very stern, and Mrs W.T. Lobb.

Rumford Methodist Sunday-school tea treat, c.1910. The tables are fully laden, the band is playing and there's water in the barrel on the cart (top right) ready for making the tea. The two girls standing in front of the cart are Philippa Hawke and Blanche Powell. Nearby are Mrs Curgenven and Mrs Parsons, standing holding a baby. Standing on the left: Mrs Arthur Strongman, and sitting are Ella Buscombe, Emma Tippett and Mrs Will Curtis. Front, just showing their heads, are from left: Alice Old, Mrs Old, ?.

John Lobb with children James Charles and Myrtle Doreen, dressed for Sunday-school anniversary, c.1915?

Tom Pearce, gardener at Primrose Hill.

The Wesleyan Methodist Sunday-school anniversary parade arrives at Mrs Sandry's, Treravel, in 1910, where they will have tea in a field behind.

with vases of flowers. A barrel of water for the tea had to be wheeled in a cart to the field, together with coals for heating the water. The men would attend to the kettles, which were suspended with crooks from an iron bar over a fire in a trench below. They ate splits and cream – clotted, of course – and saffron cake. The same sweet stalls as for Penrose Fair came out from Wadebridge.

Yet another financial effort was needed when the Methodists converted a piece of farmer Rowe's land on the side of the main road between Rumford and Penrose into the Free Church (Nonconformist) cemetery, opened on 9 April 1919. The War Memorial was erected on Tuesday, 20 December 1919.

Among the first to be buried there were two young men of the Bennetts families, William John, aged 28, and John, aged 27.

The church from the north, showing the churchyard extension, the barn (top left) *at Churchtown Farm with the school behind and the rectory* (top right).

The rectory, c.1920, in Revd Johnson's time. This postcard was sent by Emily Bennetts to her nephew Jack (John Henry Richards) to wish him 'Happy Birthday', promising a present later.

CHAPTER 13

Prebendary Johnson

Revd Johnson was the Bishop of Truro's chaplain for three years before he was put in charge of St Ervan in 1914. At 43 years old, a man of mature years, of high intellect and refined tastes, he found decay and neglect. Revd Barton, coming to the end of 60 years as rector, was 90 years old, a widower and completely alone. Even Mary Edyveane, his 'faithful servant and friend' for 50 years, had died in January.

The school, the church fabric, and the burial-ground were matters which Revd Johnson set to work on immediately. In March 1914 he wrote explaining the situation to the Secretary of the Ecclesiastical Commissionary.

Sir,
The Rector of St Ervan is of advanced age, and the Bishop has put me in charge...
The churchyard has been in use from time immemorial. Bones are frequently turned up, and both for decency's sake, and because of local feeling it is desirable to disturb the ground no more...
A level piece of glebe land is free for the suggested purpose, and is peculiarly well adapted for it... The advantage of the site is such that we shall be able to make the whole comely and even picturesque. A good deal of the necessary stone hedging exists, and we should complete it with more hedge of the local herringbone pattern.

Permission was forthcoming and work progressed. In June Revd Johnson drafted a letter from the aged Revd Barton to his parishioners:

My brethren
On Monday next, St Peter's Day, at 3.30 pm, the Bishop of the Diocese will come to consecrate the new churchyard. The churchwardens and I beg to invite you to be present.
It is a great pleasure to me that this extension of the churchyard has been made as a memorial of my more than sixty years in St Ervan. I have been glad on my part to assign the ground; and we acknowledge gratefully the subscriptions of Mr Williams, Miss Barton and Mrs Skilbeck, and the gift of stone by Mr Tremain from his quarry. Specially also do I wish to mention Mr W.H. Old of Penrose who with Mr F. Buscombe to help him has done the work; good judgment and skill of eye and hand have made it what we see...

The printing and sending of 75 of these letters was a major item of expenditure, £21.10s.1d. Francis Buscombe was paid 3s.4d. per day for hedging for five days, Tom Old 1s. per day for lopping trees and he supplied the lar, and J.K. Brewer of Glebe Farm 16s. for carting the six loads of stone from the quarry.

Hedging is an art. The hedge (or wall) in the herringbone pattern is as firm and beautiful today as when it was first constructed.

Revd Johnson decided to rescue one of the bells from the floor of the ruined tower. The local blacksmith, W.H. Old & Sons, fixed it on a tripod of elm boughs for him. The firm's account ledger has the record. In March and April 1914 William Henry and his two sons, George and Arthur, cut trees, prepared long boughs and fixed the tripod with ironwork on which the bell was hung, for a total of £2.2s.6d. In June they repaired the sundial, 'raised the cross and fixed it upright and straight' on top of the church.

The church fabric and the school were his next priorities.

Conscious of the financial position of the majority of his parishioners, he decided that rebuilding the ruined tower would be too expensive at that time, but he asked architect Harold Brakspear to submit suggestions for improvements to the rest of the church. However, he decided the estimated cost, £1,680, was too much. The whole project was abandoned and the church left as it was after Revd Barton's 1888 'restoration', with the ruined tower a ruin, exactly as it was after its crude demolition, with two bells standing forlornly on the floor.

The third bell was now suspended on the tripod outside. Revd Johnson made a flowerbed around it, with columbines and bulbs of Muscan Heavenly Blue. This was the sight that greeted the teenage John Betjeman when he cycled down the lane. He arrived just as Johnson was tolling the bell for Evensong. Betjeman was the only congregation at the service. Afterwards he was invited to tea at the rectory and treated to a learned discussion. He records this memorable experience in his autobiographical poem *Summoned by Bells*.

The new rector's efforts to gain greater authority over the school premises and right of access to the school pupils so as to be able to provide a proper standard of religious education brought him into conflict with the schoolmistress, Miss Drake, with the District Education Committee and with the County Education Secretary.

During 1915 and 1916 he waged an acrimonious campaign which involved long correspondence, seeking legal and other advice from the National

In 1914 Revd Johnson had one of the bells hung on a tripod of elm boughs by W.H. Old & Sons.

Society, from the diocesan education authorities, from the Patron of St Ervan Rectory, Mr Skilbeck JP, and from several of his ecclesiastical colleagues. The matter was finally resolved in September 1917 with the drawing up of an indenture for seven years at the same nominal annual rent for the premises, £1, giving the Local Education Authority the use of the school buildings from 9.45a.m. to 4.30p.m. on every school day except Christmas Day, Ash Wednesday, Good Friday and Ascension Day, and giving the rector or his delegates access to the premises between 9.00a.m. and 9.45a.m. for the purpose of religious instruction. The Education Secretary, Mr Pascoe, sent a note pointing out that 'compulsory attendance does not commence at 9.00a.m.'. The past three years had shown him that in his communications with Revd Johnson the 'ts' had to be crossed and the 'is' dotted.

Inevitably Revd Johnson clashed with Miss Drake. Early in the negotiations she had denied him admission to the school on Ash Wednesday and Saturdays and Sundays, even though the District Education Office claimed to have notified her that for the time the old arrangement stood.

Revd Johnson faced the difficulties early on: 'It is impossible in local conditions – the parish is practically entirely Dissenting and rather hostile – to re-open as a Church School.'

He decided that County, District and parish were in a conspiracy against him. He referred to Mr Pascoe as a braggard, and when it was suggested he should meet the County Education Officers to talk things over he replied:

I don't want to meet Mr Pascoe and Mr Oxland. I am warned not to trust him [Pascoe]. And he makes negotiation difficult because when one is supposed to be dealing with the CEA [County Education Authority] – the responsible authority – he flings the whole thing down before the District E.A. and they call meetings at which the whole matter is prejudiced and heated up, especially as it is presented by local Dissenters.

He once wrote to Pascoe about the District Committee arranging a parish meeting. He regarded this as a great pity, since:

... nothing is more likely to harden any difficulty there is in the position than a public parochial pow-wow, probably working on imperfect information tilting at windmills, and blown out with irrelevancies.

Unfortunately for the rector, the same men who were giving him so much trouble over the school also served on the Parish Council, which was exercising too much independence for his liking. He sought sympathy from the Vicar of Sithney near Helston, who replied:

What an extraordinary Parish Council you have. Really there is no limit to their impudence. They have no right whatever to appoint a Warden – that belongs to the Vestry. A non-communicant or even a non-Churchman could be elected.

The editor of the *Western Morning News*, Maurice Baily, in a private letter, gave him some good advice:

May I... express a hope that you will use all possible tact in dealing with these people? They are in many respects peculiar, and if your experience of Cornwall is not long you may easily get to loggerheads... Pardon the hint, but my acquaintance with Cornwall began in 1870, and I don't find them much changed today from what they were then.

Revd Johnson's knowledge of the English language and literature, particularly of the eighteenth/nineteenth century, was exceptional, and his sensitive, scholarly nature made it difficult for him to reconcile himself to the modern world. In the parish magazine he wrote:

Sunday Jan 30th (1949) was the three-hundredth year's mind of the martyrdom of King Charles the First, who died for high principles which greatly need assertion as against the tendencies of the modern world.

(He obviously approved of the monument to Ralph Keate in the church.)

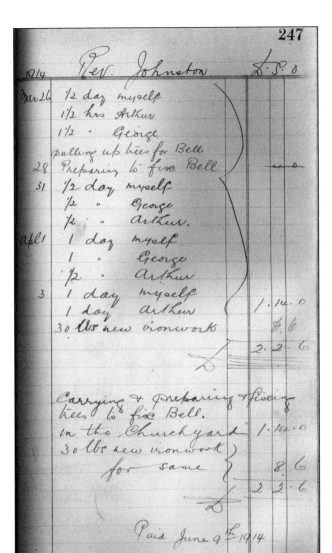

Page from accounts ledger of W.H. Old & Sons in 1914, when they fixed the church bell on a tripod of elm boughs outside the church for Revd Johnson so he could call the parishioners to services.

As an epilogue to the post-Second World War year, 1946, he wrote:

A sad and disappointing year between the nations and within the nation. May God overrule the course of a world rebellious to righteousness, wisdom, understanding and charity.

On education he had some trenchant thoughts:

... one test of education is that it leaves us eager to read, knowing what is worth reading, and able to read it. Popular education, that grandiose and expensive failure, certainly does not bear the test well... And in particular how many read the great poets and find within themselves the answer of delight?

Occasionally his cutting comment on some local matter could be amusing:

March 1951   Civil Defence
This matter in this area is the responsibility of the Wadebridge and Rural District Council, but the Council appears to be busy digging up a drain at Rumford.

Revd Johnson was a shy man. He is remembered with great affection by his parishioners as a kindly eccentric, always dressed in a long black frock coat. In 1929 the Methodists had a fund-raising drive for the Wesleyan Debt, and published a small book of *Rumford Tit-Bits*, in which are verses entitled:

That Dear Old Coat
Adam wore it, so they say,
In the Garden one Spring day,
For to drive the crows away,-
*   That dear old Coat.*

Noah had it in the ark,
Just above the water-mark,
To bring blessings on the barque,-
*   That dear old Coat.*

And so it travelled down the years,
And now in glory it appears,
We look at it and shed salt tears,-
*   That dear old Coat.*

The colour of thing is green,
It shines with such a lovely sheen,
And everywhere it may be seen,-
*   That dear old Coat.*

It has a rent two feet four
Down the back, like an open door,
And darns and patches, oh, galore,-
*   That dear old Coat*

At Concerts, Whist Drives, Garden Shows,
And everywhere the owner goes
To meet his friends, or perhaps his foes,
*   You'll see that dear old Coat.*

The 'Flutterbys' are going soon
To give a Concert on the moon,
To get funds to dye maroon
*   That dear old Coat.*

He never liked to be photographed. Only in a wedding group can he be seen at the back, peeping out between the bride and groom.

He enjoyed being with children. At Christmas he invited them all to a party in the rectory, and allowed them the run of all the rooms for their games, except his study and his bedroom. The children clambered up to the attic rooms and out on the balcony right at the top. Fortunately, none of them plunged to the ground far below.

Though it might be difficult to imagine from his skirmishes with the 'hostile' parishioners in his early days, he enjoyed a more relaxed relationship later.

July 1950 Ascension Day
A perfect day. Everybody came to church at 9 o'clock as everybody might do every Sunday if everybody tried. At Porthcothan there was no wind and the sunshine was warm but not scorching. So all was proper for paddling or building castles or just sitting on the rocks. No tears. No accidents. The grandmothers of the party looked after the tea. Yes, it was a memorable day.

Peter Sandry recalls how his father, Tom, enjoyed his discussions with the rector, from which he received much sound business and legal advice. And Harry Strongman, a great book reader, who farmed at Churchtown Farm, spent hours in conversation with him. Harry's wife, Mary, cooked his Sunday lunch.

Revd Johnson was a passionate and experienced gardener and at St Ervan he had the opportunity to indulge this to the full by creating at the rectory a garden of beauty and of horticultural interest. His gardening diary recorded the seeds and plants he put in. In one year he planted shelter belts and trees and shrubs and between January and September sowed 219 different lots of seeds. By 1938 he was harvesting 119 different fruits, including 36 varieties of apple. He grew several varieties of fig – one of the rare collections grown outdoors in this country. In 1938 he described his success:

Sept 3. Reculver fig. Two figs. There was one a year or two ago. They are medium size, rather long, pale pinkish brown skin, light slightly pink flesh, soft and delicate and sweet.

The following year he recorded wryly: 'Sept 5. Figs. A good crop, highly appreciated by the blackbirds.'

Like many other people in the parish he kept bees. '1931. Dec 26. Bees in hive by glebe gate out in a crowd this mild morning: a few from the hive by the garden doors are working at the *Berberis darwiniis*.'

He corresponded with nurseries in New Zealand, Japan, Tasmania, Australia and South Africa and with the Royal Horticultural Society in London, and sowed seeds which had been sent from all those countries in sheltered corners of his garden in order to study how well they could thrive so near the north coast and in salt winds. He took cuttings of Scotch rose from Watergate Bay near Newquay and heather cuttings and sundew from Music Water in the parish. He also experimented with sea sand and clay sand.

He had setbacks:

1938. Oct 4. Returned from London to find that a gale had bent over many fir trees in the orchard and brought much of the fruit there and in the walled garden down.
1940. April 17. The Pinius insignis *close to the Sops in Wine bush went down in a gale some weeks ago. Tony Cowling and I (mainly Tony) got it up with a pulley and set it straight and I put fresh earth and dressing of adco compost to it.*

One of his many gardening notebooks began with quotations about gardeners, including the following

Wedding of William Rabey and Edith Bawden, October 1936. Left to right, back row: *C. Harry Strongman (best man), Revd W.R. Johnson (rector), Sidney L. Bawden (father of Edith);* front row: *Madeline 'Madge' Cowling (later Mrs Keat), the groom and bride, Margaret Phillips.*

Work is about to start on rebuilding the west tower of the church, a ruin for 70 years.

from E.A. Bunyard's *Old Garden Roses* (1936): 'He is a bad gardener whose garden is kept only for himself.'

In Revd Johnson's garden parishioners enjoyed a garden party every year in June. After Sunday school he allowed the children to go into the walled garden by the lower gate and pick a piece of fruit. Sometimes he told them there was a special flower in the lower garden which they should go and look at. This walled garden was normally out of bounds to them and seemed like a jungle of rare plants. They were not allowed to pick wild flowers. They must have been the only country children who did not!

Animals were another concern of his: '1933 Dec 14: Weather very cold. Snow lying on the ground. A lame thrush taken indoors.'

And he wrote at length about his band of 'pensioners', as he called his hens:

1938 Aug 17: The hen with one leg, who has lived in the front garden for years and has slept under sheets of glass below the library window, has been off her feed for some days. Last night she seemed weak and could not get to her roosting-place, so I put her in a basket and brought her in and she died peacefully about 1.30 am... Buried her next day where she liked to sit in the sun.

The colleague who wrote Prebendary Johnson's obituary remembered driving him back from representing the diocese at a bishop's funeral up country. There was a gorse fire on the hill. Suddenly Johnson burst into tears. 'Oh, the poor little rabbits, the birds,

and all the dear things on that hill. Whatever will they do!'

In later years Prebendary Johnson enjoyed the fruits of his labours in his large garden. '1949. May 14: A lovely Rogation Sunday. A joy to be in the garden and orchard, the blossom profuse and the bees busy.'

This peace had been disturbed during the Second World War when three wartime aerodromes on its borders encroached into the tranquillity of the parish.

1940. April 17: The eve of my sixty-ninth birthday. A beautiful evening and quiet as the evenings were before the aerodromes; the proper country sounds, the birds, work in gardens, and cricket practice. So the evening was like old times till 9.00 when the aeroplanes began to come out from St Eval.

Prebendary Johnson shared his enjoyment of his garden with his parishioners at the annual Garden Show. He described the last one he would witness, in the parish magazine of September 1953:

And indeed St Ervan has had an event. It happened on the first day of August, which is Lammas Day. The Garden Show has been happening for nearly quarter of a century. Year after year there have been those loaded tables, much to look at and much to eat, with exhibitors trying to be calm and judges succeeding in being complimentary. A fine show, 'sure 'nuff, me dear'.

He died, aged 83, in 1954. Stewart Buscombe, church-warden, recalled that when the pony died that pulled the trap he used to travel in, he carried on visiting by foot. When the St Ervan School was being closed and sold by the diocese, Frank Rowe remembered Prebendary Johnson as: 'that fine, cantankerous priest of the old religion who nourished the school through five generations in St Ervan.'

He was rector of St Ervan for 40 years; Prebendary of St Endellion from 1946 and he represented the diocese as a Proctor in Convocation. He was remembered by his clerical colleagues as 'our beloved Prebendary':

For nearly 40 years now, on Committee and Conference days a well-known figure would have been seen in Truro; spare figure, lately somewhat bowed, black beard later grizzled grey, thin and thoughtful face; on the head a clerical hat of bygone form, clothed in black frock coat of like antiquity and probably torn and roughly cobbled together about the skirts; in one hand an unrolled umbrella and in the other a frail or black oilskin bag full of books and possibly a monastically frugal lunch. It was he whom we called above all others 'The Prebendary'.

If we had followed him to Conference or meeting we should have found him in some retired corner; never obtrusive until peccant English, muddled thought, modern vulgarity, or what he thought injustice brought him to his feet. Then clear voice and clear thinking, with all he said clothed in perfect if Johnsonian language, demanded and invariably won attention... One could almost see his soul shrink and shudder when he met crudity, pushfulness, vulgarism. He was pained and sad at the strident times in which, in later years, he had been called to live.

The tribute from his clerical colleagues describes him as a high scholar. By his St Ervan parishioners, with whom he settled into an affectionate relationship, he was remembered fondly. The following tribute appeared in the parish magazine:

Wilfrid Ryan Johnson, for 40 years Rector of this Parish. Many of his Parishioners will long remember with gratitude his uncompromising devotion to the Church, his zealous performance of his duty as the Parish Priest, his unfailing care in visiting the sick, his wise counsel at the service of all who asked for it.

Prebendary Johnson left his own memorial. In his will he bequeathed his life insurance – worth £745 – to the parish, to be spent on the repair of the west tower.

The little Parish Church is almost hidden among the trees in the valley.

❖ CHAPTER 14 ❖

Through the Depression Years (1875–95)
into the Twentieth Century

When the Assistant Parliamentary Commissioner visited North Cornwall in 1880 he learned of serious losses over the past years, especially on tillage lands. His report told of four bad seasons in succession. Produce in 1879 had been 50–60 per cent below average. One farmer told him he had 30 acres of wheat from which he had not one bushel of saleable corn. Yet the Commissioner had no bankruptcies to report in the district, no distraints for rent levied, no farms unlet, rents were well paid. Larger landowners had helped by making remissions of 10–20 per cent on rental.

When the protective Corn Laws were repealed in the 1840s there was an outcry that repeal would bring about the ruin of Britain's farmers. This had not happened. It was the 1870s before refrigerated storage in ships enabled massive imports from the Middle West of the United States of meat and grain to make any significant impact on Britain's farmers.

This was compounded by the bad harvests at home.

The farmers grumbled to the Commissioner about expensive labour and excessive local rates. Labour, they pointed out, cost 33 per cent more than a few years before. Wages were now 12s., 13s. or 15s. per week (for which the labourer had to work six days from 7a.m. to 5p.m. with one hour out for dinner in the middle). During harvest, meat and drink for the men had to be found by the farmer, though some preferred to pay 2s. a day extra instead. The farmers claimed that labourers were well off, indeed many had risen to become farmers!

The local rates had increased considerably, in St Ervan from 4d. in the pound in 1849 to 8d. in the pound in the 1870s.

The Education Rate was a particular bone of contention. The object was a national one, therefore why should the finance be a local burden? The rate was assessed principally on land values, so farmers took the brunt. They were a minority paying for a benefit to be enjoyed by the majority, they argued. In addition to education, there were local rates for sanitary provision, the Union asylum, police and highways, which together imposed an unjust burden on occupiers of land.

Farmers protested about the deprivation of child labour, now that pupils had to remain at school until they were 14. This added to their wage bill; boys were cheaper to employ than men and a boy of 13 could work a team (pair) of horses in the plough.

The Assistant Commissioner noted, nevertheless, that land in this district was fairly supplied with capital and farming much improved. Leases of 7–14 years were very general. Conditions of the leases were stringent and, some claimed, restricted

Isaac and Mary Parkyn. Isaac worked as sexton, among other things, and was known as 'superman' of the parish.

Bert Prynn ploughed with heavy horses at Ken Skinner's farm, Treburrick, until 1965.

117

Wedding group at Treleigh following the marriage of Albert Richards (son of William Richards and Bessy (née Hicks) and Minnie Bennetts (daughter of Bessy (née Hawke) and farmworker at Treleigh, Henry Bennetts) on 3 August 1912. 1. ? Bosinquet, 2. John Bennetts, 3. Dick Chapman, 4. Harry Bennetts, 5. Emma 'Jane' Rabey (née Hawke), 6. ? Hicks, 7. Charlie Hicks, 8. Albert Richards (groom), 9. Minnie Richards (bride), 10. Emily Bennetts, 11. Jane Chapman (née Bennetts), 12. Gladys Richards, 13. Fred Richards, 14. William Richards, 15. Bessy Richards, 16. Bessy Bennetts (née Hawke), 17. Henry Bennetts, 18. Phyllis Rabey, 19. Willie Rabey, 20. Reg Chapman.

The labourer's cottage at Treleigh, built about 1890 by the farmer, William Old. The family of farm worker Henry Bennetts was the first to move in.

Penrose village seen from the south, with Lowertown at the bottom of the hill in the valley, c.1925.

improvements in farming methods. Tenant farmers considered that the longer period of lease should more generally be given, with compensation for unexhausted improvements made by a tenant, and that, with the exception of the last three years of a lease, the mode of cultivation should be unrestricted, provided only that the land was kept in an improving state. However, the husbandry clauses, stringent as they were, were generally not enforced.

Before July 1880 there had been a great depression in Cornwall for the past three years, at its most severe during the past six months. Corn growers had suffered the most and longest, the quality of the corn which they did manage to harvest being much below average. The fact that farmers in Cornwall invested more money in machinery than usual – one with 25 acres would have a reaping machine – had not helped them enough.

Nevertheless, the depression in Cornwall was not as severe as elsewhere due greatly to the flexibility of mixed farming and the temporary ley system. In Cornwall corn-growing land decreased in letting value by 15 per cent, other land suffered no diminution and farmers could increase their pasture. However, sheep rot caused great losses, more losses resulted from a form of blood poisoning and there were losses in cattle. After three years of heavy losses, farmers were now short of capital.

At this period much of the land in St Ervan and in surrounding parishes was being acquired by J. Michael Williams of Carhayes (near St Austell in south Cornwall), who was putting the wealth he had accumulated from unpredictable mines into land which was more permanent.

Any residue of grandness from Arundell days was long since gone. Their former property, Trembleath, once the principal estate, was divided and the main farm had become a barton. Trenouth, a 'reputed manor', was now no more than a

'barton', and Treravel, once a 'gentleman's seat', was now a farmhouse. Nevertheless, the farmhouses were very different from the labourers' cottages. The farms, in this 'granary of Cornwall', had substantial stone-built farmhouses with slate roofs. At Bogee and Treleigh (Paynter properties) there were, alongside the main farmhouse, stone-built cottages for labourers.

The number of agricultural labourers continued

A steam threshing machine at work somewhere in St Ervan, c.1890. The engine was portable and had to be hauled to the field by horses. The big wheels would catch in ruts, shifting the shafts from side to side, which caused a lot of injury to the horses.

Charlie Powell's father, Albert, on his Marshall traction engine, which still stands in Charlie's yard, with brambles growing through. If Charlie wins the lottery...

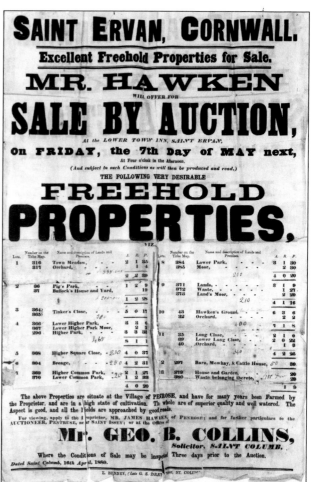

Land at Penrose for sale in 1880, divided into 13 small lots.

to decline – more and more the tenant farmers were managing with less live-in labour, more casual. Men employed continuously earned 10s. per week or more, plus grist corn and potato ground, women 7d. or 8d. per day and children 6d. Day workers could earn more per day – Josias Dawe, farming 8 acres at Penrose, paid R. Rosevear in November 1870 'for a day's work 2s.' but he was only employed that one day. They also had the disadvantage of paying a higher rent for accommodation. Cottages attached to farms were let at 1s. per week (£2.12s. per year), others at £3–£4 per year.

Labourers such as Isaac Parkyn could get by because they were strong and did many different jobs. As sexton he earned 4s. every time he dug a grave, and when the school 'offices' had to be cleaned out Isaac or his brother Jacob would do it. It was said Isaac could 'hear the dell', that is the deal boards rattling after a ship was wrecked and be down to the coast and back again before work. Known as the superman of the parish, he would mow a little meadow before breakfast. He rewarded these heroic efforts by refreshing himself on a Saturday night at Lowertown, where beer cost 1s. for six pints.

In his *Gazetteer of Cornwall*, published in 1884, Symons gave another reason for the survival of the farmer in Cornwall:

Agriculture has received a great impetus from the improvement in the machinery employed (which have largely supplanted manual labour and expedited the operations)....

The Parliamentary Commissioner agreed that farmers in Cornwall invested more money in machinery than others. Even the farmer of only 8 acres, like Josias Dawe at Penrose, could hire a reaper. On 17 September 1870 he paid £1.10s. for 'thrashing the corn by steam'. He also paid 2s.11d. for 'rabbits for thrashing the corn'. Ten days later he paid 'Stephens for thrashing the corn – 1s.', perhaps the small amount left over by the machine.

Before 1840 farmers combined to buy threshing machines, but in 1876 Peter Sandry at Rumford bought his own. Engineering was in the Sandry blood. The combination of family talents for black-smithing and farming was a valuable one at this period. (Threshing machines only came in with a rush much later, from 1902 onwards.) Peter Sandry must have been the envy of all, especially in this period of agricultural depression.

Bad times for farmers meant bad times for the middle class in the parish too, the millers. In 1883 there were still three mills in St Ervan, but only one miller, grandson of our former Bible Christian leader, Richard Brewer, at Rumford. Millingworth had passed through a series of changes of ownership and occupancy since Richard Brewer had died in 1853 and was worked only occasionally. These 'desirable flour and grist mills' changed hands twice in the 1860s for sums of over £300 but sold at auction in 1871 for only £100.

There was stronger competition for farms in Cornwall than in many other counties. In 1880 James Hawken sold high the land he had inherited from his uncle at Penrose by dividing it into small lots of one or two fields of about four acres each, and by the well-known device of giving the bidders a

Lowertown Farm, Penrose.

dinner at a public house and keeping the beer flowing. The granddaughter of the man who gave £200 for Lot 2 – 'Pig's Park' (1a.2r.9p.) and the 'Bullock's House and Yard' – said it was a ridiculously high price and that it was worth, in her father's view, only £150. Lands around Penrose, in the crux of the two streams, were mostly well watered, but the purchaser of the four-acre field,

'Breage' paid 'a high price (£250) for a field with no water', in the opinion of John Henry Lobb.

Two years later, John Binny was not so fortunate. He put up seven acres of 'rich and productive Meadows and Orchard' at Penrose for auction. The sale included a freehold dwelling-house, i.e. the Maltster's Arms Inn, plus the dwelling. In spite of a large attendance, the biddings for the four lots did not reach the reserve prices. The land was then offered in one lot, but again did not reach the reserve of £750, which was considered an extravagant one.

The inn was variously called Lowertown Inn or the Maltster's Arms, the innkeeper being a farmer and maltster as well, but about now malting ceased to be practised and the inn's name changed to the Farmer's Arms. It was the same inn which caught the eye of a less desirable visitor in the darkness of a November night.

According to a report in the *West Briton* of 6 November 1882:

On Friday night or early on Saturday last a burglary was committed at the Farmer's Arms Inn, at Penrose,

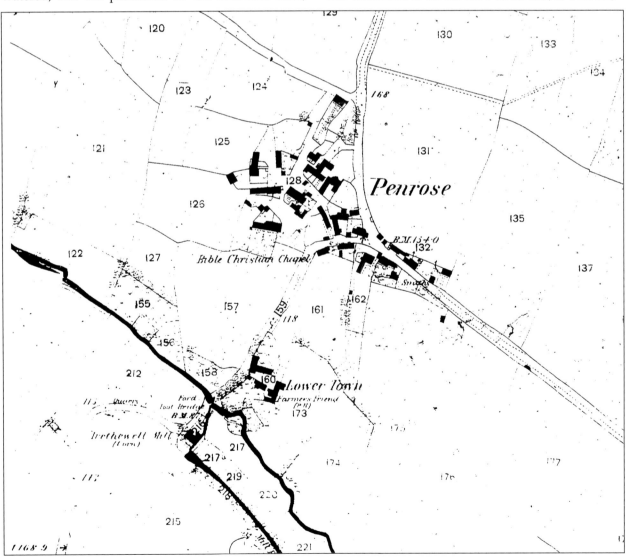

Penrose village in 1881.

Penrose Fair 2005 style: scarecrows on Penrose green.

Penrose Fair 2005 style: children's dog show assembling.

Penrose Fair 2005 style: scarecrows in a dracaena tree.

Penrose Fair 2005 style: children displaying paper and cane masks.

St Ervan, kept by Mr Charles Old. The family retired to rest about 11 o'clock on Friday night and on coming down next morning found a window leading to the bar and kitchen forced open, and a goose dressed for the market, some wine, a Cornish pasty, and other articles stolen. A strange elderly man was seen in the house during the Friday, and suspicion fell on him.

He was recognised by some St Ervan farmers attending St Lawrence's Fair at Bodmin and soon afterwards charged with committing several robberies in different towns.

Penrose had an ancient Fair held in May, supposedly on the Tuesday before Ascension, though this eventually settled on 25 May. It was principally a cattle fair. In 1888 the *West Briton* reported:

This old established fair was held on Friday last and was well attended by the principal farmers and dealers of the district. Fresh steers sold well at prices from £13 to £18 each, but inferior cows were not much in request. Lease cows were in demand, and realised good prices. The usual dinner took place at the Lower Town Inn, kept by Mr Charles Old, and there was a good attendance. It was considered the best fair that had been held for some years.

Miss Winnie Lobb's parents told her that the cattle were lined up on both sides of the hill from Lowertown into the village. Boys minded them while farmers made merry in the inn. They were bartered rather than auctioned. Gradually it became more of a pleasure fair. Traders brought sweet stalls, which excited the children.

The landlord of the inn, Charles Old, was a member of a respectable family of farmers and

Mary Winifred Ellen 'Winnie' Lobb, born December 1912, with her parents, John Henry Lobb and Bessie (née Old).

This damage to the side of Lowertown was caused by the heavy bowls used in the keel alley there.

craftsmen – his cousin farmed Treleigh, a nephew founded the blacksmiths in Rumford – and he maintained an orderly house at Lowertown. It was a different story under the Rundles. At the Brewster Sessions at St Columb in August 1899 John Rundle of the Farmer's Inn, St Ervan, was convicted for allowing gambling on his premises. He was fined 20s. and costs. In 1905 William Rundle came before the magistrates on a charge of allowing drunkenness on Penrose Fair day. A prosecution witness claimed:

... he saw two men, Mitchell and Currah, who were fined at the previous Petty Sessions for being drunk and disorderly, drinking in the public house at 7 in the evening, and at 9.45 he saw them again in the Inn, each with a pint in his hand, and they were both drunk. Mitchell and Currah both pleaded guilty at the last Petty Sessions.

Cross examined the witness said Mitchell and Currah were playing keels at 9 pm... William Rundle was acquitted since the evidence for the police was slight...

The keel or kale alley (bowling alley) at Penrose was a beauty. The balls weighed 28lbs each. The outside wall of the house has a long scooped-out furrow in the wall where, long after the alley had fallen into disuse, young lads would try their skills with one of the old balls. Keels could be played all day for a gallon of ale, purchased by the loser.

The Rundle family gave up the licence in 1913 and the inn closed. There are two stories: Revd Johnson closed the pub in 1915 when he became rector; W.G. Old, farmer at Treleigh closed the pub. Mr Old was a strongly religious Methodist and a public-spirited man. He was a county councillor for 35 years and an alderman. His grandson claims the closure of the Farmer's Arms for him, and says he and Tom Old ran the parish. Maybe church and chapel worked together to effect the closure of the last pub in St Ervan. Revd Barton closed Old Inn in Churchtown in 1895.

There were still areas of moor covered in furze which remained unbroken as late as the beginning of the twentieth century. In 1909 William George Eplett leased Bogee from the Revd F. Samuel Paynter and the following year cleared Bogee Common of its furze and broke the ground for ploughing. They positioned a traction engine either end with a rope between attached to a plough, which they pulled from end to end. They removed tons of stone. The first crop sown was rape, then oats the second year. Then followed a three to four year rotation – mostly oats in this part – a mix of oats for four years, grass for four years, and oats for four years, with a bit of rape for sheep in between.

'Jim' Rundle lived at Lowertown, Penrose, c.1920. His father was the publican.

Sketch of Bogee Farmhouse from the garden, now farmed by the Reskelly brothers.

Norah Rundle of Penrose, c.1920 (born 1913).

Bogee now incorporated a number of small tenements that had at one time been farmed independently, Higher Home Long, Lower Home Long, Lower Bogee, Middle Bogee and Outer Bogee. The cottages had already crumbled and been ploughed back into the ground, though the cottage at Pleasant Streams was rebuilt as a barn. Occasionally a rose from the cottage gardens still bloomed.

Bogee was now a farm of 290 acres. It had a large stone and slated farmhouse, another four-roomed cottage, and farm premises consisting of cattle shed,

stabling for six horses, milling house, carthouse and piggeries, calf house and large barn; also off-premises consisting of a three-horse stable, two linhays and turnip house. In 1913, when Revd Paynter put both Bogee and Treleigh up for sale, William Eplett was the Bogee tenant on a lease expiring Michaelmas 1916 at £115 per annum, and paying the Land Tax of £3.3s.6½d. per annum. A linhay erected in the Great Meadow was claimed by the tenant.

The linhay was a shelter, a night sleeping quarters, for the best cows, to protect the quality of their coats. Good shiny hair could fetch £1 an inch, so a heavy winter coat brought more profit to the farmer. The linhay had a sloping thatched roof supported on granite or wooden posts, open either end. 'Gorse brouse' (hedge trimmings, brambles, etc.) was stuck in under the thatch to absorb sweat from the cows.

William Eplett acquired a reputation for brewing some of the best beer. This was important as it helped to gain the best labour at harvest time. Men were attracted more by the quality of the beer than by a higher wage. Also, if a labourer had spent a summer's day cutting ferns, for example, there was

The Paynter family built this new farmhouse at Treleigh in 1859.

nothing better than a pot of home-brewed beer to refresh him and make him feel good towards his employer.

This was the land of malting barley. All the farmers did their own brewing. At Trevengenow Sylvester Sandry brewed up regularly in the brewing furnace, which stood in the corner of the linhay at the back of the kitchen. The copper basin was set in a brick support, under which the fire was lit to heat the contents.

The same sale particulars in 1913 describe Treleigh, too. Besides the large granite farmhouse, built in 1859, and the six-roomed cottage, the range of farm buildings comprised two cattle houses for a dozen cows each, two linhays and yard, stabling for six horses, a carthouse for four carts with barn over, a calf-house and a range of yearling houses. The only old buildings remaining from the mid-nineteenth century were the roundhouse and the barns it adjoined. William Hambly Old, first cousin to the blacksmith and cousin to William Gregory Old, was the tenant. Treleigh was a smaller farm than Bogee but more of the land was productive and Mr Old's lease, due to expire in September 1914, cost him £165.12s. per annum. Now the Old family, having farmed at Treleigh for generations as tenants, bought the freehold.

Both Bogee and Trevengenow lie more in the southern half of the parish, where it was mostly oats which were grown, but all St Ervan farms were on the edge of the best barley-growing land, the shallow soils along the coast from Newquay to Padstow. To quote *The Standard Cyclopedia of Modern Agriculture*, published in 1909:

Quality is all important. [Barley] is principally grown for malting, but inferior samples are of great value for distilling, for pig-feeding, and as a food for stock. Barley meal is the best food for fattening pigs which can be named, and is an excellent adjunct in the fattening of cattle. Whole barley is a good horse corn, especially when grown with oats, under the name of 'dredge'. 'Brewers' grains are always in request for milking cows and store pigs and malt is valued as a food for fattening lambs, so that barley in its several forms is indispensable on all farms.

Nothing was wasted! Such a farm was Trevengenow. In 1924 the farms owned by J.C. Williams, whose grandfather had bought up so much St Ervan land in the 1870s, were sold and the tenants given first refusal. Trewinnick and Trevengenow were among them. Sylvester Sandry bought Trevengenow, where he had bullocks, pigs, sheep, hay and corn, mangolds and turnips for feed, cattle and therefore rape.

Farms in St Ervan had weathered the severe agricultural depression of 1875–95 in Cornwall by practising flexibility, by producing good-quality barley and by turning to dairy farming.

At Trevengenow the dairy faced north and had long slate counters to maintain the coolness. As Miss Christine Sandry, daughter of Sylvester recalled:

Here butter was made, and here too were placed the

Harvesting at Eddystone with tractor and binder, c.1940. Note the shape of the shocks.

Harry Old driving the tractor and Dick Chapman on the binder behind, at Treleigh Farm, c.1925. The binder, a standard Fordson, cuts the corn and binds it in bundles. There's nothing to protect the driver from the iron wheels.

pans of scalded milk to cool when the cream on top could be skimmed off. The skimmer was a white enamel scoop, fairly flat with holes. It was held by a blue enamel handle. The top layer of cream became crusty and golden, while beneath that it was paler and more liquid.

When separators were introduced – you poured in the milk and turned a handle until cream came out of one spout and milk the other – this liquid cream, like the thick top of milk, was then scalded to become scalded or clotted cream.

Before churns, butter making was a lengthy business and required the tenacity and patience of the woman of the house. First, hands had to be scrubbed clean, then all the tools had to be clean and cool. The cream was placed in a very smooth curved wooden butter bowl and was turned with the hand until buttermilk came out. The remaining milk had to be washed out from the butter with the pump. Salt was added and the butter kneaded again, washed again and tasted. To make the butter into pats, all the liquid had to be battered out until the pat weighed half a pound exactly. Finally, the farm name was stamped on. In hot weather this could be a troublesome job – sometimes the milk would never come out.

Penrose Farm was also a dairy farm. When farmer's daughter, Miss Winnie Lobb, left school, she did all the dairy work for her father in the farmhouse.

Break time during harvest at Treleigh, c.1930. Left to right, at back: Minnie Bennetts, Henry Bennetts; middle row: Mr Kessell, Dick Chapman, ?, Jack, Betty and Charlie Richards; front row: four Kessell children.

Harvest at Treleigh, c.1930. The tall pole had a sling with a cross-beam suspended from the top which would go round a large amount of hay. Pulleys and ropes worked like a crane, the pulling power provided by a horse. This ingenious contraption was the means of loading hay from the wagon onto the top of a high hay rick, or mow, in Cornish.

Ayrshire cows 'Dynamite' and 'Thunderbolt' at Glebe Farm, c.1955. Beth Cowling, daughter of Jack, was milking one, her father the other, when Beth's started kicking and her father's shot a full three-gallon bucket of fresh milk over him.

She made all the butter and cream, which her father, John Henry Lobb, drove with pony and trap to market in Padstow twice weekly. Her father supplied milk to almost the whole village, though nearly everyone had a cow. It was a large dairy and operated in Penrose until October 1965. And they grew flowers to sell.

The dairy was such a normal part of a woman's work that Miss Lobb told me she 'hadn't worked after leaving school'!

In a close-knit completely agricultural community, where the substantial farmers were kinsmen of the farm workers, real poverty had been suffered by only a few, those who could not work through sickness or old age and whose links in the parish were not so close. When the harvest was poor and crops failed the majority shared the discomforts of the low standard of living. For some workers on the land in the comparatively well-off parish of St Ervan, life might still be 'narrow and brutish' but they expected no more and knew where they stood. Within their community some were of lowlier station than others, but the difference was not so marked, and no one was anonymous; everyone had some usefulness, nearly everyone had a skill, everyone could join in the enjoyment of telling and re-telling the stories of the pranks at Lowertown Inn, such as the time they put the drunken James Hawken in the trough and pumped water on to him until he woke up, or the little pricks of defiance against the rector, the one outsider. For all its limitations, the agricultural labourer's life, in a parish where everyone depended for a living on the land, and where everyone depended to some extent on everyone else, had been one of communion.

John James 'Jack' Masters pictured on a postcard sent home from France in the First World War. He died at Penrose in 1953 aged 66.

In 1944 Jack Masters paid £13 for a year's rent of meadows at Penrose which included this one, Trebells, where he and his son Leonard are haymaking.

Road gang with, second from left, *Clifford Strongman, Council Foreman.*

❖ CHAPTER 15 ❖

Between the Wars

Even a parish as remote and peaceful as St Ervan felt the impact of the First World War.

In January 1915 the *Cornish Guardian* reported:

A family of Belgian refugees have arrived at St Ervan and are being housed and cared for at Penrose in the parish. The family consists of mother, two sons and two daughters. The father is a fisherman, and is fishing off the coast of France.

In May about 70 soldiers sat down to lunch at Penrose after a 'route march'. Miss Drake gave the schoolchildren a holiday to go and see them.

The best farm horses, and farm workers except those essential to food production, were taken for the war. John James 'Jack' Masters sent home from France a *carte postale* with his photograph in uniform and in 1917 his mother and wife at Penrose received three Field Service postcards. No personal messages

were permitted, only sentences selected from those printed on the card. Jack Masters chose 'I am quite well' and 'Letter follows at first opportunity'.

Jack returned to Penrose, but not all men were content to return to the low wages of farm workers. Some found employment with the road gangs. Each gang was responsible for a section of lane, the hedging and ditching, in which these men were experienced, as well as maintaining the road surface. When Sidney Bawden had no work, Mr T.T. Strongman, St Columb Rural District Council Surveyor, took him under his wing and put him on a road gang. Bawden had no education but was a clever man, quick at complex calculations, and soon worked up to surveyor.

Stewart Buscombe's father, John, was very happy in his job but John's brothers emigrated to Canada.

John, son of Henry and Bessie Bennetts, farm workers at Treleigh, was reported missing in 1917

Harry Sloggett (1891–1973) and wife Annie, née Hawke, (1891–1973).

Golden wedding anniversary, 1968, of Harry and Annie Sloggett in their cottage at Egloshayle.

Fred and Gladys Hawke with their three eldest children, early 1927, in Leafield, Oxfordshire, where Gladys was born and Fred was posted during the First World War to man the radio station.

Chakrata was built in 1924 for the retirement of Henry and Bessie Bennetts when they finished working at Treleigh. They paid for it by pooling their own savings with savings of their son, Harry, and the savings of their deceased son, John, who was reported missing in the First World War. Harry was to inherit the bungalow and share it with John if he were ever found.

and never found. His savings were kept until 1924, when they were added to those of his brother and of their parents, to build a bungalow, Chakrata, for the parents' retirement.

Other bungalows and houses were built in the 1920s and 1930s. In Rumford William Brewer built Henley (c.1932), Endsleigh is a modern house, and Tom Old built the first bungalow, Trelawney, alongside Primrose Hill. Up at Four Turnings Jim Parsons built Kola for himself and family, on the site of old run-down cottages.

Anyone building new consulted Charlie Hambley, water diviner, so they knew where to sink the borehole or well. He lived with his wife at No. 1 Hillside and was a beekeeper. He made his own skeps from woven straw and sold many to America.

Council housing came to the parish, the first six in 1922 at Dolgey Post, and two a little later. Others followed after the Second World War, four at Penrose in 1949 and six Cornish Units in Trewinnick Lane in 1951, plus two a little later. Here water was pumped to concrete tanks between the houses, and the occupant had a hand pump in his kitchen to pump it into his house.

Although some changes occurred as a result of the First World War, which mostly affected the agricultural labourer's working conditions for the better, the village remained a hive of activity. Rumford in 1923 still presented a picture of times past.

The grocer's shop was more a centre of exchange. Farmers took in eggs and butter for sale in the shop.

Henley House, Rumford, built in 1932. William Brewer (1878–1954) married Dora Moody from Wiltshire. They lived in Penrose, then 'Birdcage Cottage', Rumford, then in the more modern bungalow Trelawney, before buying a meadow in the centre of Rumford and building this house. Dora was the tenth of twelve children born in a house called Henley, in Box, Wiltshire. She met William Brewer while working as a cook at Porth, St Columb Minor. The shop was built at the side. Henley House is now hidden by trees.

Trelawney, the first of the modern bungalows built next to Primrose Cottages in Rumford.

Endsleigh House, Rumford, built in the early-twentieth century by Samuel Paynter Sandry. The picture was taken before 1930.

In return the shopkeeper gave the farmers groceries, e.g. a bushel sack of flour. He also sold tools and other farming requirements.

William Brewer had a shop attached to the side of Henley House for more than 20 years. His father, Richard Brewer, the miller at Millingworth, had taken flour around in a pony and trap. William Brewer took his butter to Padstow in baskets on his bicycle, two on the handlebars and one behind. Known as 'the butterman', he also did some rabbit trapping in the winter before opening his shop each morning.

William Brewer emigrated once, to London, where he worked for such drapery stores as Whiteleys or D.H. Evans. He had developed a reputation as a fast 'reckoner up', and was accurate, with never a single mistake. When he returned to St Ervan his skills were put to use as rate collector for the parishes of St Ervan, St Eval, St Merryn and Little Petherick. Another turn of speed he developed was jumping over the hedge out of the path of the rector, Revd Barton, when he saw him in the distance, to avoid having to exchange formal greetings with him.

William F. Rabey, boot- and shoemaker, sold everything, it was like a mini-Woolworth's – hair ribbons, a fowl, tea and cocoa, ribbons and laces, a grater, a writing tablet, a comb and child's hosiery.

And in Rumford in the 1930s there was even a chemist, T.A. Chattock's Drug Store. He made deliveries on his bicycle, and could be heard muttering: 'Oh my giddy godfather!', much to the amusement of the children.

Charlie Hambley with the bee skeps he made, 1948. He sent many to America. With him are Pat Thomas (left) and Gillian Rabey. Mr Hambley won many prizes for his honey. He passed on his knowledge to Gillian's father, William Rabey. Harry Curtis and William Rabey kept bees together and went to all the shows, including Bath. Bees are still kept in St Ervan today.

Shopkeeper William Brewer, in his shop coat, and Dora outside Henley in 1939.

Council-houses at Dolgey Post in the 1920s. Just showing against the trees is the bungalow where Miss Christine Sandry lived.

After his store closed Mrs Old kept a little shop there which sold all sorts of iron hardware and other domestic goods, such as galvanised buckets, brushes, lamp glasses, tins of snowfire ointment, clothes pegs, huge blocks of hard kitchen soap, a disgusting perfume called 'Midnight in Paris', kits for repairing bicycle tyres, Zubes, home-perm lotions, carbide lamps, etc., etc.

There was agricultural machine owner T.H. Sandry, blacksmith Ernest 'George' Old, carpenter

William (Bill) Brewer, nicknamed 'Monty', in his ARP (Air Raid Protection) beret, 1943.

Larry Old's shop, the former Drug Store, in 1981, with Mrs Edith Rabey in her beloved garden.

Joan Brewer, c.1930, in her late teens in the garden of Henley House, showing off her fashionable fur-trimmed coat.

Thomas Astley Chattock, chemist (1871–1935), standing outside his 'Drug Store' in Rumford village. He was born at Castle Bromwich in Warwickshire, son of a 'gentleman' and was living at Brockenhurst in Hampshire before coming to St Ervan.

The sub-Post Office, opened next to Mill Cottage in Rumford in 1936, with postmen W.F. Rabey (left) and William Brewer. Above the door it reads 'W.F. Rabey Licensed to sell tobacco'.

Rumford Post Office and General Store, 1965. Long before 1965 William Rabey's shop had moved out of the corrugated-iron shed into the Post Office to which it had been attached. Left to right: Edith Rabey, William Rabey and their daughter, Gillian Fisher.

Agnes Kestle had the first Post Office at Penrose, behind Penrose farmhouse. She moved to Scotland.

Thomas Old, wheelwright Henry 'Harry' Parsons and shoemaker William Rabey, who also started a taxi service. Did the carpenter still use the sawpit at the side of the street for sawing timber for coffins?

Rumford was the first place in the district to get an automatic telephone exchange. This was requested to assist the two principal businesses, T.H. Sandry & Son and W.H. Old & Son. Ten lines were listed as live from the exchange. The ones I have identified so far are: W.H. Old & Son had No. 21, W.G. Old at Homesleigh No. 22, [? 23], Richard Salmon at Trewinnick No. 24, T.H. Sandry No. 25, John Roy Tremain at Treginegar No. 26, William H. Old at Treleigh No. 27, Sidney Bawden, surveyor, No. 28, and Stanley Kestell, lorry owner at Penrose, No. 29.

From 1914 there was a sub-Post Office in Rumford, managed for many years by the Rabey family, and at Penrose the general stores also contained a sub-Post Office. In the 1930s John Bunt ran a stationers and Post Office.

At Penrose in 1923 there were two shopkeepers, George Hawke and Miss Ellen Tippett, boot repairer Francis Old, shoemaker Joseph Thomas Old and mason William George Tippett. Again there were frequent comings and goings of butchers and pedlars of drapery goods. Most people baked their own bread, in clome ovens in the side of the open fireplaces, but each village had a bakery too.

John Henry Lobb's farmhouse at Penrose was one of the earliest to take in holiday guests. Here he is later enjoying showing two young visitors around. Trethewell Mill in St Eval can just be seen in the valley.

Robin Farbrother's parents had stayed at Penrose Farmhouse as holiday guests of Winnie Lobb's parents when Robin was a small baby. Winnie, aged 80, claimed to recognise him when he called on her at 'Springfield' in June 1995.

A butcher from the town called at the villages once a week.

There was always plenty for the children to watch, the smith at his forge, the carpenter in the sawpit, the cobbler mending shoes, the men playing keels at Lowertown, and the excitement of the steam threshing machine being hauled through the village or at work on a farm.

There were the Sunday-school treats, one for each chapel, and the church Feast Day and Penrose Fair. On Penrose Fair day the men and boys went over to Jimmy Carlyon's rock to collect the best mussels. In the next cove, Pederstroy, boys went crabbing.

With their chapels each village was a focal point of life, worship, work, trade and pleasure. The chance to chatter in the village street is what one 90-year-old was missing so much in the 1970s.

There was the annual trip to the seaside for the children. On Ascension Day Revd Johnson took them to Harlyn or Porthcothan Bay.

Everyone travelled to the big annual Summercourt Fair near Newquay, sitting on a plank of wood placed across the pony cart. It was the opportunity for buying cheap clothes. There were Fairs at St Columb in spring and autumn, and at Padstow.

Of necessity farmers started diversifying in the 1930s. In 1935 Eddystone Farm was advertised as:

... a Farm Guest House 2½ miles from Mawgan Porth, delightfully situated; rough shooting, fresh farm produce, personal supervision, garage accommodation (Mrs F.E. Old, proprietor).

In 1939 John Henry Lobb, farmer, dairy and poultry

farmer, advertised a camping ground near the sea, and accommodation at Penrose Farm. His early guests at Penrose Farm used the outside toilet just like the family. Soon the caravan site at Music Water was offering the facilities demanded by townspeople and today farmers convert their barns to a high standard for the holidaymaker.

The farmer's wife was busy in the farmhouse. At Treleigh at least two pigs were still being killed each year, to be cut up and preserved in the salter or salting keeve. This was an enormous granite trough in which the ham and bacon were placed between layers of salt, for one month. Then the surplus salt was wiped off, the meat wrapped first in newspaper, then in an old flour sack with a bit of hay inside, and hung – bacon on bacon rack, hams all around the walls, where they could dry out in the warmth rising from the cooker range. Nothing was wasted. The tripe was taken down to the river and washed clean. At Treleigh three men were employed permanently, but at harvest time casuals, known as 'slingers', were needed to help and the pig meat was needed to feed the extra workers.

At Pentruse several of the heavy hooks for hanging the hams are still fixed in a ceiling. The old kitchen had the slate floor and skirtings of slate until recently.

At Churchtown Farm Harry Strongman kept Guernsey cows and his wife Mary made the cream. She remembers the large number of separators, and filling ten or more large bowls with cream, which Harry took into Padstow and sold to cafés.

There were pleasures for the farmer, too, such as shooting pheasants, partridges, and plenty of rabbits, as well as a few hares.

Rabbit-trapping was more of a business and trappers could make quite a good living from it. A trapper paid the farmer to be allowed the exclusive right to trap on his farm for the next 12 months and he kept the

Winnie Lobb, a fashionable young woman in her fur-trimmed coat...

George Albert Hawke in May 1989, aged 97, taken at Mor-vue, built next to Trewinnick Farm in 1967.

proceeds from selling the rabbits. The agreement between landowner and tenant was carefully defined. In 1905 Gregory Brewer, tenant at Trethewey, received a letter from solicitor William Coode, steward to landowner Colonel Brune, asking which he preferred to do on fields owned by the Colonel:

... either: that Col. Brune should trap the rabbits himself giving the tenant half the cash realised by their sale after the cost of carriage and selling, taking the other half to pay his trappers' wages
or: that the tenant should make his own arrangements strictly in accordance with the Ground Game Act.

The latter, it was suggested, was the course the tenant was more likely to accept.

George Hawke, grandson of Bible Christian James Hawke, who on his marriage in 1913 moved into the little cottage wedged between the miller's house and the mill at Millingworth, was classified as an agricultural labourer, but earned his living principally as a rabbit trapper. The many small paddocks in St

Ervan's stonier area on the southern downs correspond to the area from which mother, father and children could clear stones, which they threw to the edges and disposed of in the earth-filled centre of the hedges. Many one-acre paddocks were constructed as a result, which made marvellous rabbit refuges. A rabbit could streak from the safety of one hedge to another before you could say 'Jack Rabbit'. The trappers 'buying' neighbouring farms had to agree between themselves who had the right to trap the rabbits in the boundary hedges.

In the 1950s, George Hawke 'bought' a farm for £40–£20 down and £20 towards the end of the 12 months, i.e. he bought the exclusive right to trap rabbits on that farm. In order to secure a good farm, he once paid £50 in advance. Further expense was incurred by the purchase and renewal of his steel traps. The traps had to be checked morning and evening, and from working the different farms he knew every field in the parish. He also did a bit of sheep shearing in season, and helped with harvest.

Stewart Buscombe had a gammy leg as a result of

illness at the age of four, so could not manage the heavy labouring work on the farm, but he was given the chance to learn the trade of cobbler with a gentleman at Padstow. He pedalled his pushbike five miles there and five miles back each day for the four years of his apprenticeship. Apprentices learned how to wind their own thread for hand-stitching, by rolling 4ft strands of hemp in wax. The shoemaker bought a whole skin and cut what he needed. Boots and shoes were made to measure, and a labourer's boots, even when worn every day in rain and mud, would last a full 12 months.

There was always rivalry between parishes to provide a bit of excitement:

St Ervan Hornawinks v. St Eval Peewits

It was the night of the fifth of November,
In the year nineteen twenty-eight,
When there came to the city of Rumford
Some Peewits who thought themselves great.

The squibs they raged fast and furious,
The rockets they soared to the sky,
And great was the fun in Rumford
On that night in the month gone by.

Till those Imps from St Eval got plotting,
Said one, – This beautiful spot
Would look very nice in our parish,
We will try and blow over the lot.

Let us start on this house by the drug store,
Quite close to the famous Fish Square,
And great will the shock be in Rumford
When they find themselves up in the air.

Some squibs they put under the front door,
But the house never moved, not a jot,
And soon they decided that Rumford
Was a very immovable spot,

And so they got tired of trying.
Said one – My bedtime is past,
I'm afraid my mother will spank me
If I don't go home very fast.

So they all took their bikes to hasten
Back to St Eval to roost,
But the Hornawinks of Rumford were waiting
With tabs and earth very loose.

And then the battle raged furious,
Mud flew thick and fast thro' the air;
And great were the groans of the Peewits,
In that beautiful city so fair.

Said one – If I'm dead by tomorrow,
You will know on whose head lies the blame,

The little cottage between No. 1 The Court and Steps House was known in the Bennetts family as 'Auntie Em's house'. This picture was taken in 1967, when Stewart Buscombe lived there.

Send me a wreath of dandelions,
And tell my girl I died game.

Then they took their wings and departed
And Rumford was rid of the pests.
The Hornawinks went back to their houses,
And soon they all were at rest.

Next morning a traveller to Rumford
Said – Whatever's been happening here?
That night is a date in history:
Will ne'er be forgotten, I fear.

Now all these young Peewits I warn them,
One night the Hornawinks may storm them,
One morn they'll arise, and great their surprise,
When they find St Eval
Has been blown to the devil.

(From *Rumford Tit-Bits* by 'Observer',
sold in aid of the Wesleyan Debt, 26 June 1929.)

William 'Bill' Salmon of Trewinnick Farm was a farmer who took away many prizes from shows. His father-in-law, George Hawke, was very proud that his daughter, Margaret, had married such a champion farmer.

When John Buscombe went to work as a farm labourer at Bogee Farm at the beginning of the twentieth century, he saw the first motor car come into Cornwall. His employer, William Eplett, told him the car was up at Wadebridge and would be travelling to St Columb that evening. After his day's work John walked to Winnards Perch to see it go through. He told his children years later that a man walked in front ringing a bell, and the driver was steering with a pole.

Frank Rowe had a Morris Cowley in 1938 and after the Second World War Henry Old in Rumford had a blue two-seater Morris with a dicky seat behind. William F. Rabey was the first to start a taxi service. When he could not get the car to start on a cold morning his wife would come out with a kettle of boiling water. Garfield Lobb's father had an Armstrong Siddeley which was hit by a visitor's car. Albert Harry Key proudly took his parents for a ride in his first car, a Humber, in about 1920. His daughter and her husband, Edith and David Cowling, have a prizewinning vintage car, a 1932 Austin 12/6, restored by David.

In 1992 David Cowling restored an Aveling Porter Showman's Tractor, built in 1920. His grandson Matthew is showing a keen interest.

It was the car that would bring about the biggest changes after the Second World War.

Photographed by James Hawken in 1922, at the cottage wedged between the mill cottage and mill, the child is either Mary Jane or Margaret Hawke.

The Rowe family of Eddystone in their Morris Cowley in 1938. The children in the dicky, left to right, *are Edward, Tresa, Jennifer and Dorothy. Frank and his wife, Myrtle, are in front with Diana.*

Albert 'Harry' Key, c.1925, driving his parents, Albert Henry and Anna Key, in his new Humber, his first car.

David Cowling's Aveling Porter Showman's Tractor, built in 1920 and restored by him in 1992. David's grandson, Matthew Cowling, is also keen.

Albert 'Harry' Key (born 1896) with his sister, Kathleen (born 1900), at Trenouth.

David and Edna Cowling's prizewinning vintage car in 2005, a 1932 Austin 12/6.

Treglinnick farmhouse, built c.1890.

The village of Penrose, perched on the crest of the hill, as seen from the south.

Edward Gregor of Trevilledor Farm with a prizewinning ram, c.1925.

Right: *Second World War clearance of gorse and scrub on Bear's Downs, with members of the Rowe family of Eddystone and others at work. Tractors were lent by the War Agricultural Department.*

South Devon long-wool sheep, formerly kept by the Skinners at Treburrick Farm for their very thick wool.

Keith Gregor of Trevilledor and men sheep shearing, 1970.

Farmer Frank Rowe of Eddystone with Mr James, War Agriculture Representative, preparing scrubland on Bear's Downs for potato planting, 1940.

✦ CHAPTER 16 ✦

War and Peace

In the Second World War there were three airfields on the edge of St Ervan; St Mawgan, St Eval and, most intrusive, St Merryn. Land on two farms in the north-west of the parish, Treginegar and Treglinnick, also on part of Treravel, was requisitioned for the Fleet Air Arm aerodrome of St Merryn, as it was called. But the flying fields were all in St Ervan parish. Hedges were removed, the ground reinforced with wire netting to take the weight of aeroplanes, hardcore was laid for runways and concrete for the bases of hangars.

William Hart Key and family stayed on in the farmhouse at Treglinnick, but slept at Mrs Key's father's place at Trenouth. They farmed traditionally, beef, sheep, arable, turnips and kale. Now the Eustice's have beef, South Devon sheep for wool and lamb, and corn. Wool barely pays the costs of shearing.

T.H. Sandry gained work hauling stone aggregate from his quarry at Trevose, which supplied 70–80 tons per day right through the war to the three airfields, employing first 25 men, later 40.

The bridge over the river at Lewidden was widened to take wartime traffic and heavy vehicles, an advantage today when heavy rainfall swells rivers and brings floods to other parts.

Bomber Command was at St Eval. Eddystone farmhouse, right at the end of a runway, was commandeered for officers. Frank and Myrtle Rowe moved back to Trevorrick Farm, St Issey, at night because of the danger of their proximity to the airfield. There was a gun position about 20 yards from the front of the house, a searchlight battery right on the farm and an underground War Room.

The War Agriculture Representative came out to discuss the reclamation of the downs with Frank Rowe. They lent him extra tractors to clear them of furze and scrub so potatoes could be planted.

Prisoners of war worked on local farms. John Henry Lobb had four Germans at Penrose. J.H., as he was known, was a lovely man and took cake and tea out to them in the fields. At Bogee Obed Phillips employed Italian prisoners. At harvest time they were taken around to whichever farm was busiest.

The RAF needed a source of water for the station and installed a pumping station on former common land opposite Music Water. Concerned that animals from Bogee Farm might pollute the water, they fenced off the pump with a 7–8ft fence all the way round and cemented in the posts. But they did not know that Tom Sandry had inherited a century-old

right to that piece of land following the Trewinnick Enclosure of 1839. Tom decided that the fence stopped his animals exercising their rights of access to water, so he put in a claim against the RAF and won. The fence was removed!

The war left a lasting impression on Beth Cowling at Glebe Farm. There was a lot of flying. She remembers Spitfires at St Merryn and Shackletons at St Eval. Revd Johnson sheltered frightened people in the rectory. One day a German warplane was hedge hopping and fired on Beth's father, Jack, who was in the field.

As many as 200 soldiers were billeted in tents. They were quite happy to wash in the river until a ram had a go at them. Another time their tents blew down in a storm at night and Jack Cowling gave them shelter in a barn.

An altar cloth crocheted by Mrs Edith Cowling of Glebe Farm.

Beth Cowling (later Mrs Len Carhart) of Glebe Farm, with her dog, Shep.

St Eval and St Ervan Home Guard machine-gun crew. Left to right, back row: Jack Andrew, Harry Old, two Lieutenants from down west; *middle row:* Fred Cole, the driver who brought the Lieutenants, Charlie Powell, ? Bennett from St Eval; *front row:* Sam Kent, Graham Brewer, Sergeant Tim Hore, Dick Tremain from St Eval.

Men at home joined St Ervan and St Eval Home Guard. After the war Cornwall old comrades, renamed the 'Choughs' (Cornwall's special bird) held a reunion dinner each year. Harry Old attended every one without interruption for 31 years.

Modernisation came slowly. Electricity came to Rumford village in the 1930s, and in 1965 a new series of 11,000 volt mains, tapped from the National Grid system, was laid throughout the area, which brought a big improvement in the voltage level delivered to consumers. Rumford has four street lamps and Penrose two, though the residents know their way in the dark anyway and sometimes resent the fact that street lighting obscures the stars in the sky on a clear night.

At first the water required by St Merryn airfield was taken from Rumford River. The village received water mains only in 1955. Farmers used wells, sank boreholes and piped water across to their farmhouses and other cottages. Stewart Buscombe drank the water from the spring well at Churchtown and never knew it go dry, even in the worst drought, just as the well at the 'watering-place' at Trevilledor saved the Gregors' cattle in the drought of 1976. Even today some farmers prefer the water tapped from the well.

St Eval and St Ervan Home Guard. Left to right, back row: Charlie Powell, Ronald May, A. Johnson, Clifford Brewer, Jimmy Babb, Albert Ball, Preston Rabey, Reginald Chapman, Fred Cole, Jack Brenton, Gerald Brewer; *third row:* R. Cocks, Harold Chapham (peeping through from behind), Sidney Currow, Jack Rundle, Rowe Binny, Edward Gregor, Norman Nicholas, Raymond Brewer, Eddy Hill, Frank Leverton, Stan Brewer, Denis Brewer, Frank Trebilcock; *second row:* Walter Curtis, Henry Rundle, Dick Tremain, Bobby Darke, Russell Brewer, Harry Old, Jack Andrew, Harry Bennet, Roy (?) Bennetts, George Morley, Leonard Curtis; *front row:* Bertie Sandry, Wilfred May, Graham Brewer, Harry Cowling, Warrick Cowling, William Key, Charles Curtis, Leonard Masters.

William (Bill) Brewer, shopkeeper, who had a great reputation as a wonderful singer, wearing his ARP (Air Raid Protection) badge.

Cottages in Rumford, showing the rebuilt chimney breast of Mill Cottage (left) and the conservatory porch at Ladysmith.

Three cottages, The Gardens, at Penrose.

In 2005 South West Water installed an iron mains pipe to replace the plastic one put in during 1972, which often burst.

Earth closets were still being used by a few houses in the 1960s. One cottage had its first bathroom and toilet in 1969. Before that residents bathed in a tin bath and threw the water outside. They were so excited they took a bath even before the block walls had been plastered. The cottage known as 'Granny Thatch Cottage' kept its thatched roof until mid-century and then reverted to its old name, Mill Cottage.

A beaten-earth floor still existed in one cottage within living memory.

As late as 1965 there was no public sewerage system in Rumford, each dwelling having its own arrangements for sewage disposal, some of these still very primitive.

Travelling vans with fish or meat and the mobile library no longer call as they did as late as the 1960s. Unfortunately, advances in car travel killed these businesses. Now there is just the little shop in Rumford kept by the Old family at W.H. Old & Son, stocking non-perishables for people who cannot travel to the supermarkets.

The St Ervan Garden Show was always a great event. Started in about 1925, it did not stop for the war. The 1944 show was reported at length in the *Cornish Guardian*. There were 697 entries to be judged by Mr H.W. Abbiss (vegetables, flowers, fruit), Miss A.J.W. Nicholas (farm produce and

The mobile library at St Ervan, c.1964. Alan Bennett (in white shirt) and Vilma Trenerry are choosing books.

cookery, including 21 jam sandwiches), Miss A.L. Corry (table decorations) and Mr A.F. Knight (honey).

Mr Abbiss, speaking for the judges, said the show was of a very high standard; he never remembered judging such a well laid-out show and of such good quality.

Prizewinners at the St Ervan Garden Show in 1945. Included at back: Mr Joe Prowse, Mr W.G. Old, Mr Donald Curgenven. Left to right, front: Diana Rowe, Mrs T.H. Sandry, Hilda Salmon, Dick Rabey, Nellie Key, Mrs W. Rabey, Will Rabey, Maud Salmon.

Garfield Lobb, schoolboy, proudly showing his mechanical aptitude with his Meccano model, 1928.

Arthur Lobb, Garfield's brother, at Rumford with Puss Moth – a De Havilland DH80A, 1938/9.

Miss Nicholas said she had never judged exhibits of such high class. The milk was the cleanest she had seen in any show and, as for the cookery section, it was of a higher standard than anything she had judged in pre-war days.

The rector entered his own produce and won prizes. In 1938 his diary records that he won a 2nd and a 3rd prize for honey, but nothing for his gooseberries.

Garfield Lobb's mechanical interest started early. He, Tim Hore and Mr Hugo of Wadebridge attracted great interest with their working models at St Ervan Garden Show in 1944.

Whist drives were described by Frank Rowe of

St Ervan Cricket Team toured the Isles of Scilly in about 1965. Left to right, standing: *Geoff Hawkey, Ivan Wright, Bobby Wright, Michael Old, Joe Prowse (who ran the club, a real 'scallywag'), Vernon Brewer, Roger Biddick, Alan Rodliffe, Eddy Rowe, Michael Salmon, Terry Brewer;* sitting: *Brian Salmon, Roy Menhenitt, Mervyn Sowden.*

The old corrugated-iron cricket pavilion.

Eddystone as 'the life blood of the parish'. In 1930, a drive in aid of the Cricket Club was held in the schoolroom, but later this was stopped. Frank Rowe protested:

We were forced to build our own small pavilion because there were always objections to our use of the school from the education authority... The Church never at any time gave those of us who wished to use the school any support, but sided with the education authority... the Church, over the years, far from using its school for Church functions, was always glad to use our small pavilion instead, so that the cricket pavilion became a de facto village hall.

Well, sadly, the cricket club is presently moribund and its pavilion is dilapidated.

That was in 1973. The cricket club had been thriving.

In 1965 it finished third in the County Cricket League, Division 2 (Junior-East). It was the best season for the club since 1959 and, in terms of games won, the best since the war. They were, by and large, a young side. They probably did not mind too much that they played on farmer Biddick's field, where his cows had grazed the day before. Sometimes, when harvesting was on, they could not get a team together. In later years, as young men left the parish to join the services, the club gradually ran out of members. Roger Biddick joined the team at Pencarrow, St Breock parish, which took players from a wider area.

The cricket pavilion was built of corrugated iron. There were boards on the floor covered with strips of carpet for a bit of warmth but the draught came up so strongly that it lifted the carpet around the knees. Nevertheless, many were the games of whist played there. Large amounts of money were raised for a variety of charities over the years. The people of St Ervan were unstinting in their fund-raising. At every anniversary or special occasion the profits went to charities. And when a woman in St Ervan developed multiple sclerosis, the £2,000 needed for an electric wheelchair was raised in a very short time.

St Ervan celebrated the Queen's silver jubilee in 1977 with a united service of thanksgiving in the Parish Church on Sunday, and on Tuesday 7 June there was a full programme of sports and games, a tea, the presentation of jubilee mugs to the children and the cutting of the jubilee cake in the afternoon, with a fancy-dress parade and music, dancing, games

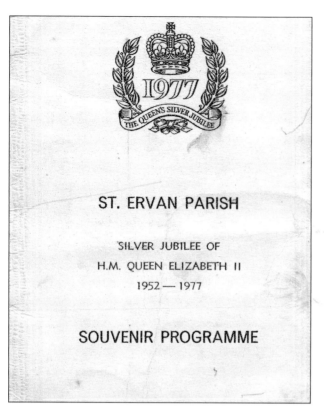

ST. ERVAN PARISH

SILVER JUBILEE OF
H.M. QUEEN ELIZABETH II
1952 — 1977

SOUVENIR PROGRAMME

Above and right: *Programme of St Ervan parish's silver jubilee celebrations in 1977.*

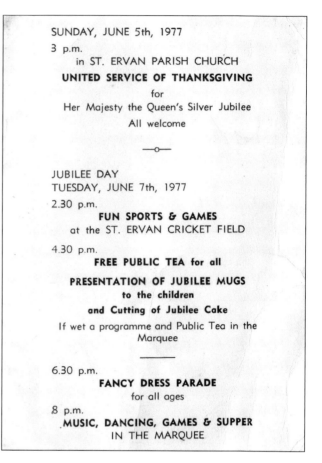

SUNDAY, JUNE 5th, 1977
3 p.m.
in ST. ERVAN PARISH CHURCH
UNITED SERVICE OF THANKSGIVING
for
Her Majesty the Queen's Silver Jubilee
All welcome

—o—

JUBILEE DAY
TUESDAY, JUNE 7th, 1977
2.30 p.m.
FUN SPORTS & GAMES
at the ST. ERVAN CRICKET FIELD

4.30 p.m.
FREE PUBLIC TEA for all

PRESENTATION OF JUBILEE MUGS
to the children
and Cutting of Jubilee Cake
If wet a programme and Public Tea in the
Marquee

6.30 p.m.
FANCY DRESS PARADE
for all ages

8 p.m.
MUSIC, DANCING, GAMES & SUPPER
IN THE MARQUEE

Fancy dress at the celebrations for the Queen's silver jubilee. Left to right: Suzanne Trevaskis, Freda Salmon, Nicholas Fisher (in barrow), Gillian Fisher, and Bertie Gregor at her right shoulder.

Celebrating the Queen's silver jubilee, at the cricket field. Among those in fancy dress were Clifford Strongman (centre front) as Billy Bunter and Pat Powell (far right).

and supper in the marquee. It was held in the cricket field, with marquees erected in place of the cricket pavilion and discreet toilets built of hay bales.

Music is a thread running through the history of this parish. They took music from elsewhere, copied sheet music and gave it their own St Ervan character. Complicated settings of music were used in St Ervan Church.

Richard Buscombe (1826–1905) played cello in church by ear for the hymns.

Gregory Tom of Trethewey has left a manuscript music book. It contains tunes for metrical versions of some psalms and other sacred pieces. The music is not complex. Some tunes are named, some with Cornish names, e.g. Falmouth, Liskeard and Zennor. 'Sound, sound' was known to local congregations. It appears in Padstow's 'Strike Sound'.

Padstow Carols are well known locally. Everyone knows 'Rouse, rouse from your slumbers' but in the 1920s it had been forgotten, except by Mrs Ellen Lobb (née Tippett) of Penrose, to whom it had been sung as a child by her Tippett grandfather.

Methodists have always been great singers. Samuel Ley Thorne, at the opening of the new chapel at Penrose in 1861, commented that 'the singing is excellent', and in 1880 the school inspector reported: 'The singing is remarkably good'.

In 1878 an amateur concert of vocal and instrumental music was given in the schoolroom to raise money for a parish library. There were songs and duets, part songs by the St Ervan Glee Singers, and a pianoforte duet. A highlight was:

> ... a concerted piece, adapted from one of Haigh's compositions for the pianoforte and flute, but... transferred to pianoforte, violin, violincello and triangle, the parties taking part... being respectively Miss Barton, Messrs Hawken, Hawke and Sandry.

Frank Rowe loved playing and had every instrument in the farmhouse.

Harry Strongman's family still remember him conducting his Sunday school in 'Onward Christian

'Pydar Pedlars' Hilda Bennett and Millicent Curgenven with their prizewinning scarecrow, October 1983, at the Royal Cornwall Showground.

Celebrating the Queen's silver jubilee, Hilda Bennett dressed as a tramp.

St Issey Band. Jim Parsons (second from right, middle row), a great bandsman for 60 years, played euphonium with St Issey. St Ervan was not large enough to have its own band.

The identity of the 'Beauty Queen' at the celebrations remained a secret for a long time. It was Roger Biddick, more recognisable in wellies driving his tractor.

Soldiers', sung very lustily. He loved his music. His nephew, Clifford Strongman, was an accomplished musician, both instrumental and as a founder of St Columba Choir. Donald Curgenven was a member.

William Brewer of Rumford had a wonderful voice and was in great demand for concerts.

Jim Parsons, 'a bandsman for 60 years', played in St Issey Band, the parish not being big enough to have its own. He played his euphonium all afternoon after Sunday lunch in the parlour. It was not appreciated by his young grandson, Charlie!

In January 1935 Miss L.D. Evans took up her duties as headmistress of St Ervan School, with 40 pupils. Miss Dorothy Tippetts was assistant teacher of the infants. In 1971 the headmistress, by this time

The old schoolhouse from the cricket pitch. Treglinnick is on the horizon (top left), and Treravel is to the right.

St Ervan Hall, completed by voluntary effort in 1982.

Mrs Arthur Strongman, reached retirement and the little school was closed. Dorothy Tippetts, now Mrs Harry Bennetts, went to Wadebridge to teach for a few years before her own retirement. At the time of writing there are people around who learned to read and write with her.

The school closure was inevitable but greeted with sadness. However, the sale of the school by auction in 1973 aroused great anger in the parish, who felt it was theirs, 'by tradition and moral right'. Unfortunately, though their grandparents had contributed, the parish had never owned it legally. It was converted to a dwelling and purchased by a London couple with small children, who ran a pre-school playgroup for a while.

Revd Steward stayed on as rector until he had secured for the parish a piece of glebe land on which they could build a hall to replace the pavilion. The highlight of 1982 was the completion of the new St Ervan Hall. In 1977 the land was purchased by the PCC from the church authorities for a nominal £5. Outline planning permission was granted in 1978, and for several years magnificent flower festivals in the church helped to raise money. The ladies not only arranged the flowers but 'baked like crazy' – the cake stall was always very popular. There were 20

St Ervan Women's Institute celebrate 50 years, 12 March 1999. Left to right, back row: *Mrs Betty Brewer, Mrs Millicent Curgenven, Mrs June Dunstan and, on right of banner Mrs Gillian Fisher (Treasurer);* middle row: *Mrs Hilda Bennett, Miss Maud Salmon (Founder Member), Mrs Mary Skinner, Miss Christine Sandry;* front row: *Mrs Pat Read (Secretary), Mrs Margaret Salmon (Founder Member), Mrs Joyce Sterling (President), Mrs Alberta Gregor. (Miss Jan Heeley was taking a guest home.)*

St Ervan School in George V's jubilee year, 1935. Left to right, back row: *Rose Cole (later Penter), Marion Ball, Margaret Hawke, Hilda Salmon, Hilda Thomas;* middle row: *Miss Lydia Evans (headmistress), Queenie Mounce, Frank Kent, Cyril Buscombe, Una Hawke, Doris Cole (went to Wales), Ruby Stephens, Peggy Tucker (married Garfield Lobb), Clifford Strongman, Charlie Powell, Mavis Powell (assistant teacher?);* front row: *Dennis Hill, Wilfred Davy, Kathleen Gagg, Margery Cole, Audrey Hawke, Phyllis Hill, Doreen or Joyce Mounce, Dick Bray, Bill Kent, Graham Brewer.*

In 1935 the junior school pupils were photographed separately from the rest of the school. Left to right, back row: *Dorothy Tippett (teacher), ?, Don Curgenven (born 1927), Mavis Johns, Joyce or Joan Mounce, ?, Ervan Ball;* front row: *Graham Ball, Tony Cowling, ?, ?, ?, George Hill, ?, ?. Note the herringbone slate hedging edging the school yard behind the group, and the church in the background.*

Headmistress Mrs Lydia Strongman (left) retired in 1971. She is pictured with three generations she taught of one family, Mrs Jennifer Old, her son Richard Old, and Jennifer's mother, Mrs Margaret Salmon.

Dorothy Tippett in the 1930s.

Arthur Strongman (1897–1971), farmer at Penrose. He was baptised at the Bible Christian chapel on 22 July 1897 by Minister H. Rundle.

Wedding of Harry Bennetts and Dorothy Tippett in the summer of 1941. Reg Chapman (on left at back) was best man, Jack Tippett the father of the bride.

St Ervan Women's Institute attend the Federation's golden jubilee rally at the Royal Cornwall Showground, Wadebridge. President Mrs T.H. Sandry holds the new banner, made in 1965. It was designed by Miss Cowling and embroidered by Mesdames D. Old, T.H. Sandry and D.E. Morley.

St Ervan WI's prizewinning exhibit at Wadebridge Fatstock Show, December 1987.

The National Federation of Women's Institutes celebrated 75 years on 11 September 1990. Members of St Ervan WI met at St Ervan Church to ring the bells, 75 peals, then walked to Rumford along the leat footpath for the celebration tea party in the garden of Ladysmith. **Left to right:** *Mrs Gina Cooper, Mrs Hilda Bennett, Miss Maud Salmon, Miss Gwen Hawke, Mrs Audrey Hawke, Miss Christine Sandry, Mrs Betty Kelly, Mrs Jenny Old, Mrs June Dunstan. Mrs Gillian Fisher was working that day.*

Dear Friend,

We give to you a cordial invitation to join us in our Centenary Celebrations. The Chapel has been a centre of Christian Worship and Witness at Penrose for a hundred years. We are grateful for the devotion of those who handed on to us a goodly heritage. We are humbly proud of those who today maintain the cause. We believe that it is God's will that we should hand on to future generations an inheritance enriched by our devotion and faithful service.

If for any reason you cannot join us at any of our meetings during the week-end but wish to associate yourself with the Centenary Celebrations with you, please offer a prayer asking God's blessing on all that is being done, and send your gift in the envelope enclosed herewith. But do come and join us if you can.

Your presence and support will be esteemed.

Yours sincerely,

WINNIE LOBB,
Trust Secretary,

ALBERT COWELL,
Minister.

J. Edyvean & Son, Printers, St. Columb 147

1861 - 1961

PENROSE METHODIST
(formerly BIBLE CHRISTIAN)
CHAPEL

Historical Note

The Chapel was built through the faith and efforts of the Bible Christians at Penrose. From the records, which alas are all too brief, we learn that the Foundation Service was held on MAY 24th, 1861 and the Opening Services on NOVEMBER 17th and 18th of the same year. The preacher for the opening services was the Rev. R. KENT of Torquay.

The original Trustees were :—

JOHN BREWER, MILLER, ST. ERVAN
JAMES TIPPETT (the younger), MASON, ST. ERVAN
JAMES STRONGMAN, YEOMAN, ST. WENN
WILLIAM TUCKER CHAPMAN, ST. BREOCK
WILLIAM BREWER, MILLER, LITTLE PETHERICK
WILLIAM BENNETT, MILLER, ST. MERRYN.

The Minister at the time was the Rev. SAMUEL L. THORNE who entered the ministry in 1851 and died in 1892.

Centenary Celebrations

SATURDAY, NOVEMBER 18th, 1961

4 P.M. DIVINE SERVICE
Conducted by
THE REV. A. R. MARTIN of Dawlish.

5-15 P.M. FAITH TEA

7 P.M. PUBLIC MEETING AND GIFT TREE EFFORT
Chairman : MR. J. NEAL of Nanpean.
Speakers :
MR. J. H. L. MORGAN of Newlyn East.
REV. A. R. MARTIN and REV. A. COWELL.
Soloist : MISS M. HARRIS of Newlyn East.
The Gift Tree to be stripped by MRS. A. COWELL.

SUNDAY, NOVEMBER 19th

SERVICES at 2-45 and 6 p.m.
Preacher : REV. A. R. MARTIN.

Penrose Methodist (formerly Bible Christian) chapel celebrates its centenary. On a scrap of paper attached to this programme is a carefully recorded note of the expenses and income from collections at the morning and evening services.

volunteers at the start. Peter Cowling used his digger to remove rubble and Len Carhart, Colin Fisher and plasterer Clarence Deacon finished it off. Howard Hawken showed them how to put up A-frames. Ladies fed and watered the workers. By 1981 work was proceeding well and the build took two years, with everyone working in their spare time. They finished it in time for St Ervan Harvest Sports and Feast in October and by December 1983 the loans to St Ervan Hall committee were repaid.

Until recently St Ervan had a very active Women's Institute. It was founded in 1949 with 37 members and celebrated 50 years in 1999. St Ervan joined in the celebrations of the Federation's golden jubilee

Rumford Sunday-school anniversary, 9 June 1952, gathering in the evening, with the band, in front of Rumford House.

The prize of Turnwrights Toffee Delight tin, refilled each year with sweets, was won in 1969 by Richard Old. Also included is Kay Sandry, teasing Richard, Clair Trevaskis, Richard Sandry, Wendy, Valerie and Michael Curgenven, John and Ruth Skinner, Christopher Parken, and Mr Billie Curgenven.

Penrose chapel front, 2005, after refurbishment.
(Courtesy Historic Chapels Trust)

Penrose chapel 2005 after extensive repairs.
(Courtesy Historic Chapels Trust)

The pews at the west end of Penrose chapel after repairs. Many of the pegs around the walls had to be replaced.
(Courtesy Historic Chapels Trust)

year at the Royal Cornwall Showground and were represented by Mrs T.H. Sandry at the Queen's Garden Party. In 1990 St Ervan celebrated the Federation's 75th anniversary by ringing the church bells, a peal of 75, then walked back to Rumford for tea at Ladysmith.

In 1965 a new banner was designed by Miss Cowling and embroidered by Mesdames D. Old, T.H. Sandry and D.E. Morley. It depicts the Methodist church and Rumford bridge, the pond at Trewinnick, known traditionally as the Lake, and the anvil at the blacksmith's shop, this being one of the few parishes where this trade was still carried on.

The Parish Church needed constant attention throughout the century. In 1989 major repairs were carried out to the walls, where damp had caused damage. The level of heating was a constant problem and three new windows were installed. In 2006 the Ralph Keate monument is beautifully refurbished. Once again it can be appreciated that 'the general balance of the design is worked out into delicate detail of ornament', which so pleased Prebendary Johnson.

The Methodist chapel at Penrose celebrated its centenary in 1961 with a service.

153

Penrose chapel, 2005. New lamps were installed but the original timber work was repaired. In front of the pulpit is an enclosed area used for meetings.

(COURTESY HISTORIC CHAPELS TRUST)

There are always fresh flowers in St Ervan Church. This arrangement was the Easter greeting in the porch in 2005.

Rumford Methodist Sunday school anniversaries were celebrated with a service and children's sports. At Rumford a large tin was filled with sweets by Tom Old and awarded to the winner each year.

In 2005 another big event took place in the parish, the completion of the refurbishment of Penrose chapel, a Grade II* listed building, by the Historic Chapels Trust with funding from the Heritage Lottery Fund and proceeds from local fund-raising events. The repairs included the reinstatement of Cornish rag slates to the roof, the introduction of a lost plaster ceiling, the eradication of rot in the timberwork and sub-structure and conservation of the Thomas Brewer's unusual timber furnishing. The chapel retains its complete and original set of box pews, arranged in tiers in the west end. The pulpit has a panelled enclosure in front that was used for meetings and is now a rare survival. The chapel dates from 1861 but appears to follow an older, more traditional plan form and stands out as a rare, intact representative of small rural chapels in the county.

The completion of the work was celebrated by a service on Easter Day and, in October, a service of thanksgiving for the harvest followed by a sale of vegetables and fruit and other goods. At Christmas, with Mike O'Connor and his fiddle leading, Penrose residents went round the village singing carols, then adjourned to the chapel for warming refreshments and more singing before going home.

Childhood here was a happy time. There was always plenty to do. Children wandered freely all

Florence and George Hawke walking down the church path to attend a wedding.

day long, exploring the fields and valleys, going off for long distances on their bicycles, racing each other, cycling to the cinema at Padstow, fishing in the rivers, enjoying the activity at harvest time, watching the blacksmith or wheelwright at work. Joan Henwood

Roger Clemens of Penrose with his pedigree South Devon bull 'Penrose Stonehedging – Summers', breed champion, at the Royal Agricultural Show, Stoneleigh, Warwickshire, in 2003. By 2004 he was breed champion nine times in nine shows.

Eddy Rowe of Eddystone Farm in 1995 (he died in 1997 aged 72). Of the five children of Frank and Myrtle Rowe, he was the only son, so although he wanted to be a librarian he had to carry on the farm. He had an extensive collection of books in the farmhouse, including some first editions. One farmer said that Eddy never learned to reverse a trailer.

Eddystone farmhouse, modernised during the twentieth century.

Old and new at Eddystone Farm.

Michael Salmon at Trewinnick Farm with a champion Limousin bull, c.1985.

tells how fascinating it was to watch the blacksmiths hammering on the anvil, the red-hot sparks from horses' shoes being made and the horses shod. William Rabey sat mending shoes in the evenings, and men gathered around to chat. His daughter, Gillian, enjoyed the smell of the glue he used! They loved to watch carpenter Harry Parsons at work. He would encourage the children to sing hymns and other songs and, if they sang well, would give them a piece of fruit from his garden or a sweet. They were given pony and cart rides around the lanes by Flo Hawke and would stand on the cart to pick crab apples off the trees. They enjoyed Sunday-school tea treats and sports, outings to Porthcothan beach, playing ghosts and hide-and-seek at Prebendary Johnson's Christmas parties. They remember the abundance of wild flowers and the beautiful and rare plants in his walled garden. In a marshy meadow above T.H. Sandry's yard was a field with flag irises and wild cotton, and 'zillions of tadpoles', but children were warned to avoid the dynamite shed. Was there really dynamite there, or was the story told to keep children away from the well in that field? The leat at Millingworth was a magical place to play. There was the stream, and lots of wild flowers. That was before the area was drained and cultivated. In winter there were water meadows; in summer, when it was dry, animals were allowed to graze there.

Harry Strongman at Churchtown Farm was great fun and the children enjoyed his magic tricks. He had a dairy herd of Jerseys, known for their bad temper. The bull once chased a young lad on his trial bike across the fields! The farmyard was just below the school and one day the children watched Harry riding round his yard on the same bull!

One boy had access to the stock of the undertaker, notably rope that was very smooth on the outside. They cut it into cigarette-sized lengths, packed five of them into an empty Woodbine packet and pretended it was tobacco. Another wanted to serve petrol at W.H. Old's, where his father worked, but was forbidden. One day he decided to serve a customer on a motorbike, lost control of the pump and doused the biker!

Many things have changed but some activities get a fresh start. The Harvest Festival at the Parish Church is again a big occasion, the church crowded for the thanksgiving service, St Ervan Hall full of vegetables, fruit, flowers, fresh-made clotted cream and butter, etc., swiftly auctioned by farmer Roger Biddick. At the chapel in Penrose a Harvest Festival is just as enthusiastically attended, with Roger Clemens as auctioneer. Penrose Fair is celebrated with such competitions as paper mask-making, dog

Champion at the St Columb Major Christmas Fatstock Show in 1982, this 20-month-old heifer, 'Snowy', is owned by Michael Salmon of Trewinnick Farm, St Ervan. Pat Morris presented the cup.

Corn at Glebe Farm. The corn has been cut by binder, which throws out bundles or 'shocks'. These are stood up in groups of nine – called 'shocking' – and left to dry out. At harvest time they are carried into the barn.

Farming can be a lonely business.

Little Trewinnick farmhouse, built c.1900, with Stephen and Susan Old.

A reed comber which prepares straw for thatching. This contraption is built on top of a threshing machine. There are big drums inside with combs protruding which comb the heads and grains out of the top and the leaves and weeds out of the bottom, leaving long clean straw. Waste drops down into the threshing machine, the loose waste is baled up for bedding straw. Grain is carried by a shute into the trailer behind. On top, their heads just showing are: Dick Wood and Lisa Grey from Penrose, feeding the wheat in at both sides. Standing lower left: Ivan Powell who has brought his trailer and baler. Lower right: Annette Wood is trimming the bundles to make them presentable for the thatcher to put on a roof.

Cattle man at Treburrick, St Ervan, Albert Francis. A farm worker's cottage built on the farm c.1900 is named after him.

Barns converted for holidaymakers at Treleigh.

competitions, pony rides and scarecrow competitions, sideshows in a field on the edge of the village (see page 122) and a St Ervan version of the furry dance composed by Michael O'Connor. An annual rounders competition pitches Penrose against Rumford. Poetry evenings in the Parish Church once a year nourish the soul with poignant and humorous verses, and the body with the renowned refreshments provided by the ladies. St Ervan challenges teams from adjacent parishes to guess the meaning of unusual words on Bluffers Night.

No sleepy village this!

The main industry is still agriculture. Farms have amalgamated under fewer owners but are still small, diverse family affairs farming beef, sheep and corn. Farming is more or less traditional, somewhere between organic and intensive, but highly mechanised. They still use sea sand to balance the acid in the soil and, though sheep are kept for meat, wool is a minor business now.

Farmers inherit generations of experience and a knowledge and understanding of the soil. As one declared: 'What's the point of higher education if you lose the sense of the soil?' But farming today is more a way of life than a profitable business. The farmer farms as though he will be farming forever and lives as though he is going to die tomorrow. But in St Ervan there are only three farms where there are sons (or grandsons) wanting to carry on farming. The townsman envies the countryman's way of life and tries to capture it for himself, but he often fails because he has no real understanding of exactly what it is.

Country people have always improvised. In St

Columb parish Dick Wood has a reed combing machine. This combs and packs the reeds ready for the thatcher to place on the roof. The comber is a drum which revolves, with flattened teeth on the outside combing the reeds. Leaf and chaff and broken straws are removed. The comber sits on top of a threshing machine which is screened for different sizes of grain, which it feeds along a chute into a trailer behind, and bundles the waste to be stacked and used as cattle bedding. The whole contraption of cogs and belts, driven by two old tractors, looks very Heath Robinson but works extremely efficiently.

The Wood brothers supply reed to roof thatchers in Cornwall and Devon. William Wood at Glebe Farm has been growing the special wheat straw – a thatcher needs a stiff reed. No. 59 is the Woods' preferred variety but it is difficult to get. A modern hybrid, Maris Widgeon, is highly suitable, and triticale, a cross between wheat and rye, is also suitable.

Some old customs survive. When Ken Skinner's cattleman, Albert Francis, got ringworm on his arm, Ken went to a charmer with a piece of cloth belonging to Albert. When Ken returned to Treburrick Albert told him that he had known the precise moment that the charm had been uttered – his arm tingled and immediately felt better.

Improvisation, innovation, moving with the times, but keeping hold of traditions that are positive, all these keep a rural parish alive.

A quiet place, St Ervan can take a little while to get to know, but once captured it is almost impossible to escape. There is still great spirit here.

As part of Radio Three's Bach Christmas, the BBC, in conjunction with the Royal College of Organists, asked that every church in the country where the organ and organist were capable should play the famous Bach Toccata & Fugue in D minor at their main service on Sunday, 18 December (2005). St Ervan Church managed this in great style with a superb performance at the end of their service – not having an organist and having to rely on a CD player can have a 'silver lining'.

June Evening, St Ervan

'Let me put on the lights', the old lady said,
'Then you can see it all so much better.'
Nine o'clock and the rain plashed down
From the ashes and sycamore arching the lane
Plunging down to the ford and holy well.
Tall as a man the cow-parsley bloomed
And foxgloves reaching for light in that lush shade
Gleamed four feet high and more as we passed
Under our streaming umbrellas, making for the church.

I remembered St Ervan from many years back:
A dim damp cell, the mildewed walls,
Musty pews and sweating slate-carved plates,
Memorials of gentry and farmers, the death's heads
Grinning upon the marble raised to one Ralph Keate.
The north chapel held a slate to William Arthur
And his lady: five sons, three daughters stiffly knelt
In ruffs and breeches. And here they all were still,
Piously praying in this hidden retreat:
Now rather less neglected, almost glorified
By newly plastered walls and floor of polished blocks,
Red carpet laid upon it, and those cheerful lights.

Betjeman came here, was welcomed and then taught
By the Rector who tolled the bell, invited him,
A shy exploring youth, to tea. And lent
Him Machen's 'Secret Glory', opening out
The world of Celtic mysticism to his poet's mind.
A framed and scripted passage, taken from
'Summoned by Bells' hangs modestly
Upon the belfry wall, reminding both
Visitors and local worshippers of this,
St Ervan's claim to fame in literature.

And who was St Ervan? We may argue over him:
Obscure as Eval and Issey and Ewe. Erbyn, perhaps,
Father of Geraint, the King of Western Celts?
Or some forgotten namesake, hermit in these woods,
Sequestered from the mainstream of religious life,
And great works of the Age of Saints, who kept
His light of faith, and by example taught
The pagan Cornish all he knew of love?

'They blew up the tower a hundred years
Ago, with dynamite,' the old lady said. 'A shocking state
'Twas in, and when St Issey was struck
By thunderbolt, that decided them.'
The two-stage tower is crowned with concrete now;
But three bells ring that had been silent here
A century.

The farming parish spreads beyond;
The schoolhouse now a residence, the Rectory
A hotel-restaurant; but at Trembleath,
Farm of the Wolf, where the last Cornish wolf was killed,
The hay is in, the crops are reaching up
To slake their thirst with this relief of rain.
At Rumford agricultural engines throb,
Serviced and repaired, and haulage lorries roar
Their baleful ways along the country lanes
To building sites and refuse tips alike.
And by the church the modern village hall,
Heart of the parish social life, receives
The young, the old, the Women's Institute
And shields beneath its roof their simple honest joys.

There you and I went to a Cornish evening once,
When Kernow Brass announced, with royal peal
On peal, their ringing marches – trumpet and trombone,
Cornet and Euphonium – to our delighted ears.
And Hilda Bennett, clad in hat and wig,
With glasses falling off her nose, gave forth
A dialect story that convulsed the throng
With aching merriment for helpless minutes then:
Bucolic humour at its ripest peak...

'The chancel,' said our guide, 'is crooked, if you will.
– Set at an angle to the nave, a fact
No-one can quite explain.' I sign the book,
After the few names penned in June, and drop
Some money in the wall-box. 'We must go,
And you will want to lock up now.' The rain
Redoubles on the slate roof and the trees
Outside, 'Can we offer you a lift back home?'
– 'I like the walk, this time of evening, thank you.' So
We left her musing in the silent chapel
By the slate memorials and the plaques.

Under our black and striped umbrellas we depart,
Along the lane with campion, vetch, herb Robert,
Hedge bedstraw dripping fleering chains of light
As evening thickens, clamming in upon us.
Yet, as moisture seeps into my knees and feet
And even sheep seek shelter in the hedge,
I hold that brave refurbishment, the will
Of those who will not let their church decay
In this unheeded corner of our land, aloft
In honour, guarding treasures of the past,
History's examples, faith of priest and flock,
A haven from the rage of modern life.

Donald Rawe, 1989

Subscribers

Mrs Joan Ackers (née Curtis), St Ervan

Shirley Aldworth (née Deacon), Guildford

Caroline Arnold, of Hawken descent, London

Art St Ives Gallery, St Ives, Cornwall

Sandra and Ian Backway, St Eval

Diana P. Ball, Killivose, Camborne

Mr Edwin Ball, Canada (Ball family originated St Ervan mid-1600s)

Mary Ball, formerly St Ervan

Fernley and Nancy Banbury

Richard and Claire Banbury, St Ervan, Cornwall

Mr Richard Banbury,

William Benallack, Lansing, Michigan

Margaret Bendle, Newquay

Pam Bennallick, formerly St Ervan

Mr Allan J. Bennett, Dolgey Post, St Ervan

David and Gillian Bennett, St Columb. Born St Ervan

Dudley Bennett, Mawgan Porth

Hilda M. Bennett (née Sowden), St Ervan. Born St Eval

Leslie and Vilma Bennett (née Trenerry), St Ervan

Maurice and Pat Bennett, St Ervan

Eric Berry, Busveal, Redruth

Mary Best (née Sowden), formerly St Ervan

Bradley Biddick, Livingston, Wisconsin, USA

Helen Biddick, St Ervan

Mr Peter Biddick, Trenoweth Manor, St Columb

Roger and Suzanne Biddick, St Ervan

Denis and Pat Billingham, Primrose Cottage, Rumford

Rachel Blackburn, Fareham

Alistair and Bridget Blake, St Columb

Elaine Bolitho, Wellington, New Zealand

W. and I. Booth

Mr and Mrs Patrick Boyd, Penrose

Ronald J. Bray, Wadebridge

Betty Brewer (née Curtis)

Collin W. Brewer, Egloshayle

Mrs Diana and Mr Jonathan Brewer

Ronald Brewer, Wauzeka, Wisconsin, USA

Vernon and Diana Brewer

Brewer & Hicks, Mrs S. Hall, Leicester

John Buckingham, Padstow

Roy and Wendy Buckthought (née Curgenven), Born St Ervan

Pet and Len Burge

K.J. Burrow, Bucks Cross, Devon

Pam Burton, St Columb

A.E. Carhart, formerly of St Ervan

Nigel Carhart

Roger Carhart

Sally Carhart, Liskeard

Pat Carson

Reg and Mary Chapman

The Chapman Family, St Eval

Bob and Lolita Christian, Atascadero, California, USA

Mrs P.M. Christophers (née Sowden)

Jimmy and Dorothy Clemence, Four Lanes, Redruth

Roger and Rose Clemens, St Ervan

Brian N. Coombe, Liskeard

Cornish Interest Group, N.Z. Society of Genealogists

Mr Peter Cowling, The Glebe Farm, St Ervan

Edna M. Cowling, St Ervan

Ann Crichton-Harris, Toronto, Canada

Julie Cruddace (née Lindsey), Padstow, Cornwall

Diana Cunningham, Newquay, Cornwall

Paul Curgenven, formerly of St Ervan

Millicent Curgenven (née Curtis), Born St Eval

Reginald L. Curtis, Wadebridge

Elizabeth Davies, Newquay

Doris Day (née Sowden), London. Born St Eval

Clarence Deacon, St Ervan

John Deacon, formerly St Ervan

Michael (Dudley) Deacon, Trewinnick Lane

Mr David Drake M.R.C.S.(Eng.), Hong Kong

Dr Francis Dunstan, High Wycombe, Bucks

Alan Ellery, St Merryn

Tom and Jean Ellis, Eagle Harbor, MI

Richard J. Farrant, St Merryn/born St Ervan 1957

Jean A. Farrant (née Curtis), St Merryn/born St Ervan 1933

Davina A. Fennemore, Harrow

Nicholas E. Fisher, St Ervan

Colin and Gillian Fisher (née Rabey), St Ervan

Andrew Foot

Francis and Pat, St Ervan

Miss May Garland, Wadebridge

R. Gilbert, Bodmin

Elizabeth Trevorrow Mallett Gladwin, Michigan, USA

Shirley Golden, Clio, MI, USA

Mike and Jeanette Green, Trevarrian

Alberta Gregor, St Ervan

Anthony Gregor, Redruth. Formerly St Ervan

Gordon and Julie Grogan, St Ervan

Jill Hagley (née Lobb), Padstow

Jean Haigh, Padstow

Eleanor Harrison (née Binny), formerly of St Eval

Michelle D. Hawke, St Albans, Hertfordshire

W.L.A. (Les) Hawke, formerly of Edmonton

Mr A.R.G. Hawke, Wadebridge

Michael G. Hawke, East Barnet, Hertfordshire

Mrs M.E. Hawke, Wadebridge

Elizabeth B. Hawken

Mr Howard J. Hawken, St Ervan

John C.P. Hawken, Port Isaac

Mrs Dorothy P. Head (née Rowe), Eddystone Farm 1937–1955

Mr E. and Mrs H. Hemmings, Treviscoe

Joan M. Henwood (née Brewer), Rumford

John Henwood, Melbourne, Australia

Mary and Mike Higman, Sutton Coldfield

Rod Hildreth, Fort Payne, Alabama, USA

Ian and Sarah Hodge (née Biddick), St Breock

Leslie and Nora Hodge (née Key), St Breock

Dave, Ruth and Michael Hollis, St Merryn

Rowena House, Newquay

Kathy Howells, London, & Rose Rabey, St Merryn

Janet Ivey, Truro

Geoffrey James, Bath, Somerset

John James, St. Columb Minor

Nick James, Chiswick, London

Pat James (née Morley), Rumford, St Ervan

Mrs D.H. Jeffery (née Sowden)

Rita Jewell (née Morley), Truro. Formerly St Ervan

Claire and Clive Keightley, St Ervan

David Kempthorne, Eddystone, St Ervan, Wadebridge

John and Angela Kent, St Merryn

Pat, Charles and Richard Kent, St Merryn
Keweenaw Kernewek, The Cornish Connection of the Copper Country
Betty and Paul King, Padstow. Formerly St Ervan
Revd Barry Kinsmen, Padstow
Rod and Anne Knight, Boscastle
Rita Bone Kopp, OPC St Stephen-in-Brannel
Roger Lacy, Newquay
Andrew G. Langdon, Truro
Vivian E. Littlefield, St Mawgan
Peter and Maggie Lloyd, Old Rectory, St Ervan. 1987–98
Arthur Lobb, Weybridge, Surrey
Stephen Lobb, Horningtops, Liskeard
The Lobb Family, Homesleigh, Rumford
Patrick and Phoebe Lockett
Catherine Lorigan, Delabole, Cornwall
Barbara MacLeish, Minneapolis, Minnesota, USA
Dennis Martin, St Day
Mrs Margaret Martyn, caretaker of the Chapel & Sunday School for 12 years
Joanna Mattingly, Truro
Muriel May, Trewithen Farm, St Merryn
Malcolm McCarthy, Padstow, descendant of Francis and Mary Brewer, St Ervan
Mick, Sarah and Billy McLachlan
Mariota Elizabeth McPherson (Campbell), Penrose
Roy Menhenitt, St Merryn
Marta Leverton Metcalf, Orlando, Florida
Mr and Mrs Geoffrey Middleton, Somerset
John Midgley, Newquay
Anthony (Mitch) and Jane Mitchell, formerly Churchtown, St Ervan
Thelma Mitchell, formerly St Eval Parish
Melanie and John Morphew, Penrose
Shirley Morrish, Truro, Cornwall
Mylor Local History Group
John Neale, St Ervan
Mrs Karen Needham (née Ackers),
Avril Newey, Coventry
Mike and Tina O'Connor, St Ervan
Flora Toms O'Hagan, Fond Du Lac
Patrick and Pauline O'Shea
Andrew and Michelle Old, St Ervan
Christine Old, Mellingey Mill

Jennifer Old, St Ervan
Susan Old, St Breock
T. Henry Old, Rosmere
Barry and Shirley Osborne, St Eval
O.J. Padel, St Neot
Mrs J.E. and Richard Parkyn, St Merryn
Mr William John Parkyn, St Issey, Cornwall
Roger and Margaret Parr, Fuchsia Cottage, St Ervan
Winnie Parsons, St Issey
Betty and Bob Partridge, St Merryn
Peter Pascoe, Camborne
Neil Pedlar, Porth
Thalben and Carrie Pedlar (née Key), St Breock
Mr and Mrs R. Peek, Clacton-On-Sea
Susan Pellowe, Chicago
H. Plester, St Ervan
Charles Powell, St Ervan
Carl and Sandra Powell, St Ervan
Dick and Jill Powell, Treburrick
Jack and Hilda Pritchard, Newquay
Mr R. and Mrs Y. Puttick, Treviscoe
Sarah D. Rabey, St Issey
Thelma Rabey, St Merryn
Donald R. Rawe, Probus
Jean Raymont, Trevean, St Merryn
Roff Rayner, Perranarworthal
David Reskelly, Helston
Jason Reskelly, St Columb
Nellie Reynolds (née Key), St Breock
Peter and Rosemarie Richardson (née Binny)
Mrs Sandra Risdon (née Martyn), born Chapel Cottage, St Ervan
Alan and Kathleen Rodliffe, Rosedinnick Farm
Jim and Jenny Rourke, St Columb Major
Diana Rowe, 1937–1961, Eddystowe Farm, St Ervan
Tresa Rowe, Eddystone 1937–1957
William J.B. Rowe, St Mawgan
Mervyn Sowden Rumford, Wadebridge
Michael and Freda Salmon, Trewinnick Farm
Mark Sandry, Padstow
Peter Sandry, Rumford
Graham and Sheila Sault, Rumford
John and Jean Shapland, Trevisker, St Eval, Cornwall
David G. Sharpe, Crantock
Jeremy and Sally Simmonds, The Old School House
Rosie A. Simpkins, St Merryn

Trevor and Linda Simpson, Penrose
Mr and Mrs John Skinner, St Ervan, Cornwall
Ken and Mary Skinner, St Ervan
Mrs Susan Sleigh (née Martyn), born Rumford, attended Sunday School & St Ervan Primary
Joan and John Smedley, St Columb Major
Elaine Sowden, Porthcothen Bay. Formerly St Ervan
Jean and Bernard Sowden, Porthcothen Bay. Formerly St Ervan
Malachi Spear
Megan Speed, Newquay
Hazel Ruth Stacey, St Austell
K. and C. Stacey, Cardiff
Robbie and Suzie Stokes, Penpol, Crantock
Grace Strongman, Porthcothen Bay
Mary Strongman and Anne Curtis, formerly of Church Town Farm, St Ervan
Charlotte and Oliver Tangye
Harry T. Tangye, Torquay
Jean Thomas, St Columb
Jean Richards Timmermeister, Spokane, Washington State, USA
The Tippett Family, Gairloch
Mrs Emily R. and Mr John M. Tonnelier, St Ervan
Sir Richard and Lady Trant, Lostwithiel
Mr John Tremain, High Lanes
R. Tremain, Trerair, Penrose
Peter Trenerry, St Ervan
Zoe and Adam Turner
John Tyacke, Toronto
K.H. Udy
Sandra and Nicky Veale, Newquay
Mrs Elizabeth J. Vegter, granddaughter of Ellen Rabey of St Ervan
J.R. Verrier, St Ervan
Gary and Catherine Vivian, Toronto, Canada
John F.W. Walling, Newton Abbot, Devon
Mr E.A. Walling, Ruislip, Middlesex
Mrs Rosemary Walters, granddaughter of Ellen Rabey of St Ervan
C.N. Wiblin, St Levan, Cornwall
Andrea W. Wildes, Auckland, New Zealand
June Williams (née Wright), formerly St Ervan
Elizabeth Wood, Penzance
W.H. and A.E. Wood, St Ervan

There are now over 160 titles in the Community History Series. For a full listing of these and other Halsgrove publications, please visit www.halsgrove.com or telephone 01884 243 242